WHO Library Cataloguing in Publication Data

Roemer, Ruth
    Legislative action to combat the world tobacco
    epidemic / Ruth Roemer ; with a chapter by Richard
    A. Daynard. — 2nd ed.

    1.Smoking – prevention & control – legislation
    I.Title

ISBN 92 4 156157 2   (LC Classification: HV 5740)

The World Health Organization welcomes requests for permission to reproduce or translate its publications, in part or in full. Applications and enquiries should be addressed to the Office of Publications, World Health Organization, Geneva, Switzerland, which will be glad to provide the latest information on any changes made to the text, plans for new editions, and reprints and translations already available.

TYPESET IN INDIA
PRINTED IN ENGLAND

92/9332 - Macmillan/Clays - 6500

Legislative action to combat the world tobacco epidemic

Second edition

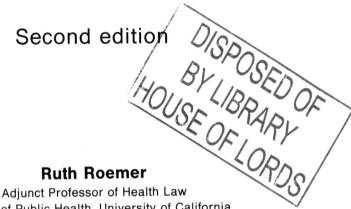

Ruth Roemer
Adjunct Professor of Health Law
School of Public Health, University of California
Los Angeles, CA, USA

with a chapter by Richard A. Daynard

World Health Organization
Geneva
1993

Contents

Foreword

Every year during the 1990s, three million people will die of the harmful effects of smoking. Over the last 40 years the role of tobacco in the causation of lung cancer has been proved beyond dispute. But tobacco also plays a part in the onset of other diseases, including cancers of the bladder, larynx or pharynx, chronic bronchitis and chronic respiratory insufficiency, and cardiovascular diseases such as arteriopathies and ischaemic heart disease. Besides the direct consequences of smoking on the smoker, passive smoking — by non-smokers exposed to tobacco smoke — has now been shown to increase the risk of lung cancer, cardiovascular problems, and respiratory diseases of children.

The smoking epidemic spread rapidly in the industrialized countries from the start of the twentieth century. In France, for example, tobacco consumption grew by over 4% per year between 1920 and 1976. The proportion of adults who smoke in France today has stabilized at 40%. However, while the proportion of men who smoke is decreasing, the proportion of women smokers is on the increase. Another alarming aspect of the current smoking epidemic is the large proportion of young people and adolescents who smoke — 30% in 1990, with as many girls as boys. Assessments at the global level predict that, if no change takes place, 200 million of today's children and adolescents will die as a result of their smoking habits.

Another alarming aspect of this epidemic is its foreseeable shift towards the developing world. At a time when smoking is tending to stabilize or even decline in the industrialized countries, the multinational tobacco companies are finding new markets in Africa, Latin America, Asia and eastern Europe. These countries will be drawn rapidly into the vicious circle of smoking, disease and death, at a time when some of them are still struggling to attain an acceptable level of health and an increased life expectancy for their population.

The World Health Organization has thrown its moral weight behind the efforts to control this epidemic. Under its leadership, many governments, politicians, public health specialists and non-governmental organizations have joined forces to develop effective protective measures against the ravages of smoking.

The control of smoking calls for complex mechanisms. One weapon, both powerful and essential, is legislation. Over 90 countries around the world have now adopted legislation to control the use of tobacco and the number is increasing. Many of these countries are also strengthening their existing legislation and arming themselves to apply it more effectively and systematically.

This is the case with France. The law of 9 July 1976 on the control of smoking aimed to restrict tobacco advertising, to ban smoking in public places and transport, to inform tobacco consumers of the risks they incur, and to teach young people through routine health education activities. But this law has proved difficult to apply: compliance with the ban on smoking in public places has been patchy, and above all the advertisers have tried every means of getting around the law and continuing their activities to encourage young people to smoke.

The law of 10 January 1991 has now strengthened the first law. It introduces a total ban, as from 1 January 1993, on all direct or indirect advertising of tobacco. It reverses the attitude hitherto predominant, by considering non-smoking behaviour as the normal behaviour; thus all public places will automatically be non-smoking and permission to smoke will be a limited exception subject to strict conditions. With the ban on advertising, France joins a number of other countries, including Canada, Finland, Iceland, New Zealand and Norway.

The comprehensive review of world legislation on the control of tobacco use contained in this book is essential information for every health official, minister, member of parliament or politician who is faced with the statistics on premature death or disease due to smoking, and with their economic consequences. By putting forward legislative measures that *can* be adopted, because they *already have been*, the book supplies additional and convincing arguments for the many countries that are looking into the possibility of introducing regulations to control smoking. It also sets out the difficulties encountered by various countries in arriving at these laws.

The figures given by WHO speak for themselves: about 500 million people who are alive on this planet today are likely to be killed by their smoking habit. There is no time to lose; only swift and energetic action can halt this epidemic before the predictions come true. Governments have a moral responsibility for their citizens' health; they must take the necessary measures quickly and formalize them by adequate legislation.

I am convinced that this book will motivate decision-makers throughout the world by showing them the fundamental role of legislation as an essential tool for achieving the objective of tobacco control that the world has to set itself.

Claude Evin
Minister of Solidarity,
Health and Social Protection of France,
May 1988 to May 1991

Preface

When the World Health Organization published the first edition of *Legislative action to combat the world smoking epidemic* in 1982, 57 countries in the world had enacted some type of legislation to control tobacco use. By 1986, when an update was released, 15 additional countries had enacted legislation, several countries had strengthened their existing laws, and many provincial or state and local governments had adopted laws to control smoking in public places and workplaces. As the decade of the 1990s begins, the number of countries and territories with national anti-tobacco legislation has reached 91, and subnational legislation has become commonplace.

Perhaps as significant as the spread of legislation are the increased strength and effectiveness of recently enacted statutes. As governments have faced the persistence of the tobacco epidemic and their young people begin smoking year after year, more and more have banned all advertising and promotion of tobacco, have substantially raised taxes on, and prices of, tobacco products, and have expanded restrictions on smoking in public places, workplaces, and public transport.

Despite much progress in adopting and implementing restrictive legislation to control the use of tobacco, the challenge ahead is daunting. Many developing countries have weak legislation or none at all. In several regions of the world, legislation is inadequate. And, as smoking declines in the industrialized countries, the multinational tobacco companies are targeting the developing countries as potential new and lucrative markets.

In the struggle to combat the tobacco epidemic, an essential tool is effective legislation. Expressing the official policy of governments, legislation reflects the commitment of policy-makers and provides leverage and support for a comprehensive programme of tobacco control. It sets the stage for the transition to smoke-free societies.

As noted in 1982, this study has been undertaken in an effort to assist governments and health officials, alarmed by the health and economic consequences of tobacco use in their countries, to develop effective legislation as part of a campaign to reduce morbidity and mortality from tobacco-related diseases and, in general, to combat what has been described as the "tobacco epidemic". More specifically, the study is designed:

— to update previous studies of anti-smoking legislation published by WHO;

— to communicate the experience of various countries with different types of anti-tobacco legislation to others contemplating the introduction of such legislation;

— to present the reasons why certain types of smoking-control measures have been adopted;

— to comment on and evaluate, as far as possible, different legislative approaches; and

— to relate legislative activity to other strategies for combating the tobacco epidemic and its consequences.

Like the original monograph and its update, this second edition is based primarily on an examination of the legislative texts on smoking control throughout the world. These are analysed in Chapters 1–12. Chapter 13, Judicial action for tobacco control, by Richard A. Daynard, deals with the attempt, through litigation, to obtain compensation for tobacco-induced diseases and death and to achieve other smoking-control goals. Information on such litigation and other types of court action has been included because of its possible usefulness in suggesting legal strategies to supplement the enactment of legislation. Chapters 14 and 15 deal respectively with the challenge to developing countries, and the development and implementation of a policy on tobacco control.

Annex 1 presents a tabular summary of legislation by WHO region. The tables are intended to assist the reader in identifying types and provisions of legislation in the different countries and regions. Knowledge of experience in other countries has proved to be helpful in encouraging governments to strengthen their laws. The tables in this second edition present a more detailed summary of the legislation than was contained in the original monograph. The 1982 edition presented merely the type of legislation and a judgement as to whether the restrictions were strong or moderate. In this edition, more specific information is offered in the tables and the notes appended to them so that readers may evaluate the legislation for themselves. Annex 2 contains the texts of resolutions of the World

Health Assembly on the control of tobacco. Annex 3 lists all the available legislation of the various countries and territories, as well as subnational legislation and Directives of the European Community, past and present, on tobacco and health. Some legislation has been amended or repealed, but citing all available legislation affords the reader an historical perspective on the legislation of each country or territory. Annex 4 presents diagrams showing the effect of legislation on tobacco consumption, while Annex 5 gives examples of the health warnings on tobacco products.

The dynamic developments in this field have produced an enormous volume of material that is continually evolving—laws, regulations, reports, and scholarly analyses of legislative strategies. While every effort has been made to present an accurate account, errors, omissions, and misinterpretations may have crept in. For this the author assumes full responsibility and apologizes.

Deep gratitude is expressed to the many colleagues in WHO, the USA, and other countries who generously furnished information on, and interpretation of, laws and policy on tobacco and health. The WHO Health Legislation unit in Geneva graciously provided expert, efficient, and reliable research support. Mr S. S. Fluss, Chief, Health Legislation, had the foresight a decade ago to identify the need for study and analysis of the legislation in this field and has continued to back up tobacco-control researchers and advocates throughout the world. Dr J. R. Menchaca and Dr C. Chollat-Traquet of the WHO Programme on Tobacco or Health were responsible for initiating this study and have extended every aid and encouragement.

It has been exciting to undertake this study at a time when several governments were making quantum leaps forward in legislative attack on the tobacco epidemic. It is hoped that this monograph will contribute in some small way to that movement throughout the world.

Chapter 1

The smoking epidemic and action by the World Health Organization

The Tobacco or Health programme is different from most other WHO programmes, in that it does not work to protect human beings against natural forces such as disease or catastrophe, but rather against other human beings peddling a dangerous drug. To sustain an addiction which would otherwise tend to die out, the tobacco industry spends thousands of millions of dollars on advertising which presents a flattering, often dazzling, image of smoking.

Dr Hiroshi Nakajima, Director-General, WHO. *Tobacco and health 1990. The global war. Proceedings of the Seventh World Conference on Smoking and Health, Perth, Western Australia, 1990*

Legislation has been enacted in 91 countries and territories (for summary, see Annex 1) in response to the tobacco pandemic that is already the main cause of avoidable disease and premature death in developed countries and will become the leading cause of preventable death in the world as a whole in the 21st century. Every year, an estimated 3 million people die from tobacco-related diseases. More appalling even than past and current deaths are the projections of future smoking-related mortality if current patterns of smoking continue. It is estimated that future smoking-related deaths among people alive in 1989 could be as high as 10 million annually by the year 2025 if no further change occurs in the proportions of young adults who become regular smokers. This will mean that more than 200 million children and teenagers alive today will be killed by tobacco, as well as a comparable number of today's adults. Thus, a total of about 500 million of the current world population will die from tobacco-related diseases; about 250 million of these deaths will strike people in middle age (35–69 years), who will lose on average 20 years of life (Peto & Lopez, 1990).

In the 40 years since the first reports linked cigarette smoking to disease, scientific knowledge of the health hazards of tobacco use has expanded beyond the wildest original fears. Over the years, epidemiological investigations in the USA (Wynder & Graham, 1950), and the United Kingdom (Doll & Hill, 1950), and reports by the relevant health authorities, have provided documentation on the magnitude of the health risks of tobacco use (Royal College of Physicians of London, 1962, 1971, 1977, 1983; US Department of Health, Education, and Welfare, 1979; US Department of Health and Human Services, 1980, 1981, 1986, 1988, 1989; US Public Health Service, 1964).

Studies in many countries have contributed to this growth in knowledge, but it is convenient here to trace the expansion in understanding of the health risks of tobacco by reference to the periodic reports of the US Surgeon General. In the 1960s and 1970s, major investigations demonstrated an approximately 70% higher death rate in male cigarette smokers than in non-smokers. By 1967, overwhelming evidence had proved that smoking was the principal cause of lung cancer. In women, lung cancer increased dramatically following the adoption of smoking by women, so that by 1988 lung cancer had outstripped breast cancer as the leading cause of cancer mortality among women in the United States and Scotland. In 1984, the US Surgeon General's report concluded that cigarette smoking was not only a cause of bronchitis but a major cause of chronic obstructive lung disease (US Department of Health and Human Services, 1984).

Successive reports of the US Surgeon General have concluded that cigarette smoking is a contributory factor in bladder, kidney, pancreatic and stomach cancer. More than 15 epidemiological studies have consistently shown an increased risk of cervical cancer in cigarette smokers as compared with non-smokers.

The evidence has mounted on the association of smoking with coronary heart disease, which was first noted in 1964 and confirmed in 1967 (US Public Health Service, 1964, 1967). By 1983 the report of the US Surgeon General concluded that cigarette smoking was a major cause of that disease and noted the decreased risk of it among former smokers as compared with current smokers. In addition, powerful evidence showed that cigarette smoking increased the risk of stroke and that smoking cessation reduced that risk. Smoking is also directly related to the incidence of atherosclerotic peripheral vascular disease.

The adverse effects of smoking by pregnant women on their

2

fetuses were first documented in 1964 in the increased incidence of low-birth-weight babies (US Public Health Service, 1964). Subsequently, maternal smoking was indicted as creating an increased risk of prematurity, spontaneous abortions, stillbirths, and neonatal deaths (US Department of Health, Education, and Welfare, 1979).

In 1972, involuntary smoking was identified as a health risk, and in 1986 the US Surgeon General's report (US Department of Health and Human Services, 1986) focused exclusively on its health consequences. It concluded that involuntary smoking was a cause of disease, including lung cancer, and that the children of parents who smoke, compared with those of non-smoking parents, have an increased frequency of respiratory infections and smaller rates of increase in lung function as the lung matures. It also stated that simple separation of smokers and non-smokers within the same air-space may reduce, but does not eliminate, exposure of non-smokers to environmental tobacco smoke.

In 1979, the report of the US Surgeon General (US Department of Health, Education, and Welfare, 1979) indicted smokeless tobacco (snuff and chewing tobacco) as a cause of cancer. In 1988, after an exhaustive review of the pharmacological and behavioural evidence, the Surgeon General's report concluded that cigarettes and other forms of tobacco are addictive and that nicotine is the drug that causes addiction (US Department of Health and Human Services, 1988). In 1990, a strong association was shown between prior cigarette smoking and the risk of developing leukaemia (Mills et al., 1990).

As the scientific evidence on the dangers of tobacco mounted, WHO launched increasingly strenuous efforts to mobilize governments and voluntary organizations in the fight against the tobacco epidemic. Its numerous expert committee reports have developed the scientific base for policy in this field (World Health Organization, 1975, 1979, 1982, 1983, 1986, 1988, 1990a). The International Agency for Research on Cancer has published detailed evaluations of the carcinogenic risks to human beings, including those associated with tobacco smoking, with tobacco habits other than smoking, and with passive smoking (International Agency for Research on Cancer, 1986, 1987a,b).

Resolutions of the World Health Assembly in 1970 and 1971 (WHA23.32 and WHA24.48) (see Annex 2), and of the WHO Executive Board in 1974 (EB53.R31) laid the groundwork for WHO's Programme on Tobacco or Health. In 1975, the report of a WHO Expert Committee, *Smoking and its effects on health*, was published (World Health Organization, 1975). In 1976, a resolution of the World Health Assembly (WHA29.55) (see Annex 2) called for

3

legislative action as a useful component of an overall anti-smoking programme. In that year, WHO published its pioneering survey of legislation to control tobacco use (World Health Organization, 1976). In 1978, the World Health Assembly, in resolution WHA31.56 (see Annex 2), urged specific strategies — increased taxation, restricting all forms of publicity and promotion of tobacco, and alternative undertakings to replace tobacco growing and processing. In 1979, the report of the WHO Expert Committee on Smoking Control, *Controlling the smoking epidemic*, was published (World Health Organization, 1979). A 1980 resolution of the World Health Assembly (WHA33.35) (see Annex 2) led to a strengthening of WHO's collaboration with Member States, other United Nations agencies, and nongovernmental organizations on tobacco and health. In 1983 the report of a third WHO Expert Committee, *Smoking control strategies in developing countries*, was published (World Health Organization, 1983).

In 1986, WHO launched a global public health approach to tobacco, urging Member States, in resolution WHA39.14, as a minimum, to: (1) protect non-smokers; (2) prevent children and young people from becoming addicted; (3) ensure that all health personnel in all health-related premises set a non-smoking example; (4) eliminate the socioeconomic, behavioural, and other incentives that maintain and promote tobacco use; (5) require prominent health warnings, including the statement that tobacco is addictive, on all tobacco products; (6) establish programmes of education, public information, and smoking cessation; (7) monitor trends in tobacco consumption and the effectiveness of national smoking control actions; (8) promote viable alternatives to tobacco production, trade, and taxation; and (9) establish a national focal point to stimulate, support, and coordinate all the above activities (see Annex 2). This global approach was reflected in the establishment in 1987, pursuant to resolution WHA40.38 (see Annex 2), of World No-Smoking Day, now World No-Tobacco Day, held on 31 May of each year.

In order to strengthen WHO's activities on smoking and health, which until then had been the responsibility of the Division of Noncommunicable Diseases, in 1990 WHO established the programme on tobacco or health as a separate programme with responsibility for implementing the plan of action for the period 1988–1995. The components of the plan of action include: (*a*) promotion of tobacco control programmes to prevent and reduce tobacco use; (*b*) advocacy and public information to promote the concept of tobacco-free societies and to establish non-use of tobacco as normal social behaviour; and (*c*) acting as a clearinghouse with a data centre to disseminate valid information on tobacco and health issues and strategies to control tobacco consumption.

Now, 20 years after WHO initiated its action on tobacco and health, one can say with confidence that many countries have made significant progress in adopting smoking-control policies. Tobacco consumption has declined in countries that have adopted comprehensive smoking-control programmes, with a consequent decline in lung cancer. But the spectre of future premature deaths from tobacco use, if current smoking patterns continue, led WHO Member States in 1990 to issue an even more urgent call, in resolution WHA43.16 (see Annex 2), for legislation to prevent involuntary exposure to tobacco smoke in public places and the workplace, to achieve progressive increases in the real price of tobacco, and to ban direct and indirect advertising, promotion, and sponsorship of tobacco. In 1991, in resolution WHA44.26 (see Annex 2), WHO urged Member States to adopt appropriate measures for effective protection from involuntary exposure to tobacco smoke in trains, aircraft, and all forms of public transport.

Chapter 2

Role and development of legislation to control the use of tobacco

It may be tempting to try introducing smoking control programmes without a legislative component, in the hope that relatively inoffensive activity of this nature will placate those concerned with public health, while generating no real opposition from cigarette manufacturers. This approach, however, is not likely to succeed. A genuine broadly defined education programme aimed at reducing smoking must be complemented by legislation and restrictive measures ...

Smoking control strategies in developing countries: report of a WHO Expert Committee. Geneva, World Health Organization, 1983

Smoking and other uses of tobacco constitute the main preventable cause of premature death and disability, and the purpose of legislation is to prevent and reduce the burden of illness, early mortality and morbidity, and human suffering caused by the use of tobacco.

Important as legislation has proved to be in combating the tobacco epidemic, it should nevertheless be emphasized that the enactment of legislation is a necessary but not a sufficient condition for an effective campaign to control smoking and reduce tobacco-related diseases. Legislation is essential to establish and promulgate public policy, to enlist the resources of all government departments, to strengthen the activities of voluntary organizations and citizens' groups, and to contribute to the development of a non-smoking environment. But legislation is only one component in a comprehensive attack on the tobacco epidemic, which includes preventive action, public information, educational programmes, smoking cessation interventions, outreach to high-risk populations, a tax and price policy based on health needs, economic strategies to decrease tobacco production, research on biological, behavioural, economic, and social aspects of tobacco use, and monitoring of the effects of tobacco-control strategies. For all these important components of a tobacco-control campaign, legislation is an essential underpinning.

Crucial to all forms of tobacco control — whether in the form of legislation, voluntary agreement, or government regulation — is the extent to which the controls are implemented. A country may have on its statute books a law that restricts smoking in public places, for example, but if it is not enforced, if the people do not obey it, the law is meaningless. Closing the gap between the letter of the law and its implementation in real life is essential if effective smoking control is to be achieved.

Specific purposes

Specifically, the purposes of tobacco-control legislation are:

— to control the growth, manufacture, promotion, and sale of tobacco and tobacco products;

— to create an atmosphere in which non-smoking is the accepted social norm;

— to promote the development of a public attitude that the use of tobacco is dangerous, unhealthy, and socially unacceptable;

— to dissuade young people from beginning to smoke and to permit children to grow up free from enticements to smoke;

— to protect the health of non-smokers and their right to breathe clean air; and at the same time to decrease the opportunities for smokers to smoke;

— to encourage all smokers to stop smoking, particularly high-priority groups, including young people, women (particularly pregnant women), parents of young children, people with medical problems, workers exposed to industrial hazards, and those in occupations where responsibility has to be taken for the lives of others (e.g. airline pilots, transport workers) or in occupations that serve as models for others (e.g. health service personnel and teachers);

— to provide the authorization, impetus, and resources for comprehensive tobacco-control campaigns.

The issue of law and liberty

Restrictive legislation inevitably raises the question of liberty. One of the responses of the tobacco industry to legislation designed to protect people from the hazards of smoking is that such legislation is an infringement of the industry's right of commercial free speech, of freedom of the press, and of freedom of choice (to smoke or not to smoke, or to choose another brand of tobacco). In fact, the industry's general response to legislation to ban tobacco advertising or to restrict smoking in public places has not been on the merits of the legislation as such but rather an appeal to fear that such legislation will open the door to allow "Big Brother" (government) to interfere in the private lives of individuals.

A subtle and sophisticated version of the industry's claim that legislation restricts its freedom was launched in the United States of America in 1989 by Philip Morris Companies, Inc. in a US $30 million campaign associating the company with the 200th anniversary of the Bill of Rights. Full-page newspaper advertisements sponsored by Philip Morris reprinted the original version of the Bill of Rights obtained from the National Archives, and warned readers not to fall into the trap of taking the rights guaranteed by the first ten amendments to the US Constitution for granted (Philip Morris Companies, Inc., 1989). Commenting on this transparent effort to convey the image of the tobacco company as a great defender of the people's liberties, John F. Banzhaf III, Professor of Law, George Washington University, and Executive Director of Action on Smoking and Health (ASH) in the United States, said: "It's ironic that the manufacturer of the only legal product that enslaves most of its users is associating itself with freedom" (Horovitz, 1990).

In all countries, the government has the responsibility to protect the health of the people, particularly of children, to preserve the quality of the environment, to regulate trade and commerce, and to promote the public health, safety, and welfare of its citizens. Government action on behalf of the welfare of society as a whole is generally upheld as valid even if it runs counter to the interests of some individuals, and particularly when there is a compelling necessity for such action. In the case of tobacco, the right of government to protect the health of its people by restricting the promotion of tobacco or controlling smoking in public places has been held to take precedence over the freedom of the tobacco industry to promote its harmful product.

As early as 1977, Finland confronted this issue in connection with its comprehensive anti-tobacco legislation, which prohibits smoking in public places unless specifically allowed, stating:

9

The question of principle is, of course, whether individuals are free to cause harm or nuisance to other individuals, and the unequivocal answer in our country was "no". But these questions were never even raised in the Cabinet or in Parliament. This suggests that the time was long overdue for introducing such measures. There was, in fact, a profound debate in Parliament on the issues of freedom and constitutional liberties but on a quite separate issue, that of advertising and sales promotion. The Parliament's Select Committee on Constitution decided, after a thorough examination of the matter, that the constitutional liberties of free speech, freedom of the press, and freedom of expression are not jeopardized by restrictions on sales promotion or advertising, and that the restrictions can be looked on as normal legal regulation of business and trade, not requiring the complicated procedure of constitutional legislation. The original purpose of these constitutional liberties was to guarantee free criticism of the Government and authorities and not of the sales promotion of life-endangering substances (Finland, National Board of Health, 1977, p. 10).

In 1988, the Canadian Parliament passed the Tobacco Products Control Act banning the advertising and promotion of tobacco products. The transnational tobacco companies immediately challenged the constitutionality of the statute, contending that a ban on advertising violated the guarantee of freedom of expression contained in Canada's 1982 Charter of Rights and Freedoms (Department of the Secretary of State of Canada, 1987). The Government's defence was that its restrictions on tobacco advertising were a "reasonable limitation" on freedom of speech, as provided for in the Charter of Rights and Freedoms (the status of this case is discussed in Chapters 3 and 13). Introduced in evidence in the pending cases are many formerly secret marketing documents of the Canadian tobacco companies that reveal how tobacco advertising is directed to young people, to non-smokers, and to smokers who may stop smoking, although the industry contends that such advertising is designed only to preserve market share. Of the numerous excerpts from these marketing documents, two may suffice to show that the aim of the industry is to recruit young smokers and to delay the cessation process (Kyle, 1990):

> Young smokers represent the major opportunity group for the cigarette industry, we should therefore determine their attitude to smoking and health and how this might change over time.
>
> Source: Imperial Tobacco's 1971 Matinee Marketing Plans, *RJR Macdonald and Imperial Tobacco Limited* v. *Attorney-General of Canada*, Quebec Superior Court, Montreal, 1989.

> It is no exaggeration to suggest that the tobacco industry is under siege. The smoker base is declining, primarily as a function of successful quitting. And the characteristics of new smokers are changing such that the future starting level may be in question . . .
> Within this somewhat alarming view of the mid-term program, Imperial Tobacco is embarking on a pro-active program. Perhaps for the first time, the

mandate under consideration is not limited simply to maximizing the ITL franchises; it is now to include as well serious attempts to combat those forces aligned in an attempt to significantly diminish the size of the tobacco market in Canada.

This is the underpinning of Project Viking. There are, in fact, two components of the program, each having its own purposes, but also overlapping with the other in informational areas:

- Project Pearl is *directed at expanding the market, or at the very least forestalling its decline ...*[1]

- Project Day represents the tactical end by which ITL may achieve competitive gains within the market of today and in the future. Unmet needs of smokers that could be satisfied by newer modified products, *products which could delay the quitting process are pursued.*[1]

> Source: *RJR Macdonald and Imperial Tobacco Limited* v. *Attorney-General of Canada*, Quebec Superior Court, Montreal, 1989, Exhibit AG-21A.

In response to the tobacco industry's efforts to entice young people to smoke and to free all Canadians from the pressures to smoke created by sophisticated advertising techniques, the Government of Canada acted to phase in the comprehensive control of the advertising and promotion of tobacco.

A total of 27 countries ban tobacco advertising completely. The countries that have prohibited all tobacco advertising and sponsorship most recently are New Zealand and France. In New Zealand, the Smoke-free Environments Act prohibiting all tobacco advertising (section 22) was adopted in 1990 following a comprehensive analysis by the Toxic Substances Board of the way in which tobacco advertising leads young people to smoke and of the marked reduction in tobacco consumption experienced by countries that have prohibited all such advertising. A number of groups put to the Board the "legal to sell, legal to advertise" argument, but it replied that freedom is seldom absolute and that, once harm from tobacco had been proven, the freedom to advertise was restricted in 1964 by voluntary action of the New Zealand Department of Health, the New Zealand Broadcasting Service, and the tobacco companies (the first voluntary agreement with the tobacco industry in New Zealand was not signed until 1973) (J. Weir, personal communication, 1992). Moreover, in New Zealand, tobacco is defined as a toxic substance, and the sale of such substances is not a right but is governed by the Toxic Substances Act of 1979. (Similarly, Canada in 1988 amended its Hazardous Products Act to include tobacco products.) In 1988, in New Zealand, the Toxic Substances Regulations 1983 were amended

---

[1] Emphasis added.

to prohibit the sale of tobacco for oral use. In 1990, the Smoke-Free Environments Act (section 30) banned the sale of tobacco to persons under 16 years of age, repealing provisions of the Toxic Substances Act of 1979 dealing with sales to minors. On the basis of its finding, after an exhaustive study, that tobacco promotion increases tobacco use and that in New Zealand on average more than 50 young people per day become daily tobacco smokers, the Board recommended the elimination of all forms of tobacco promotion. On the issue of liberty, the Board stated that:

> Where rights conflict a decision has to be made. The freedom of thousands of young people to be free from pressure to smoke harmful tobacco products would seem to be more important than the right of manufacturers to promote such products. As the title of this report implies, the choice is health or tobacco (New Zealand Toxic Substances Board, 1989, p.31).

Unfortunately, even before the effects of the New Zealand law could be assessed, a new government weakened the provisions on sponsorship.

In France, Law No. 91-32 of 10 January 1991 imposed a total ban on all tobacco advertising and sponsorship, to come into effect on 1 January 1993 in order to allow time for various sectors of society to adjust to the restrictions. This action of the French Parliament followed 14 years of experience with a strong partial ban on tobacco advertising and sponsorship but one that was found to be both inadequate in itself and inadequately enforced. The continued high prevalence of smoking among young people was a major factor in the introduction of the legislation. The proposed law caused a vigorous debate in Parliament and in the press. The tobacco industry and its publicists exerted strong pressure to defeat the bill, but the support of public opinion, strengthened by 15 years of anti-tobacco education and information, enabled the Minister of Health to emerge victorious from this struggle. The French Parliament elected to enact an unequivocal, unambiguous statute that gives clear priority to public health.

No one has seriously suggested prohibiting the use of tobacco entirely at this time. Even the most ardent advocates of combating the tobacco epidemic recognize that the custom of smoking was established long before its risks were known. In the light of current evidence that tobacco kills more people than heroin, if tobacco were a new product introduced on the market for the first time today, it would be reasonable to make its use and sale illegal. In fact, tobacco is increasingly being deemed a toxic substance, as in Canada, Finland, and New Zealand, and subject to government regulation. Nine countries have prohibited the importation and sale of smokeless tobacco. Norway, under Regulations No. 1044 of 13 October

1989, has also banned all new nicotine-containing products. The issue of law and liberty in relation to tobacco is increasingly being decided on the side of society's need, right, and duty to pass laws to protect the health of its people.

Forms of government action

Legislation

The vast majority of countries with smoking-control programmes have found legislation to be crucial in establishing official policy. As of 1990, about 90 countries and territories, as previously mentioned, had enacted some kind of smoking-control legislation. The various forms that such legislation can take are discussed below.

At the national level, the most common form of legislation consists of categorical laws dealing with one or more aspects of smoking control. Such laws may address individual issues, including restrictions on tobacco advertising, control of smoking in public places, or the banning of sales of tobacco products to minors. Many countries and territories have enacted such laws, as the tables in Annex 1 indicate. Comprehensive laws deal with many aspects of smoking control within a single statute and are designed to provide a legal basis for launching a comprehensive, multifaceted programme of smoking control. The laws of Finland and Iceland are examples of comprehensive statutes, which are less common than categorical laws.

A few laws, such as the 1983 General Law on Health of Mexico and the Law of 10 January 1991 of France banning all advertising and promotion of tobacco, deal with measures to combat the use of both tobacco and alcohol. Such laws are difficult to pass because the government faces the opposition of two powerful industries at the same time. More importantly, control strategies differ for the two products. Control of tobacco is designed to prevent all use of it, whereas control of alcohol is designed to prevent abuse of alcoholic beverages.

Some countries embody the protection of their population against tobacco use in their public health codes, particularly if these have been adopted in recent years; an example of this can be found in the legislation of Mexico. In addition, a few countries define tobacco as a toxic substance, e.g., Canada, Finland, and New Zealand, and thus bring tobacco products under their regulatory system for such substances. Laws on education often provide for compulsory health education in schools.

13

Also at the national level, and depending on the nature of the legal system, are decrees, ministerial orders, and administrative regulations that have the full force of law. Issued by the cabinet, the ministry of health, or other government agency, these regulatory instruments may be the sole or principal legislation, or they may be administrative regulations setting forth specific means of implementing the principal law.

Subnational legislation, which may be enacted at the state or provincial level in countries with a federal structure, is becoming of increasing importance. Such legislation is common, for instance, in Argentina, Brazil, Canada, and the United States. In both federal and non-federal countries, the local level of government — counties, cities, and towns — may adopt municipal ordinances or by-laws to control smoking. Such ordinances have been enacted, e.g., in Latin American countries, in France, and in North America. At the subnational level in Canada, three provinces and 114 municipalities have enacted legislation to restrict smoking in public places (Roemer, 1992; Calgary Health Services, 1988). In the USA, 43 of the 50 states and the District of Columbia have acted to restrict smoking in some manner in public places either by so-called "clean indoor air acts" or by more limited legislation (Legislative Clearinghouse, 1989). As of 1989, about 400 city and county ordinances in the USA restrict smoking in public places (Pertschuk & Shopland, 1989).

A decade ago, Gray & Daube pointed out that the effects of legislation can be subdivided as follows: (i) the effects of the publicity generated when a government announces its intention to introduce legislation; (ii) the effects of the publicity generated when a bill is being debated in a legislature; (iii) the immediate impact of legislation when it is put into force; and (iv) the long-term effect of implementing legislation as part of a smoking-control programme (Gray & Daube, 1980, p.98). Experience with the enactment of legislation over the years has confirmed the importance of maximizing the effect of legislation in each of these four phases.

Voluntary agreements

Another form of government action consists of agreements between the government and the tobacco industry. Despite the advantages of legislation and particularly that of putting the weight of government behind a non-smoking policy, a few countries continue to rely on such voluntary agreements. These agreements, sometimes referred to as "codes of practice", establish principles under which the industry agrees, for example, to abide by certain restrictions on advertising or to place health warnings on cigarette packages. Countries that still have agreements with the industry on one or more aspects of smoking control include Australia, Austria, Denmark, Germany, Sweden, and the United Kingdom. A number of countries that once relied on voluntary agreements with the industry have rejected this arrangement and have replaced it with legislation as a more effective method of control. The most recent action of this kind was taken by New Zealand, which terminated its voluntary agreement with the industry and in 1990 passed its Smoke-free Environments Act.

Voluntary agreements are weak means of controlling tobacco promotion; they are complex and difficult to monitor, and are subject to differences of interpretation which can hinder implementation. They take years to negotiate, and leave the industry free to find loopholes and to evade the restrictions by sponsoring sports and cultural events, introducing indirect advertising on television, and placing cigarette brand names on other products.

Thus, in the United Kingdom, the Department of Health and Social Security has negotiated an agreement with the industry which provides, among other things, that advertisements should not imply that smoking is associated with success in sports. However, another agreement between the industry and the Department of the Environment provides for sponsorship of sports by the industry. Clearly, the agreement on sports sponsorship is itself a violation of the first of these agreements and a device that nullifies the spirit of the restriction on advertising (Simpson, 1988).

In the United Kingdom, these agreements are negotiated in private, so that the public never knows how the industry resists proposals for meaningful restrictions but sees only the final agreement. The length of time required for negotiating the various agreements with different government departments gives the industry the opportunity to erect billboards or to install shop advertising before the new restrictions that are being negotiated take effect. Most importantly, the agreements are not enforceable. Spending more than £100 million a year in the United Kingdom on tobacco advertising, the industry derives two advantages from voluntary agreements: (a) they stave off the enactment of legislative restrictions that are enforceable; and (b) they create the impression that the industry is cooperating with government as a responsible partner in addressing public concerns. But the Director of the Coronary Prevention Group in London points out that 110 000 people a year die from tobacco-related diseases in the United Kingdom, and comments:

15

> We desperately need a campaign in the UK to dislodge the tobacco industry from its cozy position with Government and to encourage public outrage at this industry founded on death and disease ... I beg of you from other countries, especially developing countries, do not listen to the tobacco industry when they try to seduce you with voluntary agreements. These agreements have held us back in the UK from tackling the real issues (O'Connor, 1990).

Most importantly, countries that have imposed legislative restrictions have made substantially more progress in containing and reducing smoking than those that have preferred a voluntary agreement with the tobacco industry (New Zealand Toxic Substances Board, 1989, p. 64; Cox & Smith, 1984). In 1977 and again in 1983, the Royal College of Physicians of London called on the Government of the United Kingdom to substitute legislation for the voluntary agreement (Royal College of Physicians of London, 1977, 1983). In 1980, the British Medical Association called not only for legislation but also for an end to all tobacco advertising and promotion (*British medical journal*, 1980).

Development of legislation

The history of legislation to control smoking can be divided into three phases: (1) early legislation, during the period 1890–1960, designed to prohibit sales to minors and to prevent fires in public places; (2) legislation passed in the 1960s and early 1970s recognizing the connection between smoking and health and regulating specific problems, such as advertising, health warnings on cigarette packages, and other matters; and (3) beginning in 1975, the enactment of comprehensive legislation or greatly strengthened laws dealing with various facets of smoking amenable to legislation.

Illustrative of the early legislation to ban cigarette sales to minors is the District of Columbia Ordinance of 1890 prohibiting sales to minors in the capital city of the United States (World Health Organization, 1976, pp.10–12). In Norway, the Law of 19 April 1899 prohibited the sale of tobacco to children under 15 years of age. In Canada, an act to restrain the use of tobacco by young persons was passed in 1908, and prohibited the sale or furnishing of cigarettes to, and possession of tobacco products by persons under 16. In New Zealand, under the Police Offences Act of 1927, a fine was imposed on those found guilty of selling cigarettes to persons under 15. In Italy, Article 730 of the Penal Code prohibited the sale of cigarettes to persons apparently under the age of 16. A similar provision in Scotland, incorporated in the Children and Young Persons (Scotland) Act of 1937, was first enacted in the Children Act of 1908. The motivation for these measures was probably the wish to protect both health and morals. In fact, in Japan in 1900, not only were sales to minors banned but also smoking by persons under the age of 20 — a measure designed to improve the morals of young people.

Not until the 1960s and early 1970s was any significant anti-tobacco legislation enacted as a measure to protect public health. The laws of this period followed the publication of scientific studies and authoritative reports on the health hazards of smoking. Although Raymond Pearl (one of the first American demographers) at the Johns Hopkins School of Hygiene and Public Health had dramatically documented the association between tobacco use and shortened duration of life in 1938 (Pearl, 1938), his work had failed to rouse the health authorities to action. It was not until 1950, when the first studies by Wynder and Graham in the United States (Wynder & Graham, 1950) and by Doll and Hill in Britain (Doll & Hill, 1950), and further work by Doll and Hill in 1956 (Doll & Hill, 1956), linked smoking to lung cancer that the anti-smoking movement began in earnest. Then came the first report of the Royal College of Physicians of London in 1962, showing the association of smoking with serious morbidity and mortality. Further publications by Doll and Hill on the lower mortality among British physicians who had stopped smoking appeared in 1964 (Doll & Hill, 1964a,b). In that same year the first report of the Surgeon General on smoking and health was published in the United States. As mentioned earlier, it established a frightening link between cigarette smoking and several disabling or fatal diseases and pronounced cigarette smoking a "health hazard of sufficient importance to warrant appropriate remedial action" (US Public Health Service, 1964).

Stimulated by mounting evidence of the relation between lung cancer and cardiovascular diseases and smoking, various countries began to enact legislation. By Law No. 165 of 10 April 1962, Italy became the first country in western Europe to prohibit the advertising of tobacco, although this early law may have been dictated not so much by health considerations as by the need to protect the Italian State monopoly on tobacco. In 1965, the USA passed the Federal Cigarette Labeling and Advertising Act, subsequently amended to include warning notices on little cigars and smokeless tobacco. In 1970 and in the years that followed, country after country took action either by legislation or by voluntary agreement with the tobacco industry to require health warnings, restrict advertising, set upper limits on tar and nicotine, and ban smoking in public places. These laws of the 1960s and 1970s had two principal characteristics: (1) they were specifically designed to control the health hazards of

17

smoking; and (2) they were "categorical" laws addressing specific problems and objectives.

In the 1970s, a new development occurred in legislation to control smoking — the enactment in a few countries of comprehensive legislation dealing with multiple aspects of smoking control. In 1970, Singapore enacted multipurpose tobacco-control legislation. In 1973, Norway passed a law on restrictive measures in trade in tobacco products, which came into force on 1 July 1975, eight years after the first committee report recommending such legislation (Bjartveit, 1978a). France adopted multipurpose antismoking legislation in the form of Law No. 76-616 of 9 July 1976, after a campaign in 1975 and 1976 intended to prepare the public (Denoix, 1979). In August 1976, Finland enacted the most sweeping anti-smoking legislation passed until that time — its law on measures to restrict smoking. In 1980, Bulgaria also enacted multipurpose legislation — the Ordinance No. 2 on health requirements in connection with smoking.

In the 1980s, several countries continued to adopt comprehensive, multifaceted legislation, as illustrated by Law No. 74 of 28 May 1984 of Iceland and the laws and regulations of Ireland of 1986 and 1988. In 1988, Canada adopted comprehensive anti-tobacco legislation with the enactment of its Tobacco Products Control Act banning all advertising and virtually all promotion of tobacco products; at the same time its Non-smokers' Health Act eliminated environmental tobacco smoke from federally regulated workplaces and transportation. In 1990, New Zealand took similar action, under the Smoke-free Environments Act, banning all advertising and promotion of tobacco, restricting smoking in public transport and certain public places, and requiring every employer to develop and implement a policy on smoking. As noteworthy as the comprehensiveness of these laws is their stringency and clarity. The restrictions imposed on tobacco promotion and use were designed to be enforced.

In many countries the legislation enacted in the 1980s was focused and specific. The overall trend was towards identifying high-priority issues and designing legislation to match these priorities. Thus, Spain, by Crown Decree No. 709/1982 of 5 March 1982 and Portugal, by Decree-Law No. 226/83 of 27 May 1983, respectively, replaced their moderate controls on advertising with more stringent restrictions. Belgium, by the Crown Order of 31 March 1987, banned smoking in all indoor areas to which the public is admitted and provided for substantial fines and strict enforcement of this sweeping legislation. Many countries in Latin America have enacted single-purpose legislation dealing with one or two aspects of smoking control (US Department of Health and Human Services, 1992).

Numerous factors have led to this remarkable evolution in legislation to stem the tide of tobacco use. Mounting evidence of the enormous health hazards of tobacco use and the dissemination of this vast body of scientific information provided the primary, powerful impetus to government action. A significant role in the enactment of anti-smoking legislation has been played by the recommendations of international bodies calling for restrictions on the promotion of tobacco. In 1972, the Nordic Council of Ministers recommended to its members (Denmark, Finland, Iceland, Norway, and Sweden) that advertising of cigarettes be banned and that public information campaigns on the dangers of tobacco be launched, with special attention to young people (Nordic Council of Ministers, 1972). In 1973, the Consultative Assembly of the Council of Europe recommended the prohibition of the advertising of alcohol and tobacco in newspapers, on television and radio, and in theatres (Council of Europe, 1973). In 1986, the Council of the European Communities adopted a resolution on a programme of action against cancer, which included as a first priority development of measures to limit and reduce the use of tobacco, such as rules on advertising and sponsorship, rules on labelling, tax legislation, enforcement of no-smoking rules, extension of no-smoking areas, and where appropriate, the drafting of proposals for action at Community level (Council of the European Communities, 1986). Following up this resolution, the Council of Ministers of Health of the Member States of the European Communities adopted a resolution in 1989 inviting Member States to ban smoking in public places and public transport and issued Council Directive 89/622/EEC to harmonize the legislation of Member States concerning health warnings and indications of tar and nicotine yields, as discussed later. In March 1990, the European Parliament called for a total ban on tobacco advertising in the 12 countries of the European Community (Riding, 1990). In 1988, an action-oriented European Conference on Tobacco Policy was held in Madrid (World Health Organization, 1990). In May 1991, the European Commission adopted a proposal for a directive that would introduce a complete ban on the advertising of tobacco products in Europe, with exemptions for points of sale provided the advertising is not visible from outside the premises (Naett & Joossens, 1992). The governments of three States of the European Community — Germany, the Netherlands, and the United Kingdom — however, continue to oppose a ban on tobacco advertising, despite support for such a ban by 73% of Europeans (Adriaanse & Van Reek, 1992). The final decision is in the hands of the Community's Health Ministers.

Over the years, the International Union against Cancer

(UICC), a nongovernmental organization, has stimulated organizations and health professionals to mobilize for the control of tobacco. In 1990, the Asia Pacific Association for the Control of Tobacco (APACT) was organized to coordinate tobacco-control efforts among Asian countries. Most important has been the crucial role of WHO since 1970 in galvanizing actions by governments on the use of tobacco (see Chapter 1).

In many countries, the activities of voluntary organizations — cancer societies, heart associations, organizations of health professionals, and citizens' groups — have put continuing pressure on governments to enact legislation and to commit themselves to achieve a smoke-free society. As knowledge of the effects of involuntary or "passive" smoking on the health of non-smokers has increased, citizens have pressed at all levels of government for the control of smoking in public places. Knowledge of the harmful effects of environmental tobacco smoke has made control of tobacco use an issue not only for smokers but for everyone. A heightened concern with the quality of the environment has contributed to the success of these efforts. Finally, experience gained with strategies to control tobacco use has led to new and more effective legislative approaches. These are some of the factors that have led to the introduction of tobacco-control legislation, particularly in the industrialized countries.

In the developing countries, enactment of legislation to control tobacco use is in an early phase of development. Recognition of the link between health and development is clear, but, as Chapman & Leng point out:

> the most neglected issue on the international tobacco control agenda [is] the growth, and failure to control tobacco use in the world's poorest nations yet largest tobacco markets — the Third World. While the rhetoric of concern about tobacco and the Third World is in abundant supply, the overwhelming focus and resource allocations of research, lobbying and action in tobacco control remain firmly centered in industrialized nations (Chapman & Leng, 1990).

The challenge for the 1990s is to remedy this grave inequity.

Types of legislation

In 1979, the report of the WHO Expert Committee on Smoking Control, *Controlling the smoking epidemic*, defined two main categories of smoking-control measures: (1) those leading to changes in practice among those engaged in the manufacture, promotion, and sale of cigarettes; and (2) those leading to changes in practice among smokers (World Health Organization, 1979). The Expert Committee was prescient in its definition because over the years this system of classification has proved to be broad enough to encompass all the legislation that has been enacted.

Within the first type of legislation — that concerned with changes in the manufacture, promotion, and sale of tobacco, i.e., the production or supply side — we shall consider legislation on the following five aspects: (1) control of advertising, sponsorship, and promotion; (2) health warnings and statements of tar and nicotine contents; (3) control of harmful substances; (4) restrictions on sales to adults; and (5) economic strategies. Within the second type of legislation — that concerned with changes in practices among smokers, i.e., the consumption or demand side — we shall also consider legislation on five different subjects, namely: (1) tax and price policies; (2) the control of smoking in public places and public transport; (3) the control of smoking in the workplace; (4) preventing young people from smoking; and (5) health education.

For each type of legislation, we shall: (a) present the basic reasons for this type of control; (b) summarize the provisions of different laws; and (c) discuss the general experience with this type of measure, including any available evaluation of its effectiveness.

Tabular summary of legislation

Annex 1 presents a worldwide tabular summary of legislation on controlling the promotion and use of tobacco, based on information available in 1992. These tables provide information by country or territory on each of eight types of legislation, with some detail as to the content of the legislation both in the table itself and in the accompanying notes. In order to promote effective international work, the countries are grouped by WHO region. Similarities in language and culture within a region may facilitate the exchange of ideas and strategies. Summary Tables A and B show the numbers of countries and territories in each WHO region having a particular type of legislation.

Various published sources of information have been used in compiling the tables, principally texts or summaries of legislation published in the *International digest of health legislation*, and copies of laws obtained from the countries themselves. In a few cases, official communications have been used. Annex 3 lists all the legislation reviewed. To provide an historical view of the evolution of the legislation, the legislation cited in the first edition of this monograph is included.

21

Persons wishing to examine the legislation may, of course, refer to the issues of the *International digest of health legislation* cited. In addition, a convenient compilation of all the legislation on tobacco published in the *Digest* between 1978 and mid-1990 is available in a book published in 1991, *Legislative responses to the tobacco epidemic* (World Health Organization, 1991b).

Chapter 3

Control of advertising and sales promotion

The inter-relationship of tobacco advertising and tobacco consumption was examined in thirty-three countries in a study commissioned by the Board, and it covered the years 1970 to 1986...

Overall, the study found that the greater a government's degree of control over tobacco promotion, the greater the annual average fall in tobacco consumption and in the rate of decrease of smoking among young people. In total ban countries compared with the group of countries without controls, tobacco consumption fell more rapidly, and this effect could not be explained away by tobacco price or income per capita trends. The elimination of tobacco advertising, other factors being equal, more likely than not *causes* tobacco consumption to decrease.

Health or tobacco. An end to tobacco advertising and promotion, Toxic Substances Board, Wellington, New Zealand, May 1989, pp.xxiii-xxv

The importance of advertising to the tobacco industry is reflected in the size and growth of expenditure for this purpose. In 1978, global advertising costs of the transnational conglomerates amounted to US $1.8 thousand million (United Nations, 1978).[1] A decade later in 1988, in the USA alone, the tobacco industry spent $3.27 thousand million in advertising and promotion — nearly double its global expenditure in 1978 and an increase of 26.9% over its US expenditure in 1987. From 1975 to 1988, total cigarette advertising and promotional expenditure increased more than six-fold and, when adjusted by the consumer price index to constant

---

[1] All dollar figures in this monograph refer to US dollars except where otherwise indicated.

23

1975 dollars, increased threefold (Centers for Disease Control, 1990a).

The enormous amounts spent by the multinational tobacco companies worldwide on the sponsorship of sports and cultural events — a form of promotion that associates tobacco with healthy and pleasurable pursuits — are not known. Such sponsorship reaches not only the audience attending the events but also the vast audiences, many of them children and adolescents, who watch them on television. In recent years, the industry has been increasing its expenditure on sponsorship. From 1980 to 1983 in the USA, total advertising expenditure rose by 30%, but promotional expenditure nearly doubled (Warner, 1986a). Sponsorship support, including newspaper and billboard advertising of the event, is generally thought to require expenditure equal to that spent on sponsorship itself. To give some idea of the order of magnitude of expenditure on sponsorship, in 1988 in the USA, cigarette advertising and promotional expenditure related to the sponsorship of sports events amounted to $84 million (Centers for Disease Control, 1990a). In 1990, the Philip Morris Companies spent $15 million in the USA on sponsorship of the arts alone (Rothstein, 1990).

Importance of advertising

Advertising is an integral part of the corporate expansion of the tobacco industry. The industry claims that advertising is not designed to increase consumption but only to maintain market share, prevent brand-switching or maintain brand loyalty, and promote low-tar and low-nicotine cigarettes. But this is clearly false, as fewer than 10% of smokers change brands in any one year, much brand-switching is between brands of a single company, and nearly all 250 brands marketed in the USA are made by only six companies. Thus, brand-switching cannot explain the billions spent on advertising because, with 10% of 55 million US smokers switching, that would mean an expenditure of about $345 per switcher in the USA alone (Tye et al., 1987). In Hong Kong, the launching of Virginia Slims for women at a time when only 1% of women under 40 smoked was clearly not designed to prevent brand-switching but to create a market among women. Further evidence of the spuriousness of the industry's claim is the fact that, even in a country where a tobacco company holds a monopoly position, its advertising activity is intensive (Currie & Ray, 1984; Roemer, 1982).

The claim that advertising is necessary to promote low-tar and low-nicotine cigarettes is patently specious in view of findings that

24

tobacco from low-yield cigarettes does not contain less nicotine than tobacco from higher-yield ones and that smokers of low-yield cigarettes do not consume less nicotine than smokers of higher-yield ones (Benowitz et al., 1983). These findings led Claude Lenfant of the National Heart, Lung and Blood Institute at the National Institutes of Health in the United States to conclude that "despite the seductive advertisements, there is no less hazardous, safer cigarette" (Lenfant, 1983). Moreover, strategies other than advertising of low-tar brands are available to decrease the tar and nicotine contents of cigarettes, namely legislation authorizing governments to set maximum levels of tar, nicotine, and carbon monoxide yields (see Chapter 5) and increased taxes on high-yield cigarettes (see Chapter 8).

Authoritative statements of advertising executives in Australia, the United Kingdom, and the United States rebut the industry's claims and agree that advertising increases tobacco consumption (Chapman, 1985). David Abbott, a leading British advertising executive said (Daube, 1975):

> I think it's incontrovertible, though people will argue against it, that advertising things encourages people to use them. The advertising industry believes that in every other product. I don't see why the rules are different for cigarettes.

As an Australian advertising executive (Dumas, 1978) said:

> As an argument [that tobacco advertising is only aimed at brand-switching and not at attracting new consumers] it is so preposterous it is insulting. . . To claim cigarette advertising does not encourage smoking flies in the face of all advertising knowledge and experience... We have the ironic situation of the Advertising Federation of Australia, on the one hand, saying that advertising in general helps expand markets, and thereby reduces the cost of products; and on the other hand claiming that cigarette advertising keeps the market in a miraculously static state.

In the USA, Emerson Foote (Foote, 1981), former chairman of the board of the world's second largest advertising agency, commented that:

> The cigarette industry had been artfully maintaining that cigarette advertising has nothing to do with total sales... This is the public position of the tobacco industry but I don't think anyone really believes this. I am not even convinced that competition among brands is the most important purpose of such advertising. I suspect that creating a positive climate of social acceptability for smoking, which encourages new smokers to join the market, is of greater importance to the industry.

These authoritative statements have been confirmed by the industry itself. In 1986 and again in 1988, the Canadian tobacco company, Imperial Tobacco Ltd, commissioned a consulting firm to undertake a project to investigate the future of the tobacco industry.

Imperial Tobacco's instructions to the consulting firm, as quoted in Chapter 2, include the statement that Project Pearl is directed at expanding the market, or at the very least forestalling its decline.

A definitive study commissioned by the Toxic Substances Board of New Zealand on the relationship between tobacco-promotion policies and trends in tobacco consumption in 33 countries for the period 1970–1986 shows the crucial importance of advertising for increased consumption. The overall finding of this study (New Zealand Toxic Substances Board, 1989) is that:

> When countries were grouped according to the degree of government restriction of tobacco promotion, the greater the degree of restriction, the greater average annual fall in tobacco consumption. This was also true for the rate of decrease in the percentage of adults and young people who smoke.

The specific findings of this study present conclusive proof that advertising increases tobacco consumption. The amount consumed per adult fell most rapidly in the group of countries where such advertising had been totally banned and where the ban was imposed for health reasons. It fell next most rapidly where tobacco promotion was banned for political reasons, or was allowed in only a few media. By contrast, tobacco consumption increased markedly in the group of countries where tobacco was promoted in all media. Tobacco is advertised even in countries with a tobacco monopoly, often state-owned, thus indicating that the purpose of advertising is to increase consumption rather than to protect brand share (New Zealand Toxic Substances Board, 1989).

The increase in smoking prevalence among young people and women in a number of countries heightens the concern about tobacco advertising that associates smoking with youth, sport, beauty in nature, sophistication, independence, virility, femininity, and glamour. Studies in Australia indicate that tobacco advertisements probably encourage children to smoke, since "approval of cigarette advertising" was second only to having friends who smoked as the best predictor of whether a child would subsequently smoke (O'Connell, 1981). A survey in the United Kingdom in February 1984 found that children were most aware of cigarette brands frequently associated with sponsored sporting events on television, indicating the importance of this influence on young people (Ledwith, 1984). In 1991, a study in the United States reported that in just three years Old Joe Camel cartoon advertisements (a cartoon camel modelled after a well known fictional television detective and a fictional secret agent) "had an astounding influence on children's smoking behaviour". The proportion of smokers under 18 years of age who chose Camels rose from 0.5% to 32.8%, accounting for an estimated rise in sales from $6 million per year to $476 million per year, representing one-quarter of all Camel sales (Di Franza et al., 1991).

An important factor in the decision of the New Zealand Toxic Substances Board to recommend a total ban on all advertising and promotion of tobacco was its analysis of the effects of such advertising on children's knowledge and attitudes. Having found that 78% of New Zealand children aged 7–15 reported having seen cigarette advertising and that children not only see but remember the advertisements, the Toxic Substances Board commented:

> The question then becomes one of which right takes precedence — that of the tobacco manufacturers to advertise products which have been established as a grave health hazard, or that of young people, and ultimately society as a whole, to be free of social and economic costs of this hazard? (New Zealand Toxic Substances Board, 1989).

Many governments, including those of New Zealand and Western Australia, have specifically rejected the "legal to sell, legal to advertise" argument of the tobacco industry. In many countries it is not legal to sell cigarettes to minors. Certain prescription drugs and other products and services that are legal may not be advertised. But, above all, tobacco, unlike alcohol, has been proven to be harmful even in small doses, and there can therefore be no justification for promoting it.

Tobacco advertising is one of the strongest weapons of the industry. It strikes a double blow at the public's health. First, it conveys the message that it is socially acceptable to smoke and, moreover, that it is pleasurable and sophisticated. By associating tobacco with youth, sport, beauty in nature, and sexuality, tobacco advertising encourages and invites smoking, even though the industry claims that it advertises merely to preserve market share. Second, the substantial revenues that newspapers and magazines receive from tobacco advertising have a marked effect on their editorial policies and deter them from publishing articles on smoking and health. An analysis of women's magazines in the USA revealed that ten leading women's magazines that accept cigarette advertising contained only eight feature articles on smoking and health in more than a decade, although these magazines frequently cover other health-related topics, such as diet, exercise, and skin care. This meagre coverage of a topic so vital to women's health can be contrasted with the record of two magazines that refuse cigarette advertising — *Good housekeeping* and *Seventeen* — which ran 11 and five articles, respectively, on smoking and health (Whelan, 1984; Warner et al., 1986).

An exhaustive survey in 1989 of the policies of the most widely read women's magazines in Europe reported that in 11 countries more than two-thirds of the magazines accepted cigarette advertisements, although many exercised control over the acceptance of advertisements for other products or services, such as alcohol, cosmetic surgery, and pornographic images. Many of the tobacco advertisements were targeted to women, emphasizing the slimness, lightness, and elegance of the brands. Although many editors wanted to inform their readers about the health hazards of tobacco use, half the magazines had failed to cover this issue in the previous year, and the amount of space devoted to it was generally considerably less than that given to tobacco advertisements (Amos, 1990).

The same pattern can be found in magazines aimed at a general readership. A study in the USA of seven years of magazine content after 1970, when cigarette advertisements were banned from television, found that magazines that refused cigarette advertisements, namely *Reader's digest* and *The New Yorker*, carried accurate articles on the link between tobacco and disease (Smith, 1978) but that:

> In magazines that accept cigarette advertising I was unable to find a single article, in several years of publication, that would have given readers any clear notion of the nature and extent of the medical and social havoc wreaked by the cigarette-smoking habit.

Reader's digest, in fact, was punished for a strong article on the medical evidence against tobacco published in July 1957. Later that month, the advertising agency that it had used for 28 years and to which it paid $1.3 million annually, Batten, Barton, Durstine, and Osborn, said that it no longer wanted *Reader's digest* as a client. Another of its clients, the American Tobacco Company, which spent $22 million a year with the agency, had asked the agency to choose between it and the *Reader's digest* (Bagdikian, 1987, p. 171). This policy continues. In 1989, Saatchi and Saatchi, the advertising agency representing Northwest Airlines, the first US airline to become smoke-free, lost its account with R. J. Reynolds because of its representation of a smoke-free airline.

Concern about the influence of the tobacco industry on magazine coverage of the tobacco and health issue is heightened by the industry's diversification into other consumer products. It was reported that a US magazine, the *Saturday Evening Post*, was threatened with loss of non-tobacco advertising because the magazine persisted in covering the subject of smoking and health (Warner et al., 1986; *Smoking and health reporter*, 1985).

With the enactment of restrictions on advertising in many countries, the industry has sought to evade them by placing its name and insignia on other products that indirectly advertise tobacco, e.g., Camel boots in Norway, Camel matches and Marlboro lighters in Belgium, and Camel adventure travel and Marlboro leisure wear in Sweden.

Norwegian legislation prohibits this evasion of its total ban on tobacco advertising by providing that tobacco products may not be included in advertisements for goods and services (Roemer, 1988). Section 8 of Canada's Tobacco Products Control Act of 1988 specifically prohibits the sale or advertising of non-tobacco goods bearing tobacco brand names or trade marks. A minor exception is provided for goods where it can be demonstrated that the retail value of non-tobacco goods sold in 1986 was greater than one-fourth of the value of tobacco products sold retail in the same year. Only Dunhill and a few small companies qualify for this exception. Compliance with this provision is widespread, and there have been no enforcement problems.

This type of evasion of advertising restrictions has occurred in other countries as well. In France, a tobacco company advertised cigarette lighters and matches with the image of the cigarettes on the lighters. In a lawsuit brought to stop this practice, the court held this action to be a violation of Law No. 76-616 of 9 July 1976 concerning measures to combat smoking. The court stated that the advertisement conveyed to the viewer at first sight the well-known brand of cigarettes, and it was irrelevant that the word "Lighters" appeared under the brand name (De Givry, 1984), since:

> slight differences between the object, which is in fact a lighter, and a cigarette packet... cannot be noticed "at first sight" and, for their perception, require a person to stop and examine the poster, which the average observer does not do.

In the Sudan, a billboard advertising lighters under the brand name of a cigarette was placed at the entrance of a training school for nurses in Omdurman, but was subsequently removed (*Tobacco alert*, 1984, 1985).

Increasingly, the tobacco industry seeks to keep its name and products before the public and to promote a positive image by sponsoring and financing sports events and the arts. Thus, in the arts, Philip Morris has supported theatre companies, art galleries, art exhibitions, dance companies, and ballet theatre. In 1983, it donated space in the lobby of its New York building to the "Whitney Museum of American Art at Philip Morris". What does Philip Morris receive in return? As a *New York Times* journalist (Rothstein, 1990) says:

> Philip Morris is of course very concerned about letting the public know about its contributions, so it can build that positive image. As a condition of

many grants, the company's name appears in advertisements, programs, brochures and other literature put out by the arts organizations.

In exchange, though, Philip Morris often provides much more than money. "It follows up with publicity, advertising and entertaining," said Jane Hermann, the executive director of American Ballet Theater. "And in every city we play, they always buy 400 or 500 tickets".

As smoking has declined in the industrialized countries, the transnational tobacco conglomerates have intensified their promotion of cigarettes in developing countries (Lokschin & Barros, 1983; Muller, 1978; Nath, 1986). A study of smoking behaviour and the lack of knowledge of its health effects in Mexico illuminates the serious consequences of tobacco advertising in a Latin American country (Stebbins, 1987).

Marketing strategies in many developing countries are not restricted by legislation. In Kenya, mobile cinemas and billboards saturate the countryside. Radio quiz programmes offer cigarettes with cash prizes (Currie & Ray, 1984). In Pakistan, revenue from cigarette commercials on television and radio increased sixfold between 1976 and 1981 (Yach, 1986). In Malaysia, cigarettes and tobacco products are the largest advertisers of any product category, despite a ban on direct advertising on radio, television, and in cinemas (*Asian advertising review*, 1989). In Hong Kong in 1988, Marlboro spent the largest sum of any advertiser — $10.39 million, a 137% increase over its 1987 figure (*Asian advertising review*, 1989).

The graphic account in *Tobacco control in the Third World* (Chapman & Leng, 1990) of tobacco advertising and promotion in developing countries details the lack of health warnings, the promotion of tobacco sales in famine-torn areas, the brazen targeting of the youth market, the flagrant use of tobacco names and insignia on other products, the use of tobacco-sponsored lotteries to bolster sales and consumption, the pervasiveness of tobacco posters "to brighten up the squalor". Candid statements by tobacco industry representatives can be quoted, such as that by Mike Pavitt, Public Affairs manager of Rothmans Export Ltd (Chapman & Leng, 1990, p. 76):

We're just like any other business. It would be stupid to ignore a growing market. I can't answer the moral dilemma. We are in the business of pleasing our shareholders.

As pointed out in *Tobacco control in the Third World* (Chapman & Leng, 1990, p. 75) :

Tobacco advertising is the industry's frontline in its ambition to increase smoking prevalence and consumption. In many LDCs it represents some of the most blatantly lurid efforts anywhere in the world to associate smoking with dreamlike promises of prestige, power, freedom and luxury.

30

Basic reasons for restricting advertising

Public health advocates support restrictions on tobacco advertising for the same reasons that the tobacco industry spends vast amounts of money on it — because advertising increases sales and consumption of tobacco, encourages smokers to continue, induces young people to start smoking, and creates an atmosphere in which smoking is viewed as socially acceptable.

The principal reason for banning tobacco advertising is to free young people from the pressure to smoke. Forbidding the association of tobacco with sports and cultural events protects children and young people from the subliminal promotion of tobacco. Canada is encouraging people to "Break free for a new generation of non-smokers."

Restrictions on advertising and sponsorship of sports and cultural events are essential to reverse the smoking epidemic among women in the USA and other industrialized countries and to prevent the tobacco industry's assault on women in developing countries. Deploring the fact that lung cancer has become the leading cause of cancer deaths among women in the USA, the US Surgeon General, Dr Antonia Novello (Novello, 1991), indicted tobacco advertising:

> The false images that link smoking with sex appeal and depict smoking as an appetite depressant, a fashion accessory, and an essential component of a good time — all messages delivered by the tobacco industry — have been remarkably "successful". Young girls are smoking more than boys. Women are simply not getting the health message.

Restrictions on advertising free the print media from dependence on revenues from the tobacco industry and allow them to publish information on tobacco and health. Eliminating advertising accords with, and lends credence to, government health education campaigns against smoking and enhances the effectiveness of health promotion by removing counterpersuasion.

Advertising affects the rate at which the smoking habit spreads in a society, and every year that advertising is allowed more people take up smoking (Muller, 1978, p. 49). Since advertising conveys the idea that cigarette smoking is pleasurable and that tobacco is a wholesome, high-quality product, restrictions on advertising are designed to protect consumers against false or misleading advertisements and against publicity that creates false values and harms the public's health. The ultimate goal of restrictions on advertising is to help make smoking socially unacceptable and to contribute to the creation of a smoke-free society.

Total ban on advertising of tobacco products

The foregoing evidence on the effects of advertising on tobacco consumption and knowledge of the numbers of tobacco-related deaths have led increasing numbers of countries to enact total bans on all advertising of tobacco products. As of 1 January 1991, such legislation was in force in 27 countries (see Annex 1). As pointed out by the New Zealand Toxic Substances Board, bans on tobacco advertising have been enacted for health, political, trade, and religious reasons. But, regardless of the motivation for the restriction, these laws benefit the public's health (New Zealand Toxic Substances Board, 1989).

In the early 1970s, Finland, Iceland and Norway were the first countries to enact total bans on tobacco advertising for health reasons. Singapore's ban, introduced in 1970 under the Prohibition of Smoking in Certain Places Act, was almost total. As already mentioned in Chapter 2, Spain in 1982 and Portugal in 1983 replaced their moderate controls on advertising with a virtually total ban (Spain allows advertising for new low-tar, low-nicotine tobacco products for two years after their introduction on the market). Canada in 1988 and New Zealand in 1990 are the first English-speaking countries to adopt legislation outlawing both advertising and sponsorship. On 10 January 1991, France enacted landmark legislation, effective 1 January 1993, prohibiting all advertising and sponsorship of tobacco and tobacco products and imposing stringent limitations on the promotion of alcoholic beverages.

On 1 April 1992, the Australian Federal Cabinet resolved to phase out tobacco advertising and sponsorship throughout the country. This resolution is expected to be approved by the Parliament in August 1992, and complements action taken by the various states and the Capital Territory. The legislation of the states and the Capital Territory had been deficient in not being able to control national and international tobacco-sponsored events that crossed state boundaries.

According to the analysis of the New Zealand Toxic Substances Board, legislation prohibiting tobacco advertising was undertaken at first for various reasons. In eight countries of eastern Europe there was no advertising of consumables, including tobacco. In China, tobacco advertising was formerly non-existent and the situation began to change only in the 1980s. In China (Province of Taiwan), Italy, and Thailand, tobacco advertising was prohibited originally for reasons of trade, and in Algeria, Iraq, Jordan, Mozambique, and the Sudan originally for religious reasons (New Zealand Toxic Substances Board, 1989). But as active anti-tobacco programmes are being developed in these countries, the ban on advertising lends credibility and strength to their activities.

While, as already mentioned, 27 countries ban all advertising of tobacco products, only 18 restrict sponsorship of sports and cultural events by the tobacco industry. To meet the objection that sports and the arts depend on financial support by this industry, the State of Victoria in Australia pioneered an innovative strategy, now being adopted by other Australian states, namely that of imposing a state tax on tobacco to "buy out" the tobacco industry's sponsorship of sports events. In Victoria, taxes on cigarettes were increased by 50 cents a pack, with the proviso that 30% of the increased revenue be allocated to replacing the tobacco industry's sponsorship of sports events, 30% to health promotion, 10% to research, and 30% to other uses. The Victoria legislation provides for a percentage increase in the tobacco tax, which has remained constant, so that the Victorian Health Promotion Foundation, established under the Tobacco Act 1987, is protected against erosion of the income from the tax by inflation. An account of the passage of this legislation (Raw et al., 1990) concludes:

> Where top politicians used to attend sports events as the guests of the tobacco sponsors, they are now guests of the Anti-Cancer Council of Victoria.

Two other Australian states — South Australia and Western Australia — have adopted the strategy pioneered by the State of Victoria. The Western Australia Tobacco Control Act 1990 establishes the Health Promotion Foundation of Western Australia to provide alternative funds for sporting and artistic activities formerly sponsored by the tobacco industry. It will also support a wide range of sporting, recreational, and artistic activities to advance health-promotion campaigns and encourage healthy lifestyles. It will give grants to community organizations to promote good health, and fund research related to health promotion. Financing for the Health Promotion Foundation will be derived from substantial government funding that has been committed and from an increase in the state tobacco licence fee from 35% to 50% of the wholesale and retail value of tobacco products sold. The tobacco industry spends an estimated A $1.5–1.7 million annually on the sponsorship of sports and cultural events in Western Australia alone, but, as the Honorable K. Wilson, Minister for Health of Western Australia, said (Wilson, 1990):

> The Foundation will have much more money available to it than is required solely for replacement of cigarette sponsorship. This will provide a remarkable opportunity for sporting, cultural, community, and health organisations to seek new funding for worthwhile projects.

The New Zealand Smoke-free Environments Act of 1990 also institutionalizes the idea of replacing funding of sports and the arts formerly provided by the tobacco industry, although with some exceptions for multinational events, as discussed later. The Act establishes a Health Sponsorship Council, which is required to provide alternative sponsorship and financial assistance for two or possibly three years to persons deprived of financial or other assistance from manufacturers, importers, or distributors of tobacco products because of the legal ban on sponsorship by the tobacco industry.

In some countries sponsorship by the tobacco industry has been banned even in the absence of replacement funding. In Ireland, the Tobacco Products (Control of Advertising, Sponsorship and Sales Promotion) (No. 2) Regulations of 1986 provide that an event that was not sponsored by the tobacco industry prior to 1 May 1986 may not now be sponsored. In France, the Law of 10 January 1991 on measures to combat tobacco use and alcoholism provides for a total ban on all sponsorship of tobacco and tobacco products. By deferring the effective date for full implementation of the law until 1 January 1993, as previously mentioned, the Law allows time for organizations to adjust to this restriction.

Only a few countries — Bolivia, Canada, Finland, France, Iceland, Ireland, New Zealand, Norway, and Portugal, for example — have enacted legislation specifically prohibiting the indirect advertising of tobacco products by placing the name or insignia of tobacco products on other goods and services — a strategy widely used by the tobacco industry to evade restrictions on advertising. In Finland, in order to ban such indirect advertising, an amendment to the Tobacco Act of 1976 has been proposed that would require those seeking an inspection certificate necessary to market tobacco products to certify that the name of the tobacco product and other wording or features on the retail package do not refer to the name or other distinctive feature of any well-known product (T. Piha, personal communication, 1990).

It may be helpful, before turning to countries that have enacted strong partial bans on tobacco advertising, to examine in more detail the recent legislation of Canada, New Zealand, and France providing for a total ban on the advertising and promotion of tobacco products.

The purpose of the Canadian Tobacco Products Control Act of 1988, as stated in Section 3, is:

> ... to provide a legislative response to a national public health problem of substantial and pressing concern and, in particular,

(a) to protect the health of Canadians in the light of conclusive evidence implicating tobacco use in the incidence of numerous debilitating and fatal diseases;

(b) to protect young persons and others, to the extent that is reasonable in a free and democratic society, from inducements to use tobacco products and consequent dependence on them; and

(c) to enhance public awareness of the hazards of tobacco use by ensuring the effective communication of pertinent information to consumers of tobacco products.

The Act prohibits print, media, broadcasting, and billboard tobacco advertising; allows signs at the place of sale only until 1993; reduces billboards and transit posters by one-third of their dollar value annually to 1991; limits expenditure on the sponsorship of sports and cultural events to what was spent in 1987 and stipulates that only the corporate name may be used (no visual depictions of tobacco products or related trade marks are allowed); prohibits the free distribution of tobacco products; and prohibits tobacco trade marks on non-tobacco products. The Act is designed to phase out tobacco advertising gradually but completely.

The one exception is that sports and cultural events can continue to be sponsored by tobacco companies in their full corporate name only, provided that no tobacco advertising or imagery is used. Tobacco companies have taken advantage of this provision by creating shell corporations, named after major tobacco brand families. As a result, Canadians now watch the Player's Ltd Tennis Tournament and the Benson and Hedges Inc. Fireworks Festival. Major national health organizations state that the effectiveness of the Tobacco Products Control Act has been somewhat undermined as a result (Collishaw et al., 1990).

The tobacco industry fought the legislation strenuously and, as mentioned previously, has brought lawsuits to declare the Canada Tobacco Products Control Act invalid as a violation of the Canadian Charter of Rights and Freedoms (Department of the Secretary of State of Canada, 1987). On 26 July 1991, the Quebec Superior Court held the Tobacco Products Control Act unconstitutional as not within the power of the Federal Government but within provincial jurisdiction and as a violation of the provisions for commercial freedom of expression in the Charter. On 14 August 1991, the Canadian Government filed an appeal to the Quebec Court of Appeal. (See also Chapter 13, pp. 146–147)

The New Zealand Smoke-free Environments Act of 1990 was adopted after careful study by the Toxic Substances Board. The Board considered other policy options, such as health advertising to counter tobacco advertising, disallowance of tobacco advertising as a tax-deductible item, and further controls on advertising content, but concluded that a partial ban would have little effect on consumption and that only a total ban was likely to reduce it significantly. The study of tobacco-promotion policies and consumption trends in 33 countries during the period 1970–1986, commissioned by the Board, was critical in the decision to recommend the elimination of all forms of tobacco advertising and promotion and to set December 1990 as the date by which such action should take effect.

Accordingly, the New Zealand Act provides for a general prohibition of the advertising of tobacco products, with a few exemptions, such as foreign publications and retailers' displays. Use of tobacco product trade marks and brand names on goods other than tobacco products and in relation to sponsored events is prohibited. The sponsorship of a cultural, educational, sporting, or recreational activity or event by any manufacturer, importer, distributor, or retailer of tobacco products in New Zealand is prohibited. As mentioned previously, the Act establishes a Health Sponsorship Council to promote health and healthy lifestyles and to provide alternative sponsorship and financial assistance to replace tobacco industry sponsorship and support (Beaglehole, 1991).

Unfortunately, six months after the passage of the Act, the New Zealand Parliament amended it to exempt from the ban the sponsorship of multinational events, defined as those in which at least three countries participate, one of which is New Zealand. Tobacco advertising as such is still banned, and the ban on the advertising of sponsorship applies to all events other than multinational and international yachting events (the latter were exempted in the original legislation). At the time of writing, a bill is before the New Zealand Parliament that seeks to repeal all provisions banning the advertising of sponsorship but that contains new provisions concerning health warnings on signs and billboards advertising sponsorship.

In France, the law on measures to combat smoking and alcoholism, enacted on 10 January 1991, replaces as of 1993 Law No. 76-616 of 9 July 1976 providing for the strict control of tobacco advertising and will impose a total and sweeping prohibition of all direct and indirect advertising and the sponsorship of events by the manufacturers of tobacco and tobacco products. The background to the passage of this comprehensive legislation is provided by the report of the Commission on Cultural, Family and Social Affairs of the National Assembly, presented at the first reading of the bill. The Commission's report proclaimed a "public health imperative" in view of the 61 000 deaths in France, or 12% of total mortality, directly related to tobacco in 1985 (Commission des Affaires Culturelles, Familiales et Sociales, 1990). Although the report noted a 7% decline in smoking by young people from 1977 to 1988, it contained alarming statistics: 32.5% of adolescents between the ages of 12 and 18 smoke — 1.5 million young people; each year 250 000 young people between the ages of 15 and 16 begin smoking, of whom 70 000–80 000 will die of cancer between ages 45 and 50; the smoking habit is being acquired at younger and younger ages (65% of smokers began before age 13, 90% before age 20). In the light of the mixed messages that young people receive from anti-tobacco campaigns, on the one hand, and from seductive advertising associating tobacco with pleasure, success, and virility, on the other, the Report to the National Assembly states that this situation alone justifies legislative intervention.

In addition, the Law of 1976, although strengthened by Law No. 89-18 of 13 January 1989, which imposed further restrictions on advertising, was neither obeyed nor enforced. The National Assembly therefore elected to impose a total ban on all advertising, promotion, and sponsorship. A transitional period is allowed until the Law is fully implemented in 1993 in order to permit the various sectors to adjust to the ban. During the transition period, the definition of indirect advertising is expanded, a health warning is required on all advertising, and the amount of space in the print media allowed for tobacco advertising is reduced annually.

This landmark legislation is of immense significance for the fight against the tobacco epidemic. For 14 years, from 1976 to 1990, France had strong legislation restricting tobacco advertising, which was neither adequate nor adequately implemented to prevent young people from taking up smoking. A clear, unambiguous law was required if the smoking epidemic was to be curbed. This legislation also marks an innovative step in the advance of health promotion and public health. It is one of the few laws to address smoking and alcohol consumption in a single legislative approach. Although the restrictions on the advertising of alcoholic beverages are designed to prevent the abuse of alcohol, while the total ban on tobacco advertising is aimed at eliminating tobacco use altogether, the strategy of using similar legislative procedures to deal with these two problems is an important contribution to the use of law to establish public policy giving priority to people's health.

In Sweden, tobacco advertising has long been limited to the "tombstone" format, a rectangular design containing only the name, company, tar level, and price of the tobacco product, with no pictorial or theme advertising. In March 1990, legislation proposed by the Committee on Tobacco Control, appointed by the Minister of Health and Social Affairs, would impose a total ban on all forms of tobacco advertising, direct and indirect. Inside tobacco shops factual information on prices, tar levels, etc., would be available to consumers. Tobacco products, brand names, and trademarks would not be displayed in shop windows or outside points of sale, except that generic terms, such as "tobacco" or "cigarettes", could be printed on signs outside the shops. A total ban would be imposed on all forms of advertising in all media, on posters, and other outdoor advertising, direct mail advertising, free samples, and sponsorship of sports and cultural events by the tobacco industry. The advertising or promotion of non-tobacco products would not be permitted·to include depictions of tobacco products or to be designed in a way that would promote the sale of such products (Swedish Committee for Tobacco Control, 1990).

Partial ban on advertising of tobacco products

Legislation providing for a strong partial ban on the advertising of tobacco products has been enacted in Australia, Argentina, Belgium, Bolivia, Egypt, Gambia, Ireland, Luxembourg, Senegal, Spain, and Sweden. Such legislation generally limits advertising to the "tombstone" format, including only the name and address of the manufacturer, importer, or distributor, the brand name and symbol of the product, tar and nicotine levels, information on price and quality, and a health warning.

For example, in Belgium, the Crown Order of 5 March 1980 banned all advertising of tobacco and tobacco products on radio and television, in films and other visual projection in public places, on signs and billboards, except in places where tobacco products are normally sold, and by illuminated signs either within or outside places where such products are sold. Also forbidden are the house-to-house distribution of leaflets advertising tobacco, oral public promotional statements, the free distribution of tobacco samples, the use of the brand emblem of tobacco products on items not related to tobacco, and all promotion in publications for children. The representation of public figures is forbidden, as are excerpts from scientific texts or texts having any relation to health. Competitions or sporting events may not be organized in association with tobacco advertising. The advertising of each brand is restricted to a half-page in newspapers and one page in periodicals, and all advertisements must carry a health warning. On 10 April 1990, the legislation was strengthened to prohibit other forms of publicity and marketing practices, to ban all advertising aimed at minors, and to restrict advertising to the "tombstone" format (see Annex 1, note to Table D1).

In Egypt, Law No. 52 of 20 June 1981 prohibits all advertising or promotion of the sale of cigarettes or other tobacco products by state agencies, public corporate bodies, public sector units, cinemas, theatres, and sports clubs. It limits advertisements for cigarettes and tobacco products to the shape, contents, and price of the package and requires the warning, "Smoking is very harmful to health" to be displayed conspicuously in all advertisements.

In 1978, Bolivia enacted a new Health Code under which all advertising is prohibited that encourages tobacco consumption on grounds of well-being or health, as well as the use of children or adolescents in advertisements or the association of tobacco in advertisements with sporting, domestic, or occupational situations.

On 3 October 1989, the Council of Ministers of the European Communities adopted Directive 89/552/EEC banning all forms of advertising of cigarettes and tobacco products on television. Although the European Commission had proposed a Directive to limit the advertising of tobacco products in the press and by means of bills and posters, allowing only the representation of the package and the inclusion of certain facts concerning the product and requiring health warnings, by December 1990 the Council of Health Ministers had not reached a common position on further restrictions on the advertising of tobacco products (*BASP Newsletter*, 1990a,b). The action plan of the European Communities for 1990–1994 includes a proposal for regulating the advertising of tobacco products.

Two arguments have been offered in support of strong partial bans that prohibit pictorial or theme advertising of cigarettes. One contends that such bans do not interfere with commercial free speech, since tobacco companies are allowed to advertise the name and characteristics of their products. The other is that such a strong partial ban eliminates a powerful influence on young people, whereas "tombstone" advertisements, which would still be allowed, are of interest mainly to confirmed smokers.

Many countries have imposed restrictions on the content of tobacco advertising (see Annex 1). In the USA, where the free speech argument is most strongly urgUd, the US Supreme Court has upheld a restriction on commercial speech as justified by the public interest (*Posadas de Puerto Rico Associates, DBA Condado Holiday Inn* v. *Tourism Company of Puerto Rico et al.*, 1986). Commercial speech is less protected than other speech, a principle that should govern the promotion of a product as harmful as tobacco. Concerning "tombstone" advertising, one should note that partial restrictions require personnel and other resources for enforcement — resources that are often in short supply. Most importantly, the evidence from the New Zealand Toxic Substances Board, discussed above, shows that, for a ban on advertising to reduce tobacco consumption significantly, total prohibition of all advertising and promotion is necessary.

Many countries have adopted moderate partial bans on advertising. The legislation generally prohibits advertising on television and radio, and may require inclusion of a health warning, restrict sponsorship of sporting events, and prohibit the association of tobacco with healthy activities or successful achievements.

The tables in Annex 1 contain many examples of countries that have enacted moderate partial bans on tobacco advertising. For example, the United States of America prohibits advertising in the electronic media, but advertising with rotating health warnings is allowed in the print media and on billboards. No restrictions are imposed on the sponsorship of sports and the arts by the tobacco industry, and no health warnings appear on advertisements for ballet performances in which sponsorship by the tobacco industry is publicized.

The limited federal legislation in the USA restricting tobacco advertising has led local authorities to impose controls on advertising in areas under their jurisdiction. Sports stadia in several large cities have restricted tobacco advertising. The public transportation systems of the cities of Denver, New York, San Francisco and Seattle ban or restrict tobacco advertisements in buses, streetcars, subways, and public transport stations. In San Francisco, the impetus for the ban came from an organization, Parents Opposing Addictive Drug Advertising, concerned about the mixed messages children receive from cigarette advertising encouraging use of tobacco, on the one hand, and from injunctions not to use drugs, on the other. About 28 000 youth passes are sold by the San Francisco Municipal Railway system each month (Lev, 1991).

Ordinance No. 58 of 1982 of Hong Kong provides that cigarette advertising in printed publications must carry the Government health warning and the tar group designation of the cigarettes; certain exceptions are permitted in material printed outside Hong Kong. Advertisements on television and radio must comply with the restrictions on time and content specified by the Codes of Practice of the Television Ordinance. A bare two years after the enactment of these provisions, the Government of Hong Kong moved to consider a complete ban on tobacco advertising. Strong opposition from the Tobacco Institute of Hong Kong, formed in 1983, delayed action until 1986, when the Government announced the introduction of a three-stage ban on tobacco advertising on television and radio, culminating in a total ban on such advertising in December 1990. In March 1990 the Government announced that, by December 1991, it would extend the ban on advertising in the electronic media to include cinemas and require rotating health warnings in tobacco advertising on billboards, public transport vehicles, and external signboards to be displayed conspicuously.

Although some gains have been made in strengthening the moderate partial ban on tobacco advertising, the Hong Kong Government has rejected a total ban as an unacceptable interference with the print media and an infringement of property rights. The proposal to introduce a levy on tobacco to provide alternative financing of sports and the arts in place of tobacco sponsorship has been rejected as not in accordance with Hong Kong's fiscal system (Hong Kong Council on Smoking and Health, 1990). In contrast to the Government's position is the view expressed by Dr Judith Mackay, Director of the Asian Consultancy on Tobacco Control, that the freedom of children to grow up in a society without commercial pressure to smoke is more important than that of a vested commercial interest to promote a product that kills one-quarter of the people who use it (Mackay, 1986).

The need for enforcement

Once legislation has been enacted, there is a need for constant, vigilant enforcement of the law. Finnish experience illustrates this need. Law No. 693 of 13 August 1976 on measures to reduce smoking was one of the first laws banning tobacco advertising. Sections 8 and 9 provide that:

> Advertising of tobacco, tobacco products and imitations and also smokers' requisites and other sales promotion activity directed at the consumer, together with their conjunction with advertising for other products or services or other sales promoting activity, is forbidden.

> The linking of tobacco, tobacco products and imitations, and smokers' requisites to the sale or transfer of other products or to the performance of services is prohibited.

In the mid-1980s, the National Board of Health of Finland encountered increasing problems in enforcing the Law as the tobacco industry tried out new forms of sale and promotion. In 1988, the Board banned two tobacco company image advertising campaigns, and its action was sustained by the Finnish Supreme Court. In 1989, the Board banned media activities linked to a sophisticated sports sponsorship campaign for Belmont cigarettes, a decision that was not appealed. But in 1990 the Finnish Supreme Court, by a vote of 4 to 3, reversed a decision of the National Board of Health to ban the advertising (but not the sale) of Marlboro Classics men's wear. In view of this experience the first significant amendments to the

Finnish Law of 1976 are being proposed in order to restrict indirect advertising and media publicity for sports sponsorship (T. Piha, personal communication, 1990).

General experience

Experience with different types of legislation restricting tobacco advertising and promotion leads to several conclusions:

1. Legislation is essential. Voluntary agreements with the industry fail to restrict the promotion of tobacco products. The example of New Zealand has sounded the death knell of such agreements. In 1983, the New Zealand Department of Health, after having negotiated on tobacco advertising with the industry for a decade, notified the Health and Welfare Committee of Parliament that it supported in principle a total ban on all tobacco advertising. In May 1989, the New Zealand Toxic Substances Board issued its definitive report analysing the conditions in New Zealand and the impact of restrictions on tobacco advertising in 33 countries. The report called for the elimination of all tobacco advertising and promotion by December 1990. By that date, the New Zealand Parliament acted to ban all tobacco advertising and promotion. All countries with voluntary agreements with the tobacco industry must take account of the experience of New Zealand and of other countries that have found such agreements unsatisfactory (see Chapter 1). Legislation restricting tobacco advertising is an essential component of a comprehensive tobacco-control programme.

2. Partial bans on tobacco advertising are not effective in controlling tobacco consumption. Even strong partial bans are easily evaded. They permit the industry to shift resources to other forms of advertising that may still be allowed and particularly to sponsorship of sports and the arts. Annex 4, reprinted from the report of the New Zealand Toxic Substances Board, shows the annual average rates of change in tobacco consumption per adult, according to the advertising restrictions in force. The countries with a partial ban on tobacco promotion for health reasons had low rates of reduction in consumption. A rigorous regression analysis of tobacco pricing and advertising controls in 22 countries of the Organisation for Economic Co-operation and Development over 26 years revealed that the higher the prices and the

more stringent the advertising controls, the greater the decline in tobacco consumption (Laugesen & Meads, 1990).

3. A total ban on both advertising and sponsorship is essential if tobacco consumption is to be reduced significantly and quickly. In 1979, the report of the WHO Expert Committee on Smoking Control called for the total prohibition of all forms of tobacco promotion (World Health Organization, 1979). In 1990, the World Health Assembly reiterated the appeal for "progressive restrictions and concerted actions to eliminate eventually all direct and indirect advertising, promotion and sponsorship concerning tobacco" (resolution WHA43.16) (see Annex 2). It has long been clear that allowing the advertising and promotion of tobacco suggests that smoking is acceptable social behaviour, whereas eliminating it contributes to making non-smoking the norm. No longer are strong restrictions on advertising deemed adequate. In a press release issued at its fourth Executive Committee Meeting, held in Hong Kong on 9–11 January 1991, the Asia Pacific Association for the Control of Tobacco (APACT) called for total bans on all forms of advertising, sponsorship, and other promotion of tobacco products. The European Conference on Tobacco Policy, held in Madrid in 1988, urged countries to "outlaw the advertising and promotion of tobacco products and sponsorship by the tobacco industry" (World Health Organization, 1990b).

"It can be done" became the slogan of the Madrid Conference. And it *has* been done in 27 countries.

Chapter 4

Health warnings and statement of tar and nicotine content

> In 1984 a new system of rotating health warnings was introduced in Norway. Each brand has to carry 12 different warnings which are distributed equally between the packets sent out on the market. The Tobacco Act gave the Ministry of Health the authority to introduce this provision. We have now taken steps to design a new set of warnings with as strong texts as those used in Sweden, and with a similar illustrative design as in Iceland.
>
> Kjell Bjartveit, MD, National Council on Tobacco and Health, Oslo, Norway, "Fifteen years of comprehensive legislation: results and conclusions", *Tobacco and health 1990: the global war. Proceedings of the Seventh World Conference on Tobacco and Health, Perth, Western Australia*, 1990.

Mandatory health warnings on cigarette packages and tobacco advertising are a form of health information aimed at alerting the public to the dangers of smoking and use of tobacco. France requires a health warning, in addition, in sales promotion activities. As of 1991, 77 countries in the world required health warnings, but most of them (48) merely require a statement that smoking is injurious to health — a traditional warning so familiar and hackneyed that it hardly attracts the attention of the smoker any more.

Following the example pioneered by Sweden, however, increasing numbers of countries are adopting strong, rotating warnings that capture the attention of the smoker. In all, 27 countries or territories now require rotating or strong warnings — one in the African Region of WHO, six in the Region of the Americas, five in the Eastern Mediterranean Region, 11 in the European Region, one in the South-East Asia Region, and three in the Western Pacific Region.

Iceland increases the effectiveness of the warning with pictures, a strategy that was also approved by both Norway and Sweden. In Sweden, on 9 January 1991 the National Board of Health and Welfare approved a new set of strengthened warnings with pictures, contained in an enlarged "text box" (5 cm wide instead of the previous 2 cm). Four tobacco companies filed complaints against the new warnings, alleging violation of freedom of the press and trade mark law and pointing out that the new texts were not in accord with the warnings contained in the directive of the European Communities of 13 November 1989. The National Board of Health and Welfare rejected these arguments, but on 19 December 1991 the Swedish Cabinet nullified the new warnings on the sole ground that the texts differed from those in the directive of the European Communities. The Cabinet did not criticize the decision of the National Board of Health and Welfare in any way, nor did it comment on the industry arguments concerning freedom of the press and trade mark law. It is significant, however, that Sweden is applying for full membership in the European Community (M. Haglund, personal communication, 1992).

Thus, although the directive of the European Communities was designed to provide a "high level of health protection" and should be interpreted as specifying the minimum warnings required, it has served to undermine in one country more advanced warnings that were not envisaged at the time that the directive was adopted. The concerted opposition of the industry to the strengthened Swedish warnings indicates that strong health warnings are an important weapon in the fight to control tobacco use.

A further form of publicity for the harmful effects of tobacco is a statement of the tar and nicotine content of cigarettes. In 41 countries or territories, such a statement is required on cigarette packages and in some cases in advertising.

Basic reasons for health warnings

The rationale for health warnings and indications of tar and nicotine content is closely related to health education. The reasons for this type of legislation are as follows:

— to alert the public to the health hazards of tobacco use;

— to serve as the basis or starting point for a health education programme;

— to put the weight of the government and the health authorities behind a smoking-control policy and thus to assist the movement towards a smoke-free society.

These reasons for mandatory health warnings in advertising and for labels to provide information on the content of harmful substances have become more compelling as rotating warnings and other innovations in the presentation of warnings have provided more effective messages. But health warnings cannot, of course, be a substitute for a comprehensive health education programme for children or for public information for the people as a whole. Such warnings can, however, serve to reinforce educational programmes.

Nor should the statement of tar and nicotine content and carbon monoxide yield imply that cigarettes with low tar, nicotine, or carbon monoxide yields are safe. For some time, evidence has been available that smokers of low-yield cigarettes do not consume less nicotine because they tend to compensate for the reduction in yield by increasing the number of cigarettes smoked (Benowitz et al., 1983; Maron & Fortmann, 1987).

Contents of health warnings and legislative provisions

A number of innovations have characterized the development of health warnings on tobacco products, but the most dramatic development has been the replacement by increasing numbers of countries of the familiar warning, "Smoking is harmful to health, " by strong, rotating warnings. Here are some examples of such warnings:

Arab States of the Gulf Area	Smoking is a leading cause of lung cancer and of pulmonary and cardiovascular diseases.
Australia	Smoking causes lung cancer Smoking causes heart disease. Smoking damages your lungs. Smoking reduces fitness.
Canada	Smoking reduces life expectancy. Smoking is the major cause of lung cancer. Smoking is a major cause of heart disease. Smoking during pregnancy can harm the baby.
Chile	Tobacco may cause cancer.
Costa Rica	Smoking during pregnancy damages the child and causes premature births. Smoking produces lung cancer, heart disease, and emphysema.

France
> Smoking causes cancer.
> Smoking causes cardiovascular diseases.
> Pregnant women: smoking harms your child's health.
> Smoking harms those around you.
> For good health, don't smoke.

Iceland
> See Fig. A5.1, Annex 5.

Ireland
> Smoking causes cancer.
> Smokers die young.
> Smoking kills!

New Zealand
> Smoking causes lung cancer.
> Smoking causes heart disease.
> Smoking causes fatal illnesses.
> Smoking damages the lungs.

Norway
> See Fig. A5.2, Annex 5.

Singapore
> Smoking causes heart disease.
> Smoking causes cancer.
> Smoking damages your lungs.
> Smoking harms those around us.

Sweden
> Annex 5 (Fig. A5.3) contains the health warnings in effect in 1992. The strengthened warnings adopted by the National Board of Health and Welfare, but vetoed by the Swedish Cabinet on 19 December 1991 as described above, included some short and clear texts, e.g., "Smoking kills more than 20 people a day in Sweden" and "Eight out of ten patients with cancer of the larynx are smokers." Other texts were longer and contained new information, e.g., "Smoking is addictive. Nicotine makes you physically dependent in a way similar to that of heroin or cocaine." (European Bureau for Action on Smoking Prevention, 1991).

Thailand
> Smoking causes lung cancer and emphysema.
> Smoking causes ischaemic heart disease.
> Smoking is dangerous for babies in the womb.
> Please respect the right of non-smokers by refraining from smoking in public places.
> Stopping smoking decreases the risk of health hazards. For your beloved children and grandchildren please give up smoking.

United Kingdom (by voluntary agreement with the industry)
> Smoking can cause fatal diseases.
> Smoking can cause heart disease.
> Smoking when pregnant can injure your baby and cause premature birth.
> Stopping smoking reduces the risk of serious diseases.
> Smoking can cause lung cancer, bronchitis and other chest diseases.
> More than 30,000 people die each year in the UK from lung cancer.

48

USA   Smoking causes lung cancer, heart disease, emphysema, and may complicate pregnancy.
Quitting smoking now greatly reduces serious risks to your health.
Smoking by pregnant women may result in fetal injury, premature birth, and low birth weight.
Cigarette smoke contains carbon monoxide.

In Europe, the Council Directive of the European Communities 89/622/EEC requires both a general warning — "Tobacco seriously damages health" — on all tobacco products and a strong, specific, alternating warning taken from a prescribed list. The warnings are to be rotated so as to guarantee the appearance of each warning on an equal number of unit packets, with a tolerance of approximately 5%.

A subsequent Council Directive 92/41/EEC extends requirements for health warnings to tobacco for oral use and requires unit packets of smokeless tobacco products to carry the specific warning, "Causes cancer". It specifies that rolling-tobacco products (tobacco that the consumer uses to roll his or her own cigarettes) must carry the same specific, alternating warnings as cigarette packages. The list of prescribed warnings is as follows:

A. Warnings that must be included on the national lists:

1. Smoking causes cancer.
2. Smoking causes heart disease.

B. Warnings from among which Member States may choose:

1. Smoking causes fatal diseases.
2. Smoking kills.
3. Smoking can kill.
4. Smoking when pregnant harms your baby.
5. Protect children: don't make them breathe your smoke.
6. Smoking damages the health of those around you.
7. Stopping smoking reduces the risk of serious disease.
8. Smoking causes cancer, chronic bronchitis and other chest diseases.
9. More than ... people die each year in ... (name of country) of lung cancer.
10. Every year, ... people are killed in road accidents in ... (name of country) — ... times more die from their addiction to smoking.
11. Every year, addiction to smoking claims more victims than road accidents.
12. Smokers die younger.
13. Don't smoke if you want to stay healthy.
14. Save money: stop smoking.
15. Smoking causes addiction.

Unit packets of cigars, cigarillos, pipe tobacco, and other smoking products (other than cigarettes and rolling tobacco) are required to carry one of the following specific, alternating warnings:

1. Smoking causes cancer.
2. Smoking causes fatal diseases.
3. Smoking damages the health of those around you.
4. Smoking causes heart disease.

A number of items of legislation provide that the warnings must be displayed prominently on cigarette packages. For example, the Canadian warnings are required to be prominently displayed in contrasting colours and to occupy 20% of the area of each of the front and back of the package, in English on one side and in French on the other. Health warnings are also required on the two faces of cigarette cartons. Canada also requires warnings on packages of cigarette tobacco, pipe tobacco, and cigars (Canadian Department of National Health and Welfare, 1989). Proposed revisions to the regulations would increase the number of warnings in use from four to eight, require that they be in black and white, and also that they be positioned at the top of the package and occupy at least 25% of each of the front and back surfaces of it. Under these proposed revisions, warnings would also be required on all six faces of cigarette cartons (Canadian Department of National Health and Welfare, 1990).

Research in Australia undertaken before rotating warnings were adopted found that, for maximum effect, warnings should be in large letters, contain few words, be on the back rather than on the side panels of packages, in colours contrasting with those of the package, and be surrounded by a black border (M.M. Daube, personal communication, 1991).

In view of the importance of package design in promoting tobacco products, the Seventh World Conference on Tobacco and Health endorsed the concept of mandatory generic (plain-wrap) packaging of all tobacco products, and urged all countries to require generic packaging in their tobacco-control legislation (Durston & Jamrozik, 1990, p. 966).

The size of health warnings on billboards is also important. In India, huge billboards advertise tobacco; the warnings are placed in the margin and are minute and virtually illegible. The relatively small warnings on billboards in the USA are similarly illegible.

Both Canada and New Zealand have pioneered the innovation of establishing the legislative authority to require leaflets giving detailed information on the health effects of tobacco to be inserted inside each cigarette package. Similar to inserts in packages of prescription drugs, these leaflets would be designed to provide more information than can be presented in a mere warning. Neither country has yet chosen to make use of this legislative authority, however, although a proposal has been made in Canada to require leaflets in packages.

The National Board of Health and Welfare of Sweden has proposed that accounts of typical smoking-related deaths and illnesses be printed on the outside of cartons of cigarettes, but the decision of the Swedish Cabinet to nullify the strengthened warnings has prevented this proposal from becoming law.

The Canadian Tobacco Products Control Act of 31 May 1988 also addresses an issue that has arisen in tobacco liability suits in the USA, namely whether the existence of health warnings relieves the tobacco company of liability for damage caused by an inherently dangerous product (see Chapter 13). The Canadian legislation explicitly states that the health warnings required by law do not exempt tobacco companies from any further liability they may have under common law or any provincial law.

In the 1980s, recognition of the danger of oral cancer caused by the use of smokeless tobacco led a number of countries to ban its importation and sale, as discussed in Chapter 10. Other countries enacted legislation to require health warnings on snuff and smokeless tobacco. In the WHO Region of the Americas, both Canada and the USA require health warnings on smokeless tobacco, and in the European Region health warnings on smokeless tobacco are required in Greece, Iceland, Luxembourg, and Sweden. The Swedish warning states that snuff and smokeless tobacco contain nicotine and therefore may be as addictive as tobacco. One of the following warnings is required in the USA:

> This product may cause mouth cancer.
> This product may cause gum disease and tooth loss.
> This product is not a safe alternative to cigarettes.

A comprehensive analysis of smokeless tobacco — its chemical constituents, health effects, prevalence, patterns, and trends, and control strategies — led the WHO Study Group on Smokeless Tobacco Control (World Health Organization, 1988) to recommend, among other measures, legislation to require rotating warnings on the products themselves and also on all promotional material, the latter warnings to be prominently displayed at the point of sale. Suggested warnings (World Health Organization, 1988, p. 50) include the following:

> Smokeless tobacco causes mouth cancer.
> Smokeless tobacco is addictive.
> Smokeless tobacco causes gum and mouth disease.
> Smokeless tobacco is not a safe alternative to cigarette smoking.
> Smokeless tobacco kills.
> For better health, stop using smokeless tobacco.

51

Package labelling of harmful substances

Although the number of countries requiring a statement of the tar and nicotine contents on cigarette packages has grown, in many areas of the world such legislation is rare. For example, only three Latin American countries — Ecuador, Mexico, and Uruguay — require the disclosure of tar and nicotine contents. In Uruguay, Law No. 15361 of 24 December 1982 requires manufacturers and importers of cigarettes to publish the tar and nicotine contents of each brand once every three months in the major advertising media — hardly an effective method of informing smokers of the tar and nicotine yields of the brands they smoke.

Elsewhere in the Americas, two jurisdictions — Bermuda, and Trinidad and Tobago — require statements of tar content. In Trinidad and Tobago, the indication of both the average nicotine content and the tar group on cigarette packages is encouraged by voluntary standards. Regulations of the Bureau of Standards specify that low-tar cigarettes are those with less than 10 mg of tar per cigarette, medium-tar those with between 10 mg and 18 mg, and high-tar those with 18 mg and above. These standards apply only to cigarettes manufactured in Trinidad and Tobago. The regulations prohibit the use of the phrase "low tar" in a brand name, as in "Success Low Tar" (Trinidad and Tobago Compulsory Standard, 1989). These regulations, however, are voluntary and do not have the force of law. Accordingly, the local tobacco company, the West Indian Tobacco Company, a subsidiary of the British-American Tobacco Company, has chosen not to comply with the standards for tar and nicotine labelling, and no such labelling appears on packages of locally manufactured cigarettes.

In the United States, the display of information on tar and nicotine levels on cigarette packages is a response by the industry to the regular publication by the Federal Trade Commission of the tar, nicotine, and (later) carbon monoxide yields of different brands of cigarettes. Similarly, the manufacturers agreed to a voluntary plan to disclose tar and nicotine levels in their advertising only after the Commission had proposed a Trade Regulation Rule that would have made it an unfair or deceptive practice not to disclose those levels in advertising, based on the most recent test results (US Federal Trade Commission, 1981).

In 1989, a study of the types of information related to tar and nicotine yields provided on cigarette packages in the USA found that such information is provided selectively and at times is ambiguous or inconsistent. Five brands claimed to have the lowest yield. As tar yield increased among the brands, the package was less likely to

52

show it. Various terms were used to describe tar and nicotine yields, such as "ultra low tar", "ultra lights", "lights", "smooth", "mellow", and "full flavor" (a euphemism for high tar), so that consumers received mixed and confusing messages. Suggestions for remedying this confusing and perhaps deceptive practice include: (a) requiring uniform disclosure on packages; (b) developing a standard coding system for tar-yield terminology, such as that used in the United Kingdom; (c) requiring retailers to display at the point of sale a table showing the yields of all brands from lowest to highest, as is done in South Australia; and (d) requiring warnings that any health benefits of switching to lower-tar brands are minimal, as compared with the benefits of giving up smoking (Davis et al., 1990).

By contrast, the Tobacco Products Control Act of 31 May 1988 of Canada requires lists of toxic constituents on packages of tobacco products. Currently, Regulations made pursuant to this Act require information on yields of tar, nicotine, and carbon monoxide to be printed on packages. The Act also offers the option of requiring the reporting of other toxic constituents on packages in the future. Manufacturers of tobacco products are required to report quantities of selected constituents of tobacco products or tobacco smoke to the Minister of Health and Welfare. Reporting of sales data is also required. Maximum penalties range from Can $10 000 to Can $100 000 and/or six months in jail depending on the offence. Subsequent offences would result in fines of up to Can $300 000 and/or one year in jail.

In the European Region, legislation requiring a statement of tar and nicotine yields exists in 15 countries. Denmark and Germany have introduced legislation to replace their voluntary agreements with the industry on tar and nicotine yields.

An important factor in promoting legislation on disclosure of harmful substances in Europe has been Council Directive 89/622/EEC of the European Communities of 13 November 1989 requiring the tar and nicotine yields that must be indicated on cigarette packages to be measured in a specific, uniform way and the accuracy of the indications to be verified in accordance with a specified standard. The Directive further provides that the tar and nicotine yields and the health warning must be printed on the side of cigarette packages on a contrasting background in the official language or languages of the country of final marketing, so that at least 4% of the surface is covered for countries with one language, 6% of the surface for countries with two official languages, and 8% of the surface for countries with three official languages. In January of each year the Member States of the European Communities are required to forward to the European Commission lists of the tar and nicotine

53

contents of cigarettes sold on their markets, and the Commission is required to publish this information in the *Official journal of the European Communities*. The specificity and clarity of this Directive reflect the importance attached to the disclosure of tar and nicotine yields of cigarettes.

General experience

The most significant development concerning health warnings has been the imaginative innovation of strong, rotating warnings made even more effective by pictures. The recent requirement for adding package inserts is a promising strategy. The original, traditional warning, "Smoking is hazardous to health", is obsolete and no longer effective. Experience indicates that introduction of strong, rotating warnings in conjunction with a media campaign on television and in newspapers increases public awareness of the new warnings.

This approach, however, is not universally available because: (*a*) countries have been slow to amend their legislation to require strong, rotating warnings; and (*b*) legislation in some countries exempts cigarettes for export from the requirements.

The US Federal Cigarette Labeling and Advertising Act of 1965, which requires a health warning to be placed on every package of cigarettes, exempts from the Act cigarettes for export (other than those intended for members of the US Armed Forces stationed outside the United States); no health warning is thus required on cigarettes manufactured in the United States and exported to any other country (US Department of Health and Human Services, 1989, p. 486). It is true that, in developing countries, cigarettes are often sold in ones and twos, and in such cases a package warning would not be seen by the smoker; nevertheless, once a health warning is required, one would expect it to be required on all cigarette packages and in all sales-promotion activities regulated by the producing country.

In India, the Cigarettes (Regulation of Production, Supply and Distribution) Act, 1975, which requires a health warning on cigarette packages throughout the country, also exempts exported tobacco products from the requirement, but with an important exception. When the cigarettes are exported from India to a country requiring the same or a similar warning, there is no exemption; the exported cigarettes must in that case carry the same health warning as is required in India.

Remedial action can be taken by importing countries or territories, as has been done in Bermuda, where, under the 1988 Regulations, the warning required in the case of imported cigarettes is that required in the country of origin. But, as a matter of equity, an exporting country should ensure that the same information is provided to consumers everywhere as is mandated for its own citizens. A reasonable suggestion is that the US Congress should pass a law requiring US cigarette companies operating overseas to comply with the same safety restrictions as those applicable at home, including the use of warning labels in the language of the receiving country and compliance with maximum tar and nicotine levels (Heise, 1988; see also Chapter 7). Such warnings and labelling should be in addition to any warning required by the importing country.

Information on tar and nicotine yields displayed on tobacco products and in tobacco advertising is a more specific form of health warning. It is of greater assistance to smokers than the health warning in deciding whether to change to a low-tar brand for perhaps minimal benefits or as a step towards cessation, or to stop smoking altogether. Moreover, publicizing the harmful contents of tobacco products contributes to government action to control the composition of tobacco products, as discussed in Chapter 5.

Chapter 5

Control of harmful substances in tobacco

> There is no hope of finding a safe cigarette. The enormous, commercial tobacco interest in the industrialised countries clings to its lucrative home market by these marginal devices which may slightly reduce the risks, and does not hesitate to sell the supposedly more damaging products abroad. If reduction of tar and nicotine levels gives some slight gain, it is trivial compared with the benefits from cessation of smoking.
>
> Sir George Godber, former Chief Medical Officer of the Department of Health and Social Security, United Kingdom, at the Fourth World Conference on Smoking and Health, Stockholm, 1979 (Ramström, 1980, p. 18)

There can be no gainsaying the basic truth of Sir George Godber's statement quoted above on the infinitely greater benefits of stopping smoking as compared with smoking low-tar brands. Nevertheless, a study in 1988 indicated that smokers of filter cigarettes experience some reduction in lung cancer risk relative to smokers of non-filter cigarettes. Wynder & Kabat (1988) found that male long-term smokers who switched to filter cigarettes had a statistically significant reduced risk of lung cancer, and female long-term smokers who switched had a non-significant reduced risk. Hypothesizing that smokers of filter cigarettes did not fully compensate by puffing more frequently, inhaling more deeply, or increasing the number of cigarettes per day, the researchers concluded that reduction of exposure to tar leads to a reduction in lung cancer risk and that the magnitude of that reduction in risk for long-term smokers appeared to be of the order of 25–35%.

If it is true that lower tar and nicotine emissions carry a reduced health risk, then a range of tar levels in cigarettes of between

5 and 15 mg (or lower) per cigarette may be less noxious than one of 24–45 mg, frequently found in developing countries (Gray, 1984). In this connection, it has been urged that some of the reduction in cancer mortality in the United Kingdom may be attributed to the influence of low-tar cigarettes (Wald et al., 1981).

There is nevertheless serious doubt whether lowered tar and nicotine contents offer any protection. Examination of the records of 1190 smokers and non-smokers who died in a clinic in Germany found that smokers of filter cigarettes, who smoked a mean of 3.7 fewer cigarettes a day for fewer years than other smokers, nevertheless died on average four years earlier than those who did not use filters. This result is explained by the deeper inhalation and shorter pauses between puffs to compensate for the reduced nicotine content. Relevant to these findings is the overall experience in Germany from 1960 to 1975, when smokers more than doubled their mean daily cigarette consumption. The lung cancer death rate rose each year, at a time when sales of filter cigarettes increased to 90% of the market. The study concludes that the cigarette industry benefits most from "light" smoking as a result of the marked increase in cigarette consumption (Schmidt, 1990). As the Royal College of Physicians of London stated in 1977, "the only safe cigarette is one that is not smoked" (Royal College of Physicians of London, 1977).

Basic reasons for control of harmful substances

It has been said that smoking low-tar cigarettes is a stage in the process of stopping smoking. The American Lung Association urges the adoption of a tapering-off approach, moving to progressively lower tar and nicotine levels in order to stop smoking. But it is also contended that low-tar, low-nicotine cigarettes encourage young people and women to start smoking and may influence smokers to continue, in the belief that such cigarettes are less dangerous. Evidence presented in the tobacco industry's suit challenging the Canadian Tobacco Products Control Act (see also Chapter 13) indicates that smoking low-tar cigarettes may in fact prevent people from stopping smoking, as indicated by the following quotations:

> The desire to quit smoking altogether and the rationalization offered by many consumers that their going down in tar and nicotine brings them closer to the inevitable step of giving up smoking may actually increase the market considerably.
>
> Extract from document prepared by Marketing Systems, Inc. for Imperial Tobacco Ltd. Exhibit AG-40

We have evidence of virtually no quitting among smokers of those brands [low tar and nicotine] and there are indications that the advent of ultra-low tar cigarettes has actually retained some potential quitters in the cigarette market by offering them a viable alternative.

> Extract from "The response of the market and of Imperial Tobacco to the smoking and health environment", Imperial Tobacco Ltd. Exhibit AG-41

Further evidence is needed to resolve these questions.

The reasons for which legislation to control harmful substances is enacted are:

— to convey to society the information that tobacco is a toxic substance harmful to health;

— to make cigarettes less harmful for those who are unable to stop smoking;

— to enable governments to lower the levels of harmful substances progressively and as rapidly as possible through their power to set upper limits on emission products of cigarettes; and

— to enable developing countries to ban the importation and manufacture of cigarettes with high tar and nicotine contents.

Legislation has been enacted to control harmful substances in tobacco by: (1) controlling the composition of tobacco; (2) authorizing the government to inspect and approve tobacco products; and (3) authorizing the government to set maximum tar and nicotine levels. In addition, voluntary agreements have been reached with the industry on tar and nicotine levels not only in countries lacking legislation to control use but also in those with comprehensive legislation.

Government power to control composition

The general power to control the composition of tobacco products may be assigned to the government under a consumer products statute, a law to regulate toxic substances, or legislation concerned specifically with the control of tobacco.

In Germany, the Tobacco Ordinance of 20 December 1977 contains details of the substances that may be used in the manufacture of tobacco products. Similarly, in Belgium, the Crown Order of

28 December 1979 on the manufacturing of tobacco, tobacco products, and similar products prohibits the manufacture or marketing of any such products that contain substances other than those listed in the Annex to the Crown Order or in which levels of substances exceed those specified. On 30 March 1981, a Crown Order was issued amending and strengthening the Order of 1979, and regulating the content of tobacco products and specifying the substances that they are authorized to contain.

In New Zealand, the Toxic Substances Act 1979 defines "toxic substance" as including "any tobacco prepared for smoking, chewing, or snuffing". Section 73 empowers the Governor-General to make regulations prescribing methods of testing tobacco to ascertain its composition, and prescribing the maximum amount of specified toxic substances that may be present in any tobacco or class of tobacco. The New Zealand Smoke-free Environments Act of 1990 provides in Section 31 that no tobacco product may be offered for sale or export that contains or generates in its smoke a harmful constituent specified in regulations made under the Act or that contains harmful constituents in excess of the limits prescribed by regulations made under the Act. Thus, New Zealand now regulates tobacco both as a toxic substance and also under its legislation specifically on tobacco.

In Norway, the Law on restrictive measures in trade in tobacco products, which came into force in 1975, authorizes the Ministry of Social Affairs to make regulations governing the content, weight, filters, etc., of tobacco products. This makes it possible to ban the marketing of tobacco that contains more than certain amounts of substances considered to be dangerous to health. No such regulations have thus far been issued.

In Finland, Law No. 693 of 13 August 1976 authorizes the State Council to issue requirements for substances that are dangerous and harmful to health. Below the maximum permissible limits, tobacco products may be classified as "extremely harmful" or "harmful", based on factors such as the levels of tar, nicotine, and carbon monoxide. In 1977, the tar yield of cigarettes varied but in some brands was as high as 40 mg per cigarette. Since 1977, the State Council has issued four regulations, gradually lowering the maximum permissible limits, so that in 1985 the maximum limits for "extremely harmful" cigarettes were: tar, 15 mg; carbon monoxide, 12 mg; and nicotine, 1.2 mg. For "harmful" cigarettes, the corresponding figures, were: tar, 10 mg; carbon monoxide, 8 mg; and nicotine 0.7 mg (Piha, 1990). In 1989, all cigarettes on the Finnish market were "low tar" (less than 9.9 mg) or "moderate tar" (10–14.9 mg) cigarettes.

In the Soviet Union, the Ministry of Food was required to convert the tobacco industry to the production of filter cigarettes and to reduce significantly the level of harmful substances in tobacco products. However, in 1989, only 30% of cigarettes had filters, and the average tar level was 20 mg per cigarette (A.V. Prokhorov, personal communication, 1991)

In Sweden, a proposed comprehensive Tobacco Act, recommended in March 1990 by the Committee for Tobacco Control appointed by the Minister of Health and Social Affairs, contains provisions on toxic constituents of tobacco. Under this proposed law, the Government would be authorized to require producers of tobacco products to report toxic compounds (tar, nicotine), additives, and other substances in tobacco and would be empowered to ban the sale within Sweden and the export of tobacco products that are not in conformity with certain standards. Initially, cigarettes that deliver more than 15 mg of tar would be banned (Haglund, 1990).

A problem in regulating the composition of tobacco products on which further work is needed concerns tobacco additives. In 1981, the US Surgeon General's Report stated that use of additives may be greater in low-tar brands to compensate for loss of "flavour" due to tar reduction (US Department of Health and Human Services, 1981). In 1984, this question was again discussed, particularly because manufacturers were not required to disclose the nature of any additives used (US Department of Health and Human Services, 1984). Under the US Comprehensive Smoking Education Act of 1984, manufacturers are required to provide the Secretary of the Department of Health and Human Services with a list of all ingredients in tobacco, but no authority was given to restrict or eliminate ingredients found to be harmful (US Department of Health and Human Services, 1989, p. 613). The Canadian Tobacco Products Control Act requires manufacturers and importers to report additives and their quantities together with tar, nicotine, and carbon monoxide yields. The requirement to report additives prompted all except one of the large tobacco companies in the USA to stop exporting cigarettes to Canada. The sole exception, R. J. Reynolds, continues to export cigarettes but claims that the cigarettes have been reformulated so that the additives in use do not correspond to those in use in the neighbouring USA (Collishaw et al., 1990). Regulations governing the use of additives in tobacco have been in force in Germany since 1977 and in the United Kingdom since 1979 (International Agency for Research on Cancer, 1987).

The International Organization for Standardization in Geneva, Switzerland, has issued standards governing various constituents, including pesticide residues and the tar and nicotine content of tobacco, but no international standards have been promulgated specifically for tobacco additives.

As recognition grows of the right of consumers to know what is in the food and other products that they use, it is reasonable to require the disclosure of tobacco additives, such as benzene and formaldehyde, which are generally known to be toxic.

Government power to inspect and approve tobacco products

More specific legislation providing for the control of harmful substances is that giving governments the power to inspect or approve tobacco products. In France, the Order of 30 January 1978 specifies the substances that must be indicated on cigarette packages and the methods of determining whether such substances are present. For each type of cigarette package, the producers, manufacturers, or traders must obtain and send to the Ministry of Health a certificate issued by the National Test Laboratory stating the results of the quantitative determinations carried out by the Laboratory and confirming the statements on the cigarette packages. The latter may not differ by more than 15% from the results determined by the Laboratory. The cost of the Laboratory's work is borne by the producer, manufacturer, or trader.

In Finland, the Law of 1976 previously mentioned provides for the inspection of tobacco factories, authorizes the government inspecting agency and the customs authorities to obtain samples of tobacco and tobacco products for investigation, and provides for the revocation of a certificate of approval if a substance used in the manufacture of a tobacco product or released by smoking, although permissible at the time the certificate was issued, has thereafter been prohibited as harmful to health. The costs of the investigation or of quality control are charged to the manufacturers and importers.

While Finland has been successful in eliminating all high-tar cigarettes from the Finnish market, its classification of cigarettes into "harmful" and "extremely harmful" has allowed the tobacco industry to give some of its products a "light" image—an outcome that the health authorities did not intend. Since this classification no longer has any significance with the ending of high-tar cigarettes, the health authorities are planning to withdraw it. However, in order not to give any false impression that all cigarettes are less harmful, careful attention will be paid to the words and images referring to the "lightness" of cigarettes (Piha, 1990).

In Ireland, the Tobacco (Health Promotion and Protection) Act of 1988 requires manufacturers and importers of tobacco products to notify the Minister of Health, when the Minister so requests, of any constituent of tobacco products other than tobacco, water, or reconstituted sheet made wholly from tobacco, and of the amount of each such constituent contained in the tobacco product.

Among non-European countries, several have provided for government inspection and approval of tobacco products. In Saudi Arabia, the Central Laboratory in Riyadh analyses samples of cigarettes sold on the market to determine the nicotine and tar contents. In Hong Kong, the Government Chemist is required to determine the tar group to which each brand of cigarette belongs, and the Customs and Excise Service has authority to take samples of cigarettes for analysis by the Government Chemist (Hong Kong Smoking (Public Health) Ordinance, 1984). In Canada, the Tobacco Products Control Act requires manufacturers and importers of tobacco to report on the toxic constituents of tobacco products (tar, nicotine, and carbon monoxide) and to determine, by the methods specified in Regulations made under the Act, the quantities of toxic constituents present in the smoke produced by the combustion of cigarettes. The New Zealand Smoke-free Environments Act of 1990 requires every manufacturer and importer of tobacco products to conduct annual tests to determine the constituents of each brand of tobacco product sold and the respective quantities of these constituents present, and to report the results of these tests and specified information concerning the weight of tobacco and additives to the Director-General of Health, who may require further testing at the expense of the manufacturer or importer.

Government power to set maximum tar and nicotine levels

In 25 countries and territories, the tar and nicotine emissions of cigarettes are controlled by legislation. In two countries — France, which has legislative controls on tobacco, and the United Kingdom, which has little legislative control — a voluntary agreement with the industry regulates allowable levels of harmful substances. The maximum tar and nicotine levels and the dates on which these came, or will come, into effect are given below for selected countries:

Arab States of the Gulf Area: By a resolution of 10 May 1980 of the Health Ministers of the Arab States of the Gulf Area, the maximum permitted levels set were: tar, 15 mg; nicotine, 1 mg.

Australia: By voluntary agreement in 1988, the following maximum levels were set: tar, 14 mg;   nicotine, 1.4 mg;   carbon monoxide, 15 mg.

Belgium: 31 December 1992:   tar, 15 mg;   nicotine, 1.5 mg.
31 December 1997:   tar, 12 mg;   nicotine, 1.2 mg

Finland: 1985, "extremely harmful":   tar, 15 mg;   nicotine, 1.2 mg; carbon monoxide, 12 mg.
1985, "harmful":   tar, 10 mg;   nicotine, 0.7 mg;   carbon monoxide, 8 mg.

France: Under the Decree of 26 April 1991, the maximum tar level is 15 mg as of 1 January 1993 and will be 12 mg as of 1 January 1998.

Luxembourg: 1992:   tar, 15 mg.

Singapore: 1989:   tar, 15 mg;   nicotine, 1.3 mg.

Spain: "low nicotine and tar":

1992:   tar, 15 mg;   nicotine, 1.3 mg.
1993:   tar, 13 mg;   nicotine, 0.8 mg.

USSR: 1991:   tar, 25 mg;   nicotine, 1.3 mg.

An important influence on the European countries will be Council Directive 90/239/EEC of the European Community dated 17 May 1990 providing that the tar yield of cigarettes marketed in Member States shall not be greater than 15 mg per cigarette from 31 December 1992 and 12 mg from 31 December 1997. The Directive does not regulate nicotine or carbon monoxide yields.

In the European Community, cigarettes must be tested by the methods specified by the International Organization for Standardization. The same is also the case in Canada. Other countries have adopted different testing methods that differ chiefly in the length of cigarette butt to be left after machine smoking of cigarettes. The use of these different testing methods means that the results obtained in one country are not strictly comparable with those obtained elsewhere.

Government action to ban new tobacco products

In 1988, the WHO Study Group on Smokeless Tobacco Control undertook an exhaustive study of the extent of death and disease caused by smokeless tobacco throughout the world. It recommended that countries where a smokeless tobacco habit did not exist should, as a matter of urgency, ban the manufacture, importation, sale, and promotion of smokeless tobacco products before they were introduced into the market or became an established habit (World Health Organization, 1988). So far, eight countries and territories have acted to ban smokeless tobacco — one in the WHO Eastern Mediterranean Region, three in the European Region, and four in the Western Pacific Region (see Annex 1).

Acting on the recommendation of the European Conference on Tobacco Policy held in Madrid in 1988, Norway became the first country to ban the introduction of new tobacco products. Under Law No. 79 of 11 June 1976 on product control, administered by the Department of Environmental Protection, Regulations issued on 13 October 1989 prohibit the importation, sale and supply of new forms of products containing tobacco and nicotine. However, this prohibition does not apply to products traditionally marketed in Norway. Thus snuff, which has been available for many decades on the Norwegian market, is not covered by these Regulations. However, the Norwegian National Council on Tobacco and Health has undertaken a campaign to alert the public to the dangers of this product. Strong health warnings are being sought and also annual increases in taxes far exceeding the expected rise in prices (Norwegian National Council on Tobacco and Health, 1990).

In Sweden, the proposed comprehensive law on tobacco control contains a provision authorizing the government to ban new tobacco products, such as tobacco chewing gum. The Canadian Tobacco Products Control Act allows new tobacco products, but they can be advertised only if their safety can be demonstrated to the Minister of National Health and Welfare. To date, no such product has appeared.

General experience

The strategy of adopting legislation setting maximum tar and nicotine levels for tobacco products has forced the tobacco industry to market cigarettes with lower levels of harmful substances. The advantage of such legislation is that setting upper limits for harmful constituents leads to phasing out of the high-tar, high-nicotine brands, and governments can progressively lower the allowable limits.

Where governments have not yet taken action to require lower tar and nicotine contents, as in many developing countries, the industry is free to market high-tar and high-nicotine cigarettes. In 1981, the average tar content of cigarettes was: China, 26 mg; Philippines, 31 mg; Indonesia, 49 mg; USA, 13 mg; United Kingdom, 15 mg; Australia, 17 mg (*Tobacco alert*, 1986). Control of harmful substances is closely related to health warnings and labelling of cigarette packages. Once legislation is enacted to require health warnings and a statement of tar and nicotine contents, as in many developing countries, a logical next step is to provide for regulation of the upper limits of harmful substances.

Because of lack of resources, many developing countries are unable to test cigarettes for their tar, nicotine, and carbon monoxide yields. In such cases, a requirement could be imposed on the manufacturer or importer to provide evidence of testing (and information on levels of harmful substances) by an approved laboratory of another country.

Increasing concern about the many chemicals that occur naturally in tobacco or are added during processing has led to a recommendation that a package insert that lists the entire contents of the cigarette should be made obligatory (Daube, 1990).

Legislation authorizing the government to set maximum levels of tar, nicotine, and carbon monoxide yields is an ideal public health measure that improves the environment of the community without the need for behaviour change or individual action. In countries where strong consumer pressures against smoking have not yet emerged, legislation to control harmful substances may be the most effective way to reduce tar, nicotine, and carbon monoxide levels in both domestic and imported cigarettes.

Chapter 6

Restrictions on sales to adults

> Restrictions on places where cigarettes may be sold make a strong statement to the public with respect to a product that has been more widely available than any other product.
>
> Ruth Roemer. *Recent developments in legislation to combat the world smoking epidemic,* unpublished WHO document WHO/SMO/HLE/86.1.

Legislation banning sales of tobacco products in government buildings, hospitals and health centres, and schools and universities contributes to the creation of a smoke-free environment. Such legislation can be introduced with relative ease because it is eminently rational and engenders little opposition. In fact, the elimination of sales of tobacco products in these settings is often accomplished by voluntary action of the institution concerned without the need for legislation.

Basic reasons for restricting sales to adults

The reasons for enacting legislation imposing restrictions on tobacco sales to adults are:

— to discourage adults from smoking;

— to reinforce legislation restricting smoking in public places and the workplace;

— to keep hospitals free of smoke for the sake of patients whose condition may be adversely affected by it, and to reinforce the message about the benefits obtained from not smoking for patients and their visitors, at a time when they are particularly health-conscious;

— to contribute to a smoke-free atmosphere in educational institutions and public buildings and thus to convey a strong educational message on smoking and health;

— to promote the development of a smoke-free society.

Types of legislation imposing restrictions on sales to adults

Two principal types of legislation impose restrictions on sales of cigarettes to adults: (a) laws prohibiting the sale of cigarettes on the premises of hospitals and health centres, schools, colleges, and government buildings; and (b) laws prohibiting or restricting the use of cigarette vending machines. Control of cigarette vending machines is discussed in Chapter 10 in connection with preventing young people from smoking, as cigarette vending machines make cigarettes readily available to them, despite legislation banning sales of tobacco products to minors. Here, only legislation banning sales in government buildings and health and educational institutions is reviewed.

Very few countries have enacted legislation banning sales of tobacco products in specified places. In the WHO Region of the Americas, Chile bans sales of tobacco products in all establishments of the Chilean National Health Service, and Cuba does the same in health establishments and schools. In the European Region, Malta bans sales in health establishments; the Netherlands in health care, social welfare, sports, sociocultural, and educational establishments administered by the State; and Spain in health and educational establishments and institutions primarily for the care of children and adolescents. In the South-East Asia Region, the Government of India has ordered removal of cigarette shops from government buildings or compounds where smoking is prohibited. In Thailand, the Ministry of Health has directed all trading units in health establishments to refrain from selling cigarettes (see Annex 1). Singapore has pioneered a new strategy in prohibiting the sale of duty-free cigarettes at the airport. The ban applies to both foreign visitors and citizens of Singapore (*New Straits Times*, 1991).

Canada and the USA are two of only a very few countries in which cigarettes are sold in pharmacies. In Canada, 22% of cigarettes are sold through retail pharmacies. In several Canadian provinces, the Colleges of Pharmacy, the professional licensing bodies for pharmacists, are giving serious consideration to abolishing this practice. It is noteworthy that the company that owns the largest chain of pharmacies in Canada, accounting for about one-third of retail pharmacy sales, also owns the country's largest tobacco company, accounting for 60% of tobacco sales.

General experience

Legislation prohibiting sales of tobacco products in government buildings, hospitals, and schools has not increased over the past decade. A possible explanation may be that establishments have voluntarily terminated such sales. Another, more likely, one is that a ban on sales is a far weaker strategy than a ban on all smoking inside these establishments. In fact, once legislation banning smoking in these public places has been enacted, sales there probably automatically cease.

Nevertheless, there can be no justification for allowing sales in a hospital or health establishment of a product proven to be so harmful to health. Prohibiting sales in government buildings and in educational establishments is both feasible and appropriate. Making cigarettes less readily available conveys a strong educational message.

Legislation imposing restrictions on sales of cigarettes to adults may, in isolation, have only a limited impact. When combined with a total campaign designed to discourage smoking among adults, however, restrictions on sales acquire importance as a visible component of the campaign, reflecting the official desire of the government to create a smoke-free environment.

Chapter 7

Economic strategies

> Thoughtful examination reveals that care must be exercised in determining the true contribution of tobacco to a nation's economy and that most estimates provided by the tobacco industry are grossly inflated. Tobacco's contribution to national economy is typically measured by the total employment, output and taxes associated with the tobacco sector, but resources devoted to tobacco production are diverted from other productive activities. Accordingly, measurement of the net contribution of tobacco to an economy requires that the value of these productive resources be deducted from their value in the tobacco sector. Moreover failure to adequately account for subsidies to tobacco producers and the external costs of production may also lead to an overstatement of the net benefit of tobacco.
>
> Eugene M. Lewit, Economics of tobacco in developing countries: telling it like it is. In: *Tobacco and health 1990. The global war. Proceedings of the Seventh World Conference on Tobacco and Health, Perth, Western Australia,* 1990

In an address to the opening session of the Seventh World Conference on Tobacco and Health in Perth, Western Australia, on 1 April 1990, the Director-General of the World Health Organization, Dr Hiroshi Nakajima, expressed concern about the economic implications of tobacco consumption (Nakajima, 1990), saying:

> We are convinced that, while it is crucial for demand to be curbed in order to reduce tobacco consumption, such a reduction cannot be sustained if there is no parallel reduction in production. Without this, the deadly spiral of production, trade, advertising, sales and consumption will annihilate any efforts we make in the areas of health education and of cessation.

The economics of tobacco production is beyond the scope of this study, but the spread of the tobacco epidemic to developing countries, many of which are heavily dependent on tobacco production, makes imperative some examination of economic strategies to curb tobacco production and at the same time to assist national development. We turn here, therefore, to the legislative aspects of the following economic issues — tobacco subsidies, tobacco trade policies, and decreasing tobacco production.

Tobacco subsidies

In a number of countries, government programmes subsidize tobacco production, while other programmes of the same governments seek to curb tobacco consumption. This contradiction is puzzling to citizens, to whom government tobacco subsidies appear to be at cross-purposes with public health programmes. How can one reconcile a policy of tobacco subsidies with an antismoking policy? The answer to such questions is complex.

In Australia, tobacco growing has received substantial government assistance. According to a 1981 report of the Industries Assistance Commission, in the 1970s an estimated net subsidy equivalent of over A$20 000 per farm was paid or A $3000 per hectare of tobacco grown (Industries Assistance Commission, 1981). By 1987, assistance to tobacco growing had declined, but the Industries Assistance Commission found that it was still high by comparison with that received by other rural or manufacturing industries. The Commission recommended the phasing out of the programme by 1993 (Winstanley, 1989). It remains to be seen what the impact will be on the price and consumption of tobacco. In recognition of the problem of government subsidies of a product that is the leading cause of preventable death in Australia, the State of Victoria decided in 1984 to phase out state funding for tobacco research on the grounds that such research is inconsistent with the antismoking campaigns in Victoria (Government of Victoria, 1987; Winstanley, 1989).

An astute analysis of the tobacco subsidy programme in the USA pointed out that the direct effect of this price support programme may be the opposite of the common perception because, by guaranteeing a minimum price for tobacco in exchange for the farmers' agreement to limit production to quantities set by the Government, it raises the price of tobacco and tobacco products, and may actually discourage consumption. But the indirect effect, as is commonly supposed, is at cross-purposes with the effort to combat tobacco consumption because it sustains tobacco production, farmers become dependent on inflated prices, holders of tobacco allotments rely on income from a non-productive subsidy, and this

72

economic dependence creates a political constituency that supports tobacco production and promotion. Warner (1988) concludes that the system of government subsidies for tobacco:

> serves entrenched and nonproductive economic interests. It tarnishes the image of a government committed to bettering the public's health. It impedes legislative progress toward a society freed of tobacco-produced lung cancer, heart disease, and emphysema. In recent years, it has created an economic nightmare that taxes Americans to the tune of $5,000 per tobacco farmer. While the struggling farmer is surely a sympathetic figure, the tobacco program is not clearly the best means of demonstrating concern for the farmer's plight. . . .
>
> In the grand scheme of things, the practical health importance of the tobacco subsidy falls short of that of other tobacco policy issues ... Still, the subsidy looms large as a symbol in the battle against tobacco-related disease and death. As such, it is also a totem in the struggle to conquer cancer. It serves to remind us of the multifaceted strategy with which that goal must be pursued.

During a debate in the European Parliament in March 1990, concern was expressed that the large and increasing subsidy of tobacco production by the European Community is at cross-purposes with its public health policy. Tobacco is the most heavily subsidized agricultural commodity in the Community, and its expenditure on tobacco has increased fivefold since 1979. At the same time, 440 000 people in the Community die each year from tobacco-related diseases. This conflict of policies has led to a recommendation that the tobacco price support policy of the Community should be revised (*Tobacco alert*, 1990).

An exhaustive analysis of the common agricultural policy of the European Community, which heavily subsidizes tobacco production (US $1500 million per year or £900 million), reveals that, although the purposes of the subsidies were to expand production to disadvantaged farming areas, maintain farmers' incomes, and reduce unwanted surpluses, in fact the results have been quite different. The effects of the policy have been an enormous increase in expenditure for subsidies, production of unmarketable tobacco which is then sold at giveaway prices to eastern Europe and north Africa, and failure of production to. adapt to demand. Concluding that the common agricultural policy on tobacco is utterly discredited and deploring the selfish disregard for the health of people in developing countries that this policy entails, the authors call for abolition of all tobacco subsidies (Joossens & Raw, 1991).

An editorial in the *Lancet* of 27 October 1990, entitled "Europe ~~against~~ for cancer", expressed concern about the policy of the Commission of the European Communities in providing subsidies for tobacco production. The Commission spends £5 million per year campaigning against smoking and £740 million in subsidies. Whereas in 1970 France and Italy were the only tobacco-producing countries in Europe, eight European countries now produce tobacco, much of it of poor quality and exported to developing countries. Taking the view that the EC subsidy policy makes no sense on economic grounds, promotes disease and death in Europe, and helps to boost the ruthless export of cigarettes to developing countries by the multinational conglomerates, the editors of this influential medical journal called for the abolition of financial support for tobacco growing in Europe.

Tobacco trade policies

Reference was made in Chapter 4 to legislation that fails to require health warnings on exported cigarettes. An even more serious disregard for the health of people in developing countries is reflected in international trade policies that push use of tobacco overseas and promote smoking throughout the world.

In the 1960s, as cigarette sales declined in the United Kingdom and the United States of America in response to publicity on the adverse health effects of smoking, cigarette manufacturers in those countries expanded their market operations in Latin America. First they achieved the elimination of barriers restricting sale of foreign brands, and then they launched aggressive advertising to increase cigarette sales throughout the region (Shepherd, 1985). By the mid-1970s, the transnational tobacco companies had taken over most of the Latin American national cigarette companies, and an alarming increase in smoking rates and smoking-induced disease and death occurred (Connolly, 1988; Taylor, 1984; US Department of Health and Human Services, 1992).

A new effort by the transnational tobacco companies to penetrate the markets of Asian countries has been assisted by US trade policy. Under Section 301 of the revised 1974 US Trade Act, the US Trade Representative has broad discretionary powers to impose trade sanctions against any nation whose trade policies are "unjustifiable, unreasonable or discriminatory". Under threat of such sanctions, several Asian countries have been forced to open their markets to US tobacco products. With the opening of markets, aggressive tobacco advertising is introduced, contributing to soaring cigarette sales (Chen & Winder, 1990).

In 1986, threat of Section 301 sanctions forced Japan to eliminate its 28% tariff on foreign cigarettes and to resolve distribution problems. By the end of 1988, cigarette advertising in Japan had risen from fortieth to second place in total television advertising time. Sales of Japanese cigarettes had increased by 2%, reversing a 20-year downwards trend, and US tobacco companies had a 12% and growing share of the Japanese market (Heise, 1988). About 90% of Japan's new smokers are adolescents (Cockburn, 1989). These young people are recruited to smoking by the advertising of cigarettes during baseball games and feature films, by free distribution of samples, and by the reduction of the price of imported cigarettes in 1987 to bring imported brands into line with local ones (Connolly, 1988).

In 1986, China (Province of Taiwan) was confronted with threatened sanctions on its exports if it did not drop its quotas and tariffs on imported cigarettes and agree to lift its restrictions on cigarette advertising. Concerned about the health effects of vastly increased promotion of cigarettes, it offered to import any US product or products other than tobacco, but to no avail (D. Yen, personal communication, 1987). The US Government contended that this was a trade issue and that, if cigarettes were sold at all, marketing of imported cigarettes should be allowed under the same conditions. In 1987, the Province of Taiwan was forced to allow the importation and advertising of US tobacco. Huge billboards advertising imported cigarettes were erected, even near school yards, and free samples of cigarettes were distributed on the streets of Taipei. The most brazen example of cigarette promotion was the advertising of three concerts sponsored by R. J. Reynolds featuring a popular Hong Kong rock singer, Hsow-Yu Chang, for which the price of admission was not money but five empty Winston cigarette packages. Enormous public protest forced the cancellation of the concerts (Schmeisser, 1988). The tragic outcome of this campaign to promote tobacco has been a sharp increase in smoking. In 1987, on average, the number of cigarettes smoked per person was 80 more than in 1986 (Chen & Winder, 1990).

In the Republic of Korea, per capita consumption of cigarettes was high but fairly constant from 1972 to 1987 (World Health Organization, 1991a). In 1988, the Government was informed that trade sanctions would be applied against its textile exports unless US tobacco products were accepted, tariffs were reduced on imported cigarettes, and cigarette advertising was permitted. In order to protect its own exports, the Government capitulated to these demands. Foreign cigarette companies obtained permission to take 1% of the market and then gained concessions on cigarette taxation. As a result, consumption of imported cigarettes, formerly available only in duty-free shops, increased. From 1980 to 1986, the average annual increase in cigarette consumption was less than 1.5%, but since then it has averaged 4.7% per year (World Health Organization, 1991a).

The next chapter in this saga concerns Thailand. In response to charges filed by the United States Cigarette Export Association under Section 301 of the US Trade Act that the Government of Thailand was unjustly discriminating against the importation of US cigarettes, the US Trade Representative announced on 2 June 1989 the commencement of a formal investigation of the Thai Government's policies concerning tobacco importation. Members of Congress and US health organizations reacted with strong opposition to a trade policy that increased promotion of US tobacco overseas and pressured countries to accept tobacco products. Just three months earlier, on 2 March 1989, a bill had been introduced in Congress to require American tobacco companies to operate under the same guidelines in marketing their products abroad that they are required to observe in the United States. The proposed legislation required all exported tobacco products to carry the Surgeon General's warning or a comparable warning established by the importing country. It strongly discouraged the executive branch of the US Government from actively assisting tobacco industry efforts to open up new markets. It requested the General Accounting Office to study the economic costs and benefits of the tobacco export trade for US tobacco farmers, the effect of the US Trade Representative's activities on tobacco consumption, and the use of US funds to open foreign markets (H.R. 1249, 101st Congress, 1st Session).

In the face of the opposition to its policy from members of Congress and US health advocates, the US Trade Office filed a petition with the General Agreement on Tariffs and Trade (GATT), which established a panel to decide whether Thailand had discriminated against the importation, distribution, and sale of US tobacco. The GATT Panel examined issues related to quantitative restrictions on tobacco and tariffs and also those related to the advertising and distribution of tobacco. The Governments of Thailand and the United States presented submissions to the Panel. WHO was asked by GATT to testify, and its evidence was crucial in presenting the health consequences of this decision on a trade issue. On 5 October 1990 the Panel issued its recommendations, which were thereafter sustained by the GATT Council. The Panel ruled that, under international agreements, Thailand's ban on imported cigarettes was illegal, since Thailand produces and sells tobacco to its own people. But, at the same time, confronted with the dramatic evidence submitted by WHO, the Panel recognized the health implications for the Thai people of opening the Thai market to foreign tobacco companies.

Article XX of the General Agreement on Tariffs and Trade provides that nothing in the Agreement shall be construed to prevent the adoption or enforcement by any contracting party of measures "necessary to protect human . . . life or health". This provision, the Panel said, clearly gives priority to human health over liberalization of trade. The Panel concluded that restricting the importation of foreign cigarettes was not "necessary" if alternative measures were available, and noted that other countries had introduced measures requiring labelling and disclosure of the content of cigarettes. As far as regulating the quantity of cigarettes consumed in Thailand, particularly by young people, was concerned, the Panel noted that a ban on advertising applying to both domestic and foreign cigarettes would be justified under the Agreement, even if it created unequal competitive opportunities between domestic and foreign firms, because additional advertising rights would risk stimulating demand for cigarettes. The Panel also upheld Thailand's excise tax of 55% imposed on all cigarettes, domestic or imported, and the right of the Thai Tobacco Monopoly to regulate the overall supply of domestic and foreign cigarettes in the country (General Agreement on Tariffs and Trade, 1990; Murphy, 1990).

The opinion of the GATT Panel was a validation of the action taken by the Thai Government in 1988 and 1989 to restrict tobacco use as the prospect of the entry of the multinational tobacco companies into the Thai market loomed. On 13 March 1992, Thailand enacted two laws: the Nonsmokers Health Protection Act, banning smoking in public places to be designated by the Ministry of Health, and the Tobacco Products Control Act. The provisions of the Tobacco Products Control Act are as follows (H. Chitanondh, personal communication, 1992) :

- Article 4 bans sales to persons under age 18 and imposes a fine for violation of the ban.

- Article 5 bans sales of cigarettes from vending machines.

- Article 6 bans free samples, exchanges, and gifts of cigarettes.

- Article 7 prohibits giving cigarettes for commercial purposes.

- Article 8 prohibits all tobacco advertising in electronic, printed, and other media, including billboards, with two exceptions — international magazines and live telecasts from abroad. Advertising is defined in the Thai law as any act that enables people to see or know the wording for commercial purposes, thus including logos, T-shirts, etc.

77

- Article 9 prohibits advertising of products with the same name as tobacco products.

- Article 10 bans production, import, advertising, and sales of products that imitate tobacco products, e.g., candy, toy savings banks, etc).

- Article 11 requires producers and importers of tobacco products to disclose the ingredients of their products, as specified by the Ministry of Health.

- Article 12 provides that the Ministry of Health shall determine the labelling required on tobacco products, including health warnings.

- Article 13 bans the sale of cigarettes that do not have the required health warning and labelling.

The Governments of Thailand and the United States have complied with the recommendations of the GATT Panel. Thailand has dropped its ban on imported tobacco, and the US Government has ended its efforts to pressure Thailand into allowing tobacco advertising and easing other constraints on tobacco. The tobacco companies, however, are pressing the Thai authorities to allow them to sponsor sports activities (W. Chintana, personal communication, 1991). The response of Thailand in adopting and enforcing strong multifaceted restrictive legislation, as described above, is a model of what countries can do when faced with invasion by multinational tobacco companies and their advertising (Connolly, 1991).

Decreasing tobacco production

Tobacco is probably the most widely grown non-food crop in the world. It is produced by more than 120 countries, of which at least 90 are developing countries. While the area under tobacco cultivation declined between 1976 and 1986 because of technological improvements and rising productivity, production rose by 15% to 6.1 million tonnes. Although the area devoted to tobacco production is much smaller than that devoted to food grains and cash crops, in some countries, such as Bulgaria, China, Malawi and Zimbabwe, a significant amount of arable land is devoted to tobacco. The share of world tobacco production accounted for by developing countries increased from 53% in 1962–64 to 68% in 1986 because of increased production in Bangladesh, Brazil, China, India, Indonesia, Republic of Korea, Thailand, and Turkey, and a sharp decline in production in the USA (Malhotra, 1988).

Associated with this increased growth in tobacco production in the developing countries is a sharp rise in tobacco consumption in these countries. Consumption among people aged 15 years and above in the developing countries has increased by nearly 2% annually, while in the industrialized countries it declined by about 1.5% during 1984–86 (Malhotra, 1988). Surveys conducted during the 1980s indicated that, in almost 60% of developing countries, more than half the men smoked, as compared with fewer than 30% in the industrialized countries (World Health Organization, 1991a).

In view of these stark facts, WHO has explored the short-term benefits of tobacco production and its adverse economic effects. Tobacco is a lucrative short-term cash crop, and tobacco prices tend to be stable in comparison with prices of other commodities. Some of the profitability, however, is the result of price support policies and benefits provided by the tobacco companies to induce farmers to grow tobacco. Tobacco provides rural employment and jobs in processing and manufacturing. It generates tax revenue for the government and foreign currency from exports, although some of that foreign currency is used to buy imported cigarettes. In the Sudan, for example, imported cigarettes in 1982 cost at least £S 40 million of badly needed foreign exchange (World Health Organization, 1985, 1991a).

Tobacco production also has negative economic effects (Taylor, 1989). The enormous profits from tobacco go mostly to the transnational tobacco companies and only a small amount goes to the developing countries. Tobacco cultivation may have an adverse effect on food production and nutrition, as in Nigeria, where the high price offered for tobacco has meant that it has displaced rice, which then has to be imported (Femi-Pearse, 1983). Tobacco growing requires expensive inputs, such as fertilizer to combat soil degradation, and pesticides, which create the risk of crop contamination.

In the developing countries, large amounts of firewood, needed for fuel and heating, are used in the curing of tobacco. The deforestation caused by the use of wood for tobacco curing is accelerating desertification and causing ecological imbalances which, especially in the drier areas, can be disastrous (Taylor, 1984). In many countries, including Bangladesh, Brazil, Kenya, Malaysia, Malawi, Pakistan, Sierra Leone and the United Republic of Tanzania, firewood is the only effective fuel for tobacco curing (Economist Intelligence Unit, 1983; World Health Organization, 1985).

Moreover, the outlook for tobacco production and prices may not be so favourable to developing countries in the future as in the past because of the reduction in consumption by the industrialized countries. In 1985, the World Health Organization pointed out that:

> World leaf trade is no longer expanding rapidly and on occasion it slumps. The overall trade fell by 3.4% in 1983 owing to very large surpluses on the world market, to reduction in consumption in the developed countries, and to new manufacturing techniques which have reduced total leaf requirements. The long-standing price stability of tobacco in otherwise unstable agricultural commodity markets, which has made tobacco production so attractive to the developing countries, may therefore not continue.

Reduced demand in the USA, the countries of the European Community, and the Nordic countries will decrease the amount of foreign currency earned by developing countries that export tobacco. This loss of hard currency, combined with increased imports of foreign cigarettes, will impose additional burdens on the economies of these countries, which are already struggling with serious balance-of-payment problems. In view of the unfavourable long-range economic outlook for developing countries dependent on tobacco production and the environmental losses that these countries will probably suffer, WHO stated in 1991:

> When these negative effects are superimposed on the ill-health and mortality consequent on tobacco consumption, the problems are severe and far-reaching.

For some years the idea of decreasing tobacco production was only a hope. But as the human and economic costs of tobacco production and consumption are more widely understood, imaginative approaches to decreasing tobacco production are being proposed and tried.

Crop substitution

As part of its national programme to reduce tobacco use, Canada has pioneered the strategy of providing incentives for the growing of alternative crops. The Federal Government of Canada has provided more than Can $30 million in economic assistance to tobacco growers to assist them in giving up tobacco production and in developing alternative agricultural and other enterprises. With help from the Tobacco Adjustment Programs, many farmers have substituted alternative crops, including flowers, tomatoes, peanuts, and peppers. The number of farms in Canada producing flue-cured tobacco decreased from 2916 in 1981 to 1463 in 1988 — a 50% decline in eight years. But the amount of tobacco grown decreased by only 25% because of consolidation into a smaller number of larger tobacco farms (Collishaw et al., 1990).

In a number of other countries, studies are under way to investigate the possibility of crop diversification. In a joint project of the US National Cancer Institute and WHO, studies are being conducted on the health and economic implications of tobacco production and consumption in selected countries. The European Community is carrying out research into crop production and agricultural diversification by the Mediterranean members of the Community. Research in Brazil has shown that two crops — sweet potatoes and manioc — have a gross margin in excess of that for tobacco. In India, the production of high-yield hybrid cottons can be more profitable than the production of tobacco (World Health Organization, 1991a).

Two factors are necessary before a policy of crop substitution for tobacco can be implemented: (1) agricultural conditions that permit the growing of alternative crops; and (2) market conditions that support the sale of such crops. Considerable progress is being made on the technical agricultural problems, but alternative crops do not at present have the market support enjoyed by tobacco. Thus far, tobacco has an advantage because of the subsidies provided by governments and the technical aid and distribution system provided by the multinational tobacco companies.

Alternative off-farm work

Many of the Canadian farmers who have given up tobacco production have found employment in automobile and steel plants or in other off-farm work. Federal funding has assisted this type of change of occupation as well as crop substitution.

In developing countries, such as China, rural industry provides an opportunity for employment that is not associated with the adverse health and economic effects of tobacco production.

World strategy for decreasing tobacco production

The seriousness of the tobacco epidemic in the developing countries has led WHO to discuss with other international agencies and national governments the idea of a world strategy for diversifying into crops other than tobacco and for supporting employment alternatives to tobacco production. Such a strategy would be appropriate for developing countries that depend on tobacco production as a major source of income. In various ways, a number of agencies and bodies in the United Nations system are concerned with tobacco production and its effects — the Food and Agriculture Organization of the United Nations (FAO), the United Nations

Development Programme (UNDP), the United Nations Children's Fund (UNICEF), the Economic Commission for Europe (ECE), the Economic and Social Commission for Asia and the Pacific (ESCAP), the International Labour Organisation (ILO), the World Bank, and GATT.

The experience of Canada demonstrates that, in an industrialized country, paying farmers not to grow tobacco can be worth while. Now the benefits of such a policy need to be demonstrated in a developing country. The decision of the Thai Cabinet on 6 March 1990 to reduce the area in which tobacco is grown may provide such a demonstration (General Agreement on Tariffs and Trade, 1990). Such a policy could serve as an effective complement to the Thai Government's programme, now well under way, to decrease the use of tobacco.

General experience

The issue of tobacco subsidies is part of the larger issue of the relation of governments to tobacco production (Taylor, 1984). Economic analyses of the true impact of tobacco production on the economies of developing countries are beginning to explode the myth that the economic benefits of tobacco production outweigh the burden that it imposes on the people, the economy, and the environment (Goss, 1990; Lewit, 1990; Nath, 1986; Warner, 1990b). Urgently needed are further creative studies and real-life demonstrations of how government interventions can assist farmers to replace tobacco production with remunerative crops of benefit to health.

The efforts of multinational tobacco companies to gain entry to the markets of developing countries where smoking has not as yet taken full hold make the enactment of restrictive legislation that applies to both domestic and imported tobacco products a matter of extreme urgency. An important response to the worldwide operation of the multinational tobacco companies would be the formation of a coalition of health organizations united to prevent the expansion of tobacco use throughout the world.

With respect to economic strategies, such as crop substitution and employment alternatives, there is as yet only limited experience, principally that of Canada. New approaches, however, are in the offing. The Government of the United Kingdom has announced that it is ending aid for tobacco industries in developing countries. Concerned that the dangers to health of tobacco use in poor countries will increase the burden on already inadequate health budgets, the United Kingdom will offer help to tobacco growers to diversify into other crops (*The Times*, 1991). Finally, the WHO proposal that a world strategy for encouraging crop diversification should be developed is promising and should be implemented (see Annex 2).

Chapter 8

Tax and price policies

> Every tobacco price decision is also a health policy decision: a decision as to the amount of tobacco-related illness and premature deaths in the future. In making such a decision, the needs of the State Budget, developments in the profitability of the tobacco industry, and inflation control objectives have all traditionally come before public health objectives, despite the fact that purely economic viewpoints also speak for a reduction in smoking.
>
> The Advisory Committee on Health Education. *An evaluation of the effects of an increase in the price of tobacco and a proposal for the tobacco price policy in Finland in 1985–87,* Helsinki, March 1985.

We turn now to the consumption or demand side of legislation to control smoking — to legislation designed to achieve change in the use of tobacco by individuals. While this was at first thought to be the most difficult type of legislation to introduce because it infringes on the right of smokers to smoke as much as, or wherever, they please, it has proved to be one of the most widely adopted and rapidly growing types of legislation aimed at controlling the use of tobacco.

The tobacco industry has a major interest in defeating efforts to control the tobacco epidemic. The tremendous concentration of economic power in the transnational tobacco conglomerates presents a formidable obstacle to governments struggling to discourage their young people from taking up smoking and to persuade smokers to free themselves from tobacco dependence. Ranged on the side of the tobacco interests are their enormous financial resources, their control of industrial technology for producing, manufacturing, and packaging tobacco products, their mastery of sophisticated marketing techniques, their ability to diversify into other consumer products, and what is probably their most powerful weapon, the physically addictive nature of tobacco.

At the same time, governments have the ability to adopt fiscal and economic measures designed to protect the public's health. Increasingly, attention is being directed to the capacity of such measures to decrease both the consumption and the supply of tobacco, so as to promote the achievement of a smoke-free society. WHO has provided leadership in this process by urging the adoption of policies to achieve progressive increases in the real price of tobacco (resolution WHA43.16; see Annex 2) and by its efforts to explore with other international agencies and national governments economic and agricultural strategies that take account of the effects of tobacco on people's health.

Tobacco tax policy

Exhaustive research on the effect of tax and price increases on the consumption of cigarettes has shown repeatedly that increasing taxes on cigarettes serves two purposes: (1) it increases government revenue; and (2) it decreases tobacco consumption, particularly among young people. The vast amount of research on the health effects of tax changes will not be reviewed here; it will be sufficient to point out that, as noted by Warner (1984) in the USA:

> for adults, the price elasticity of demand for cigarettes — a measure of the responsiveness of cigarette demand to a change in price — has been estimated to be − 0.42. This means that a 10 percent increase in the price of cigarettes should produce a decrease in the quantity consumed of about 4.2 percent. Furthermore, a large majority of this response represents individuals' decisions not to smoke (i.e., to quit or not to start); the remainder is a decrease in the quantity of cigarettes consumed by continuing smokers. For teenagers, the price elasticity of demand is − 1.4 — a 10 percent increase will produce a 14 percent consumption decrease — and the vast majority represents decisions not to smoke (the elasticity of demand for smoking participation is − 1.2).

In connection with a proposed change in the federal excise tax in the USA in 1985, Warner estimated that a $0.08 tax increase, maintained in real value over time, would avert 450 000 premature deaths in the cohort of Americans 12 years of age and older in 1984 and that this number would rise to 860 000 following a $0.16 increase. A $0.08 tax decrease would result in an increase of more than 480 000 premature smoking-induced deaths (Warner, 1986b; US Department of Health and Human Services, 1989, p. 540).

86

In an important review article published in 1989, econometric studies of the effect of the price elasticity of tobacco on aggregate or per capita consumption were analysed and other studies on smoking behaviour discussed (Lewit, 1989). In these latter studies, based on data from two national surveys in the USA, it was found that: (*a*) cigarette prices affect smoking primarily by reducing the participation rate rather than by decreasing the number of cigarettes per smoker; and (*b*) there are differences in price elasticity in different groups, e.g., adult males are more responsive to price changes than adult females, and people aged 20–25 are more responsive to price changes than other age groups (Lewit & Coate, 1982). Most importantly, teenagers are more responsive to price changes than adults (Lewit et al.,1981). Lewit (1989) concludes that:

> The principal message of the Lewit, Coate & Grossman research is that an increase in the excise tax can be a potent policy to curtail smoking. This is because teenagers are more responsive to changes in the price of cigarettes than adults and because the price elasticity of smoking prevalence is much larger than the price elasticity of quantity smoked by those who smoke. These factors suggest that any tendencies for smokers to compensate for reductions in the number of cigarettes consumed by switching to higher tar and nicotine brands, inhaling more deeply, or reducing idle burn can be ignored in evaluating the impact of excise tax changes. More importantly, the large teenage smoking participation elasticity implies that excise tax increases are very effective tools to prevent the onset of an habitual behavior in this age group.

Evidence from the United Kingdom also shows that the effect of raising cigarette taxes is to increase government revenue and decrease consumption, particularly among young people and manual workers. (Manual workers in the United Kingdom have the highest smoking and mortality rates.) Between 1980 and 1984, cigarette prices in the United Kingdom, determined largely by the tax, rose by as much as 26% in real terms, and consumption fell by 20%. At the same time, cigarette tax revenue rose by 10% and yielded an extra £436 million of revenue to the Government (Townsend, 1987, p. 150). Two-fifths of the decline in consumption was attributed to taxation and three-fifths to health education (Reid & Seymour, 1987).

Applying her calculations to Europe, Townsend stated that, if cigarette prices throughout the WHO European Region were raised to the level of Norway's (US \$4.17 per package of 20 cigarettes in 1987), cigarette smoking throughout the Region would fall on average by 40%. This would make a major reduction, she added, in the grim statistics given by Richard Peto that, if there is no change in smoking patterns, 2 million Europeans will die every year from smoking at the beginning of the 21st century (Townsend, 1990).

87

Canadian experience confirms the finding that a decline in tobacco consumption is associated with price increases. Analysis of Canadian statistics from 1980 to 1989 shows that real tobacco prices doubled during this period, while per capita consumption among those 15 years of age and over declined by 29% (Collishaw, 1990). This agrees closely with earlier regression analysis of tobacco prices and consumption in Canada, which showed tobacco demand to be inelastic in the short, medium, and long terms (Collishaw et al., 1985).

In view of the concerted drive by the transnational tobacco companies to market their products in developing countries as smoking declines in the industrialized world, an important question concerns the effect of cigarette tax increases on tobacco consumption in such countries. Analysis of the impact of increased taxes on the consumption of cigarettes and non-cigarette tobacco in Papua New Guinea for the 14 years 1973–1986 shows that such consumption is even more responsive to prices than is the case in the USA and other developed countries. The excise elasticities of demand for cigarettes and non-cigarette tobacco were calculated to be − 0.71 and − 0.50, respectively. This means that 10% increases in excise taxes are associated with an estimated 7.1% decrease in demand for cigarettes and a 5% decrease in demand for tobacco (Chapman & Richardson, 1990). Commenting on this first analysis of tobacco consumers' response to price changes in a developing country, Warner (1990a) says:

> the article provides important empirical evidence that expectations generated by theory hold true in practice. Tobacco users in Papua New Guinea appear to be highly sensitive to the price of their products. Taxes seem to significantly decrease consumption. Health policy makers have valuable new information and tobacco-and-health activists have an effective new weapon.

Various objections to tax increases on tobacco products have been raised, the most common being that such taxes are regressive, placing a heavier burden on the poor than on the rich. Economists have pointed out, however, that for an overall tax system to be fair not every component of the tax system need be progressive. A regressive tobacco tax can be balanced by progressivity in another tax in the system or by benefiting low-income groups in other ways. The high prevalence of smoking among low-income populations in many industrialized countries — a condition aggravating other health handicaps — makes an incentive to give up smoking particularly important. Since smokers who are poor are more responsive to changes in price than higher-income smokers, higher cigarette taxes may benefit their health by encouraging more of them to stop smoking. Moreover, many persons on low incomes are teenagers who are only temporarily poor, and they benefit particularly from stopping or not starting to smoke because of higher prices (Lewit, 1989; Warner, 1986b).

Another objection to increases in tobacco tax is that they are inflationary. Generally, taxes take money out of the economy, and therefore increasing them is usually deflationary. But if cigarette prices are included in the cost of living index, which is the basis for wage or pension increases, then higher tobacco taxes, like any price increase, could be inflationary. For this reason, the Commission of the European Communities, Italy, and France publish retail price indices that exclude tobacco and alcohol prices (Townsend, 1990). For example, in Canada, for the first quarter of 1991, if tobacco and alcohol taxes are excluded from the consumer price index, the annual rate of inflation falls from 6.2% to a mere 0.3% (*Globe and Mail*, 1991).

Three countries in Europe have excluded tobacco from the consumer price index — Portugal on 25 July 1990; Luxembourg as of 1 January 1991, and France as of 1 January 1992 (*BASP newsletter*, 1990c). The French Law of 10 January 1991 on measures to combat tobacco use and alcoholism prohibits as of 1 January 1992 inclusion of the price of tobacco in calculating the retail price index published by the state, specifically by the National Institute of Statistics and Economic Studies. On 28 March 1991, however, the Ministry of Consumer Affairs proposed revoking this provision.

Still another objection to increasing tobacco taxes is governments' fear that they will lose revenue if higher taxes substantially reduce demand for cigarettes. While one might hope that this would happen and that governments would then be forced to find other sources of revenue, in fact the price elasticity has not been so great as to bring about this result. As Townsend (1990) points out, "tax revenue not only rises with a tax rise but . . . can fall dramatically if tax does not keep up with inflation". As the Finnish analysis found, an increase in the price of tobacco products will not decrease government tax revenue even if consumption is decreased. Moreover, Finnish experience shows that, unless the real price of tobacco is raised, that is, unless the price keeps pace with inflation and takes into account increases in real income, there will be no decline in smoking (Finland, Advisory Committee on Health Education, 1985).

Basic reasons for increasing taxes

The basic reasons for increasing tobacco taxes are:

— to discourage smoking in general and smoking of high-tar, high-nicotine brands in particular;

— to discourage smoking by young people;

— to maintain the real price of tobacco products;

— to ensure compatibility with tobacco prices in neighbouring jurisdictions and thus discourage smuggling;

— to finance education on tobacco and health, smoking cessation activities, and research on smoking;

— to accelerate achievement of a smoke-free society.

Types of taxation

Three types of taxing policies are described in *Guidelines for smoking control* — a general tax increase, differential taxes favouring low-tar and low-nicotine cigarettes, and inclusion in the tax structure of a levy to finance smoking education, smoking cessation, and research (Gray & Daube, 1980).

General tax increase

The evidence, discussed above, makes abundantly clear the need for repeated and substantial tax increases on cigarettes and tobacco products if tobacco consumption is to be reduced. No country that seriously wishes to reduce the toll of smoking can afford to ignore this evidence.

Information from the New Zealand Toxic Substances Board, although focused primarily on the prohibition of tobacco advertising, provides an insight into experience with tobacco tax and price increases. An interesting contrast is provided by the experience of Norway and Finland, both of which have had total bans on advertising since the early 1970s. In Norway, higher taxation on cigarettes has raised the price by as much as 20–25% in certain years since Law No. 14 of 9 March 1973 became effective. These increases, making Norwegian tobacco prices among the highest in Europe, took place during a period of rising incomes, so that the cost of cigarettes as a fraction of daily income fell. Nevertheless, tobacco consumption per adult declined by about 9% over the period 1975–85 (New Zealand Toxic Substances Board, 1989, pp. 78–79). Among young people aged 16–20, smoking declined by 38% in males and 48% in females over the period 1973–84 (Bjartveit, 1985). Also during this period, Norway implemented a total ban on tobacco advertising, and introduced strong rotating health warnings and an effective education programme, so that the high price of cigarettes was only one factor, if an important one, in a comprehensive attack on the problem of tobacco dependence.

In Finland, where reliance was placed primarily on a total ban on advertising and on control of smoking in public places but tobacco prices were raised only slightly, tobacco became a cheap luxury and, as a result, consumption declined but not to any great extent. Over the period 1977–85, smoking rates declined by 8% for 14-year-olds, 7% for 16-year-olds, and 22% for 18-year-olds. Tobacco consumption per person aged 15 and over fell only slightly — by 5.2% from 1977 to 1986. In analysing the Finnish experience from the point of view of the effect of the total ban on advertising, the New Zealand Toxic Substances Board (1989, p. 85) echoed the recommendations of the Finnish Advisory Committee on Health Education, discussed above:

> Very few price increases for tobacco have occurred since passage of the Act, as the pricing policy of the Government has, in fact, been designed to avoid inflation and safeguard tobacco industry employment (cigarette prices have been raised no more than 5 percent per annum). This is not a weakness of the advertising ban, but a result of the fact that the Government's policy has been primarily to serve economic, not health, goals.
>
> Finnish health officials in no way want to return to the days of tobacco advertising, but advocate that an advertising ban should be supported with sufficient tobacco taxation to counteract the twin effects on consumption of inflation and rising incomes.

In Italy, tobacco prices were unchanged from 1963 to 1974. In 1975, they were increased for the first time since 1963, and by 1980 tobacco consumption per adult had fallen by 10.1%. In 1981, tobacco prices increased by more than the rate of inflation, and smoking decreased among all age groups, including young people. Italy did not introduce strict controls on tobacco advertising until 1983, so that the effect of price increases on tobacco consumption is clearly apparent (New Zealand Toxic Substances Board, 1989, pp. 89–90). This same phenomenon was observed by Laugesen & Meads, whose regression analysis of data from 22 countries of the Organisation for Economic Co-operation and Development over 26 years demonstrated that increased prices, advertising bans, and strict warning requirements all played a role in reducing tobacco consumption (Laugesen & Meads, 1990).

An additional insight into the effect of general increases in tobacco taxes concerns the importance of excluding the price of tobacco from the cost of living or retail price index. As discussed above, one of the reasons that governments are reluctant to raise tobacco taxes is that the price of tobacco is included in the cost of living index, which may be used as the basis for indexing wage and price increases. If, however, tobacco is excluded from the index, then any possible inflationary effect is avoided. As already noted, the legislation of France, Luxembourg, and Portugal excludes tobacco prices from the cost of living index.

The association between a decline in tobacco consumption and increased taxes can be seen in other areas of the world besides Europe. In Singapore, although restrictions on tobacco advertising were enacted in 1970, tobacco consumption increased until 1974 and began to fall markedly only after tobacco taxes were raised in 1984. By 1986, tobacco consumption had fallen to 1970 levels (New Zealand Toxic Substances Board, 1989, pp. 91–92). Singapore has continued to increase taxes on cigarettes and other tobacco products to add impetus to its national effort to discourage smoking. From 1972 to 1989, the tax on locally manufactured cigarettes rose 13-fold from S $13 to S $40 per kg and imported cigarettes nearly three-fold from S $31 to S $85 per kg (Vaithinathan, 1990). In January 1991, Singapore became the first country to ban the importation of duty-free cigarettes by incoming travellers (M. Yu, personal communication, 1991).

As mentioned earlier, in Canada, before the enactment of the total ban on advertising, the real price of tobacco products, allowing for inflation, doubled from 1980 to 1989 largely because of successive federal and provincial tax increases. Consumption dropped by 29% during the same period (Collishaw et al., 1990). This trend continued into the 1990s. In February 1991, the federal tax was raised by a further Can $0.03 per cigarette. Subsequent provincial budgets further raised cigarette prices by amounts ranging up to Can $0.02 per cigarette. The Federal Finance Minister specifically described the federal budgetary measure as a contribution to the National Strategy to Reduce Tobacco Use. Several provincial finance ministers also invoked health protection as a principal motivation for tax increases. As a result of these 1991 tax increases, it is estimated that real tobacco prices will increase by about 25% in 1991, resulting in about a 10% decrease in tobacco consumption (N.E. Collishaw, personal communication, 1991).

An illuminating study of cigarette tax policy in the Canadian Province of Ontario from 1984 to 1988 found that that province, which in 1984 ranked second among the ten Canadian provinces in total tobacco taxes, by 1988 had declined to next to last. At the same time, the rate of consumption of cigarettes in 1986 in Ontario actually increased by 2.35% as compared with the figures for 1984 and 1985 and remained stable in 1987, whereas in the rest of Canada consumption decreased by 22.8% from 1984 to 1987. With adjustment for the effects of immigration and population change, it was determined that provincial tax policy was an important factor in tobacco consumption and a 20% increase in the provincial tax on cigarettes was recommended. A Gallup Survey in 1987 found that approximately 90% of the Ontario population of voting age favoured a tax increase on cigarettes if the additional funds were to be used for the sponsorship of sports or the arts, helping tobacco farmers to find another means of earning a living, public health education, or sponsoring medical research. Concluding that the health implications of fiscal decisions on tobacco are of major importance, the authors of this study estimated that a 20% increase in price would lead to a 28% decrease in the consumption of tobacco and a 24% decrease in the prevalence of smoking among children and adolescents in Ontario (Canadian Cancer Society et al., 1988).

In 1991, the Province of Ontario increased the tax on tobacco further by 1.67 cents per cigarette, raising the price of a standard package of 25 cigarettes from Can $4.80 to Can $6.60. This tax increase, when combined with the federal increase of 3 cents per cigarette, is expected to reduce tobacco sales in Ontario by 15% (Canadian Cancer Society, Ontario Division, unpublished information, 1991).

In March 1991, the Government of Hong Kong announced an increase of 200% in the tax on tobacco, raising the price of a package of cigarettes from US $1.5 to US $2.5–3.0. The press reported panic buying of cigarettes, anguished protests by the tobacco industry, and an attitude among smokers of "resignation and a newly determined effort to quit". In announcing the tax increase, the Financial Secretary of Hong Kong said (*South China Morning Post*, 1991):

> It has been put to me persuasively that for health reasons a hefty increase is now justified. So, with a particular view to reducing the attractiveness of smoking to young people, I am proposing an increase of 200% in the rate of duty. Incidentally, although the proposed increases are for health and not fiscal reasons, it has not escaped my notice that the estimated additional revenue yield after allowing for consumer resistance will be about HK $1.9 billion.

After intense lobbying by the tobacco industry and in spite of support for the tax increase from 70 international organizations, the Hong Kong Government retreated from its original proposal to a 100% tax increase, but this is still expected to lead to a significant decline in tobacco consumption in Hong Kong. As Dr Judith Mackay, director of the Asian Consultancy on Tobacco Control, pointed out, the enormous publicity generated by these events heightens the likelihood of enacting pending comprehensive anti-tobacco legislation and "hopefully, many smokers who quit two months ago will not re-start" (J. Mackay, personal communication, 1991).

Finally, general tax increases on tobacco are an attractive means of raising revenue because they are easily administered and politically acceptable, as noted above in the Ontario study. Experience in the USA has shown that, with the wide knowledge of the dangers of smoking, the public is willing to accept increased tobacco taxes. In 1989, voters in the State of California passed an initiative imposing an additional tax of $0.25 on each package of cigarettes. As of 1990, many other states in the USA have increased cigarette taxes or are contemplating such increases. Even if imposed as a means of offsetting state budget deficits rather than with the aim of decreasing smoking, they provide an opportunity, in the words of Kenneth Warner, for "doing good by doing well" (Warner, 1984).

Differential taxes

The most dramatic example of the use of tax increases to discourage the consumption of cigarettes with high yields of tar, nicotine, and carbon monoxide comes from the United Kingdom. Between 1978 and 1981, cigarettes yielding more than 19 mg of tar were subject to a supplementary tax in the United Kingdom. Within three months of the introduction of this tax, the market share of such cigarettes dropped from 15% to 3% (World Health Organization, 1983). This tax surcharge on high-tar cigarettes was abolished in March 1981 as a result of tax harmonization under the terms of directives of the European Community, but the manufacturers agreed to maintain the existing price differential.

New York City enacted an ordinance imposing higher taxes on high-tar and high-nicotine cigarettes that was upheld as constitutional (*People* v. *Cook* 1974).

A Canadian analyst has suggested that raising taxes on tobacco products with high tar and nicotine contents could be accomplished by one or a combination of the following methods: increasing customs duties on imported products; increasing the licensing fee for tobacco dealers; increasing the excise tax and excise duty paid by manufacturers; increasing the corporation tax by making promotion costs non-deductible; and increasing the sales tax at the federal and provincial levels (Buchholz, 1980). As *Guidelines for smoking control* recommends, high-tar cigarettes should become more expensive, rather than low-tar cigarettes cheaper (Gray & Daube, 1980). Perhaps a base tax on each package of cigarettes should be increased with each increased mg of tar and nicotine.

94

Levy for anti-smoking activities

Surprisingly few countries and subnational jurisdictions earmark a portion of tobacco taxes for education on the hazards of tobacco and other health purposes. In Finland, Law No. 693 of 13 August 1976 required that 0.5% of the tobacco tax be allocated in the national budget for health education, research, and the evaluation of smoking control. This law was never fully implemented, however. As a result of the economic decline in Finland in the 1970s, the government enacted a temporary law, Law No. 1147 of 31 December 1976, reducing the amount allocated to anti-smoking activities. Subsequent temporary laws gradually increased the amount each year, so that by 1985 the amount was 0.45%. Finally, a permanent law, Law No. 1037 of 11 December 1987, required that as from 1988, 0.45% of the revenue from tobacco taxes be allocated to health education and anti-smoking activities (T. Piha, personal communication, 1992).

In Iceland, Law No. 74 of 28 May 1984 requires the State Agency for Trade in Alcoholic Beverages and Tobacco to spend 0.2% of the proceeds from gross tobacco sales on information on television, radio, in newspapers, cinemas, and other places warning against the hazards of smoking. In Peru, the Law of 20 October 1982 allocates a 9% tax increase on cigarettes made from blond tobacco to constructing and equipping a cancer hospital, the development of cancer detection centres throughout the country, and research on neoplastic diseases. In the State of California, USA, a \$0.25 increase in the tax on each package of cigarettes, voted by the people, is allocated to health education and research on tobacco control and to support of health services. The most innovative use of tobacco tax revenue for the control of tobacco is the creation of health sponsorship councils in several states of Australia and in New Zealand to provide funding for sports and artistic events formerly sponsored by the tobacco industry (see Chapter 3). Because a special tax levied on tobacco products is both reasonable and feasible, the European Conference on Tobacco Policy, held in Madrid in 1988, recommended that a 1% levy should be imposed on all tobacco sales in all countries in addition to existing and future taxation, the proceeds of this levy to be used for health promotion and tobacco control (World Health Organization, 1990b, p. 43).

General experience

The most important lesson that emerges from experience with tobacco tax policies is that every fiscal policy related to tobacco has major health consequences. Moreover, the wide dissemination of knowledge about the adverse health effects of tobacco makes it easier to bring this linkage to the attention of policy-makers.

The extensive research on tax policies and their effect on smoking rates has clearly demonstrated that an effective way to decrease smoking is to increase taxes and thus the prices of tobacco products. In this process, governments earn revenue that can be used to fund health education and other anti-tobacco activities. Moreover, the experience of Australia indicates that, if tobacco taxes are increased and the extra revenue thus obtained is used to fund health and sports, public support for such action is increased. Above all, increased taxes on, and prices for, tobacco products constitute a powerful weapon for discouraging the use of tobacco by young people.

Chapter 9

Legislation on smoke-free public places and public transport

This Report . . . identifies a chronic disease risk resulting from exposure to tobacco smoke for individuals other than smokers. It is now clear that disease risk due to the inhalation of tobacco smoke is not limited to the individual who is smoking, but can extend to those who inhale tobacco smoke emitted into the air . . .

This Report also documents a relationship between parental smoking and the respiratory health of infants and children (under 2 years of age). Infants of parents who smoke have an increased risk of hospitalization for bronchitis and pneumonia when compared with infants of nonsmoking parents . . . As a former pediatric surgeon, I strongly urge parents to refrain from smoking in the presence of children as a means of protecting not only their children's current health status but also their own . . .

The growth in our understanding of the disease risk associated with involuntary smoking has been accompanied by a change in the social acceptability of smoking and by a growing body of legislation, regulation, and voluntary action that addresses where smoking may occur in public.

C. Everett Koop, US Surgeon General. *The health consequences of involuntary smoking. A report of the Surgeon General*, 1986

The number of countries or territories in which smoking in public places is controlled by legislation rose from 47 in 1986 to 90 in 1991. Moreover, numerous subnational jurisdictions — states, provinces, counties, cities, and towns — have adopted legislation to ban smoking in public places. As of 1987, all but seven states in the USA had enacted legislation restricting smoking in public places (US Department of Health and Human Services, 1989, p. 560). In Canada, the Provinces of Manitoba and Quebec have enacted provincial laws restricting smoking in public places.

Many local communities in Argentina, Bolivia, Brazil, Canada, France, New Zealand, and the USA have enacted ordinances, some by popular vote, to make public places and workplaces within their jurisdictions smoke-free. In 1986, only 39 Canadian municipalities had smoking by-laws, but by 1988, 114 municipalities in all ten provinces had enacted legislation to control smoking in public places and the workplace (Calgary Health Services, 1988). In the USA in 1989, a total of 397 city and county smoking ordinances covered a total population of 52 471 053; of these, 297 cities and counties make adoption of workplace smoking policies mandatory; 368 cities and counties control smoking in restaurants; and 298 local ordinances limit smoking in enclosed public places and/or retail stores (Pertschuk & Shopland, 1989).

Several forces have given rise to this avalanche of legislation at all levels of government and similar actions by private organizations. Initially, bans on smoking in cinemas and theatres were enacted as fire prevention measures, and bans on smoking in places where food is prepared as safety and sanitation measures. Then, tobacco-free common environments were sought in order to protect non-smokers from the nuisance of tobacco smoke regarded as a violation of their right to breathe clean air. But when evidence of the danger to health of passive smoking increased, legislation aimed at ensuring that public places were smoke-free also increased. The evidence, initially from Japan (Hirayama, 1981) and then confirmed in other countries — a 30% increase in lung cancer among non-smoking wives of smokers as compared with non-smoking wives of non-smokers — led governments and local communities to see the right to breathe clean air not only as a matter of aesthetics but also as one of public health (Trichopoulos et al., 1981; Correa et al., 1983; Garfinkel et al., 1985; International Agency for Research on Cancer, 1987b; US Department of Health and Human Services, 1986; US National Research Council, 1986; Fielding & Phenow, 1988; Janerich et al., 1990). Exposure to passive smoking also increases the risk of cervical cancer. A controlled study in 1989 found that women exposed to passive smoking for three or more hours a day were nearly three times more likely to have cervical cancer than those not so exposed (Slattery et al., 1989).

Alarming new evidence links passive smoking to an increased risk of cardiovascular disease. A 20-year longitudinal study of non-smoking wives of smokers found an increased risk of death from cardiovascular disease associated with passive smoking (Humble et al., 1990). A review of 11 studies on passive smoking found that exposure to other people's smoke was a major factor in heart disease (Glantz & Parmley, 1991). Finally, legislation to control smoking in

98

public places has escalated against the background of the worldwide concern with the quality of the environment.

Basic reasons for controlling smoking in public places

The reasons for enacting legislation to control smoking in public places are:

— to minimize and eventually to eliminate the risks of passive or involuntary smoking and to protect the right of non-smokers to a smoke-free environment;

— to deter young people from smoking by conveying the idea that smoking is unhealthy and socially unacceptable;

— to encourage parents of young children to stop smoking or to refrain from smoking in the presence of children;

— to provide support to the large number of smokers who want to stop smoking;

— to contribute to an agreeable setting for many activities of daily living, public events, travel, and work;

— to reduce the risk of fire;

— to reduce damage to structures and furnishings;

— to lead to the voluntary extension of smoke-free areas; and

— to introduce a type of smoking control that has wide public support.

Overview of legislation

Countries have used various legislative approaches to ensure smoke-free public places. These approaches, with some examples of countries that have adopted them, include:

— banning smoking in all public places unless specifically allowed (Finland);

— imposing a general, comprehensive ban on smoking in all public places (Belgium, Finland, France);

— combining a general requirement restricting smoking in public places with the designation of specific places where

99

smoking is prohibited, e.g., places where children congregate and banks or post offices where people stay for a short time (Iceland, Norway, Sweden);

— prohibiting smoking in certain public places and authorizing the designation of additional places by administrative regulations (Ireland);

— stating the general objective of banning or reducing smoking in places used by the public and authorizing administrative authorities to implement the legislation and designate the places where smoking is prohibited (Algeria, Ireland, Malta, Netherlands, Papua New Guinea, Senegal, Sweden);

— specifying particular public places where smoking is prohibited and authorizing or urging named agencies to prohibit smoking in other public places (Brazil, Poland, Romania);

— specifying by statute or regulations particular types of places where smoking is prohibited (Bolivia, Burkina Faso, Canada, Chile, Colombia, Costa Rica, Cyprus, Honduras, Ireland, Israel, Luxembourg, Malaysia, New Zealand, Nigeria, Saudi Arabia, Singapore, Spain, Thailand, Uruguay, Viet Nam, USA).

Types of smoke-free public places

The legislation varies in its comprehensiveness: it may cover only a few public places or a wide variety. The places where smoking is most commonly prohibited are government buildings; hospitals and health centres; nurseries, schools, and colleges; trains, buses, and aircraft; and indoor public places, such as cinemas, theatres, libraries, museums, lifts, and indoor sports arenas. For example, in India, a Memorandum of the Cabinet Secretariat of 1990 states that:

> In order to protect the non-smoking public from the hazards of passive smoking, at least in public places where large numbers of people are expected to be present for prolonged periods, it has been decided to prohibit tobacco smoking to start with, in a few selected places, namely, hospitals, dispensaries and other health care establishments, educational institutions, conference rooms, domestic airflights, air-conditioned chaircars and air-conditioned sleeper coaches in trains, suburban trains and air-conditioned buses.

As non-smoking in public places has increasingly become the norm, amended legislation often extends the range of places in which smoking is restricted to include retail stores, commercial establishments, food stores, banks, airport waiting and ticketing areas, and parts of hotels and restaurants, as in Belgium, France, and Singapore. In France, under section 16 of the Law of 1991 on measures to combat tobacco use and alcoholism, a decree of the Council of State dated 29 May 1992 prohibits smoking in all premises intended for use by groups of people. The decree applies to all closed and covered premises that are open to the public or that are workplaces. The ban also applies to public transport and, with regard to public and private schools and colleges, to non-covered premises frequented by pupils and students. Provision is made for smoking areas in certain categories of educational establishments, trains, aeroplanes, waiting rooms of railway stations, and restaurants.

The resolution of 18 July 1989 of the Council of the European Communities and the Ministers of Health of the Member States invites Member States to ban smoking in enclosed premises open to the public that form part of public or private establishments and to extend the ban to all forms of public transport. The public places covered include:

— establishments where services are provided to the public, whether for a charge or free, including the sale of goods;

— hospitals and health care establishments;

— establishments where elderly persons are received or housed;

— schools and other premises where children or young people are received or housed;

— establishments where higher education and vocational training are given;

— enclosed establishments for entertainment (cinemas, theatres) and radio and television studios open to the public;

— enclosed establishments where exhibitions are held;

— establishments and enclosed places where sports are practised;

— enclosed premises of underground and railway stations, ports, and airports.

Restaurants

Restaurants present a special problem because of the strong desire of some customers to smoke and the interest of restaurant

101

owners in accommodating them. At present, a compromise between the interests of non-smokers and smokers is to require the designation of separate areas for these two groups of people, as the legislation of Belgium and Ireland, for example, provides. The State of New York (USA) in its Act of 5 July 1989 requires food service establishments "to provide a contiguous non-smoking area sufficient to meet customer demand. Demand will be deemed met if at least 70% of the food establishment's seating capacity is reserved for non-smokers." Norway's Regulations No. 563 of 8 July 1988 encourage the gradual introduction of non-smoking environments in common areas of restaurants and hotels and urges that new construction take account of this factor. The goal is that, within five years of the entry into force of the Regulations, not less than one-third of the tables, seating accommodation, and rooms shall be non-smoking and that common areas shall also be non-smoking. As people increasingly demand smoke-free public environments, it is reasonable to predict that the percentage of space in restaurants designated as non-smoking will increase, and that ultimately smoking will be entirely banned in restaurants.

Public transport

Smoking on public conveyances — buses, streetcars, trains, and aircraft — has been banned or restricted in many countries. Smoke-free travel has been achieved both by legislation at the national and subnational levels and by voluntary action of mass transit and railway companies and airlines. Assigning a high priority to the further expansion of smoke-free travel, the WHO Executive Board in January 1991 adopted resolution EB 87.R8 urging all Member States to encourage the banning of smoking in public conveyances where protection against involuntary exposure to tobacco smoke cannot be ensured. In May 1991, the World Health Assembly adopted resolution WHA44.26 on smoking and travel (see Annex 2), urging Member States to adopt measures for effective protection from involuntary exposure to tobacco smoke in public transport.

With respect to air travel, the requirement for non-smoking sections on aircraft has become commonplace, and 23 countries in the world have gone further and imposed a total ban on smoking on all their domestic flights (Geizerova & Masironi, 1990). China banned smoking on its internal flights as early as 1983. Australia bans smoking on all internal flights, including those by foreign airlines. Malaysia bans smoking on flights within the country and to Singapore. In the USA, when a ban on smoking on domestic flights of two hours or less came before Congress for renewal, Congress instead passed legislation making smoke-free all flights of six hours or less within the continental United States, within Alaska and Hawaii, and connections between points in the continental United States, Alaska, Hawaii, Puerto Rico, and the Virgin Islands. This sweeping prohibition applies to both domestic and foreign airlines.

Five countries — Bulgaria, Czechoslovakia, India, Israel, and Poland — ban smoking on both domestic and international flights lasting up to two hours (Geizerova & Masironi, 1990). In 1990, Air Canada became the first airline to prohibit smoking on all its flights, including those on its transatlantic routes. Before adopting this policy, the company consulted its customers. A survey in 1990 of 1000 customers on transatlantic flights, 23% of whom were smokers, showed strong support for a complete ban on smoking. Most of the smokers said that they did not mind giving up smoking during a long flight, and 35% of them admitted that they had booked a non-smoking seat. Similar market surveys in France and the USA have shown that both smokers and non-smokers support smoking restrictions on aircraft.

The voluntary action taken by Air Canada was followed by Regulations under the Canadian Non-smokers' Health Act of 1988 phasing in smoke-free international travel on Canadian carriers. As of 1 January 1990, all flights by Canadian commercial carriers of up to six hours' duration were made smoke-free. Each year, from 1 July 1990 onwards, smoking seats on international flights have to be reduced by 25%, so that, in 1992, 75% of seats on international flights by Canadian carriers will be non-smoking, and a figure of 100% will be reached in July 1993.

The benefits of smoke-free aircraft in terms of protecting the crew and passengers from exposure to smoke, minimizing the risk of fire, and reducing cleaning costs, are being increasingly appreciated. The acceptance initially of non-smoking sections on aircraft and more recently of total bans on smoking is an indication that smoke-free air travel will be the rule everywhere in the future.

Judicial and administrative action

In addition to legislation and regulations, court decisions and administrative actions of government agencies on the effects of environmental tobacco smoke are contributing to smoke-free public places and workplaces. As discussed in Chapter 13, the landmark decision of 7 February 1991 of a federal court in Sydney, Australia, held advertising by the Tobacco Institute of Australia containing a statement effectively denying that passive smoking causes disease in

103

non-smokers, misleading and deceptive and in violation of Australia's Trade Practices Act (*Tobacco on trial*, 1991). In the USA, in June 1990, the Federal Environmental Protection Agency released a draft report which recommended classifying environmental tobacco smoke as a Class A carcinogen, the category containing the most lethal environmental hazards, such as asbestos, benzene, and radon (*Tobacco on trial*, 1990).

Voluntary compliance

Legislation to restrict smoking in public places has a ripple effect in that it impels additional institutions and commercial establishments to ban smoking voluntarily. The existence of legislation, and particularly legislation restricting smoking in a wide range of public places, highlights the issue and leads to a voluntary extension of the policy. In this way, non-smoking becomes the social norm.

Voluntary action is particularly important where no legislation or only limited legislation exists. Some countries have relied principally on the voluntary approach, for example, Denmark, Germany, and the United Kingdom.

In the United Kingdom, smoking in public places and public transport is controlled either by rules imposed by the owners or operators of the accommodation or transport, or, in some cases, under by-laws enacted by local authorities. No national legislation exists. When the United Kingdom Government asked the proprietors or operators of railways, subways, bus services, airports, cinemas, theatres, concert halls, public buildings, waiting rooms, and shops to restrict smoking, the number of smoke-free areas in public places increased greatly. Smoking in health institutions and government buildings is regulated by the management, not necessarily at the local level (D. Simpson, personal communication, 1987). The Department of Health and Social Services has issued guidelines to help hospital administrators confine smoking to specified areas and restrict the sale of cigarettes in health institutions. In 1988, the report of the Government's Independent Scientific Committee on Smoking and Health heightened public awareness of the problem of passive smoking and strengthened the non-smokers' rights movement (D. Simpson, personal communication, 1991).

In Germany, restrictions have also been voluntarily imposed on smoking in public places by the action of Government agencies, institutions, schools, hospitals, and transport companies. In Denmark, the Ministry of Health issued a circular on 23 March 1988 banning smoking in all workplaces and meeting rooms under its jurisdiction and requiring other ministries to do likewise; voluntary action has restricted smoking in other public places.

General experience

The dynamic growth of legislation to restrict smoking in an ever-widening range of public places expresses the desire of people for smoke-free common environments. A non-smoking environment has already become the social norm in a number of industrialized countries.

Reflecting this determination to ban smoking in public places is the innovative approach of local communities unwilling to wait for legislation by higher levels of government. In Canada, the USA, and a few Latin American and European countries, by popular vote or decision of local government bodies, local communities have taken the issue into their own hands and adopted local ordinances and by-laws to ensure that public places in their communities are smoke-free.

Moreover, legislation to restrict smoking in public places has generally been implemented without difficulty. Even the most comprehensive legislation, such as that of Belgium and New York City banning smoking in virtually all indoor public places, has met little resistance from the public. To assist in the implementation of its 1988 amendments to the Tobacco Law, the Norwegian National Council on Tobacco and Health produced a detailed analysis of how the new law should be put into effect; exceptions from the restrictions should be reduced as time passes and the new legislation does not prevent owners of premises or means of transport from imposing more stringent requirements concerning smoke-free air than are required by the Law. Five months after the new provisions on smoke-free environments became effective in Norway, a nationwide study showed that 70% of people who had been asked to comply with the new rules at their place of work thought that these rules had not given rise to any problems (Norwegian National Council on Tobacco and Health, 1990).

Provisions in legislation often authorize the setting aside of smoking areas, particularly in trains and restaurants, and these provisions have minimized objections from smokers. A legal requirement that signs be posted to indicate smoking and non-smoking areas tends to avert violations. In countries where smokers continue to flout the law on smoking in public places, a concerted campaign by the enforcement agency generally suffices to ensure compliance. In Israel, under an Order of 1986, "tickets" similar to those given for parking offences are issued for violations. Substantial fines, as in Ireland, and an occasional well-publicized case of enforcement yield dividends in terms of compliance with the law.

While the tobacco industry recommends "common courtesy" as a means of avoiding potential conflicts over smoking in public places, a 1987 study shows that only about 5% of non-smokers ask smokers to put out their cigarettes; the rest try to move away from second-hand smoke. Though no one could object to common courtesy, the researchers conclude that legislative or administrative mechanisms are probably the only effective strategies to eliminate exposure to environmental tobacco smoke (Davis et al., 1990).

Success in adopting and enforcing legislation to control smoking in public places should not blind us to the obstacles that had to be overcome before such legislation was introduced and accepted as the most appropriate way of ensuring the peaceful co-existence of smokers and non-smokers. The principal obstacle has been the opposition of the tobacco industry, which has invested large sums in advertising and publicity to oppose such legislation. In the USA, in opposition to ordinances on smoking in public places, industry advertisements have asked, "Do you want 'Big Brother' looking over your shoulder?"

In these campaigns, an obstacle that had to be overcome was insufficient knowledge on the part of the public concerning the magnitude of the adverse effects of involuntary smoking on health, from which the industry sought to divert attention by its specious attacks. Another obstacle has been the concern of public health officials with other pressing problems, so that enacting anti-tobacco legislation was sometimes not assigned a high enough priority. Fortunately, successful experience with this legislation, exceeding even the early expectations of its proponents, has encouraged community after community and country after country to adopt legislation designed to ensure smoke-free common environments.

The principal strategies available for this purpose are education and advocacy to promote legislation providing for, and voluntary expansion of, smoke-free public places. No legislation can be enacted without education of both the general public and policy-makers on the dangers to health of passive smoking and the advantages of creating a smoke-free common environment. The support of the media is crucial in this effort. Mobilization of citizens' groups, community organizations, and professional associations is also essential. Educational activity on the broadest scale should be conducted before the legislation is introduced, while it is being considered and acted on by policy-makers, and after enactment during the grace period while warnings are being issued before penalties are imposed. Enactment and enforcement of legislation in themselves have an educational impact.

Effective advocacy is needed to support educational efforts. The cooperation of scientists, public health officials, and citizens in approaches to legislators makes a powerful statement as to the importance and feasibility of achieving smoke-free public places. Wide community support strengthens the political will necessary to achieve and enforce legislation.

Chapter 10

Legislation on smoke-free workplaces

> The work place has attracted special attention in the call for smoke-free spaces. Many people spend more of their waking time at work than at any other place, and those who work in offices or other places where smoking is not confined to break-time can be exposed to environmental tobacco smoke for the duration of their working day. Considering that many people have a working life of 40 or more years, one's lifetime exposure to tobacco smoke at work can be considerable.
>
> *It can be done — a smoke-free Europe, Report of the first European Conference on Tobacco Policy, Madrid, 7–11 November 1988* (World Health Organization, 1990)

Control of smoking in the workplace is a particular aspect of restrictions on smoking in public places. Public places are also workplaces, so that laws banning smoking in public places also protect employees who work there. Similarly, laws banning smoking in workplaces may protect people in public places. Recognizing that people spend much more time at work than in a cinema or on a bus, many jurisdictions have enacted legislation to provide specifically for smoke-free work environments. Both legislation and policies are increasingly reflecting the realization that restricting smoking in the workplace benefits both smokers and non-smokers. For workers exposed to certain hazardous materials, such as asbestos, smoking greatly increases the risk of lung cancer in both cigarette smokers and non-smokers. Even in the absence of synergistic interaction between smoking and workplace exposure, as the 1985 US Surgeon General's report points out (US Department of Health and Human Services, 1985), elimination of the disease and disability at the worksite caused by smoking is a major contribution to occupational health.

109

Employers are increasingly concerned with smoking control not only to improve the health of their workers but also to reduce the health and related costs to them associated with the higher morbidity, mortality, and sickness benefits of employees who smoke as compared with non-smokers and the costs of higher absenteeism rates among smokers (Fielding, 1991). In the USA, a 1985 study estimated that the cost of smoking-related lost productivity was between $27 000 and $61 000 million annually, of which approximately 90% was accounted for by those below the age of 65 (Office of Technology Assessment, 1985). The US Department of Health and Human Services estimated that, in 1985, the total direct health care costs associated with smoking were $34 000 million per year (US Department of Health and Human Services, 1990a).

In the 1980s, both legislation and voluntary policies to restrict smoking at the workplace increased in numbers and strength. While some legislation applies only to government worksites, other items cover both government and private ones. Legislation and policies may restrict smoking in common areas, such as cafeterias and meeting rooms; allow smoking only in special smoking areas; and require accommodation of the interests of both smokers and non-smokers, priority being given to the wishes of the latter (Fielding, 1986).

Basic reasons for restricting smoking in workplaces

The reasons for restricting smoking in the workplace are:

— to protect all workers, both smokers and non-smokers;

— to provide particular protection for workers exposed to hazardous materials because combined exposure to tobacco smoke and to certain hazardous substances creates special risks;

— to recognize that exposure to environmental tobacco smoke at the worksite is involuntary and makes nonsense of the concept of a safe work environment;

— to reduce the amount smoked by smokers and encourage them to stop smoking;

— to reduce sickness among employees, medical claims, and absence from work;

— to reduce the risk of fire and the cost of fire insurance;

110

— to reduce damage to property;

— to contribute to the achievement of a safe, smoke-free work environment.

Three types of legislation prohibit or restrict smoking at the workplace. The first prohibits smoking in specific kinds of institutions, such as government worksites, hospitals and health care institutions, schools and colleges, and premises where food is stored, handled, prepared for consumption, or offered for sale. The second restricts smoking where it presents an increased risk, as where hazardous materials are used or where pregnant women work. The third restricts smoking in private worksites, often requiring the negotiation of smoking policies with the employees, priority being given to the wishes of non-smokers.

Restrictions on smoking in specific institutions

Restrictions on smoking in government buildings are common, and may be imposed by statute or by administrative regulation of the government agencies concerned. Canada has enacted sweeping national legislation. The Canadian Non-smokers' Health Act of 1989 restricts smoking in all workplaces under federal jurisdiction, where about 900 000 workers are employed in both the public and private sectors. Smoking is either banned completely or allowed only in a few designated smoking rooms. In new buildings, these smoking rooms must be independently ventilated to the outside (Collishaw et al., 1990). In the USA, most federal workers are covered by administrative regulations that restrict smoking in the workplace. State legislation has extended similar restrictions to public and private worksites. At the state level, laws in 31 of the 50 states restrict smoking at public worksites; in other states, smoking at public worksites has been restricted by action of the executive branch of government (US Department of Health and Human Services, 1989). Many other countries, for example Brazil, Costa Rica, Denmark, Malaysia, and Thailand, restrict or prohibit smoking in government buildings and worksites.

Particularly common are legislation and administrative orders of the ministry of health banning smoking in hospitals, clinics, health centres, and other health institutions. In Poland, under an Ordinance of 4 June 1974, smoking was banned in all organizational units under the jurisdiction of the health and welfare services. Many Latin American countries, including Brazil, Chile, Cuba, Honduras, Mexico, Peru, Uruguay, and Venezuela, ban smoking in health

111

institutions. Similarly, smoking is generally prohibited in schools, either by legislation or by regulation of the authorities. Several items of legislation, as in Mauritius, Singapore, and Spain, specifically prohibit smoking where food is prepared.

Restrictions where smoking aggravates other health risks

Occupational health programmes are increasingly concerned with the synergistic effects of smoking and exposure to hazardous materials, and therefore with the need to regulate smoking in worksites where such materials are in use. The Norwegian Regulations of 14 December 1984 on asbestos prohibit the assignment of certain persons, including those who smoke, to work where they may be exposed to the effects of asbestos dust. In Spain, the Crown Decree of 4 March 1988 prohibits smoking in any place where a greater risk to the health of the worker exists through the combination of the harm caused by tobacco and the adverse effects of industrial contamination. Spain also prohibits smoking in any occupational area where pregnant women work.

Restrictions on smoking in private worksites

Increasingly, legislation restricting smoking at the worksite is being expanded to cover private offices, factories, stores, and businesses. A number of countries — France, New Zealand, Norway, and Sweden — have enacted such legislation at the national level. The 1991 French Law on measures to combat tobacco use and alcoholism prohibits smoking in all places assigned for community use, and in particular schools and public transport vehicles.

The New Zealand Smoke-free Environments Act of 1990 requires every employer to prepare a written policy on smoking for every workplace of that employer, and to consult with the employees affected or with a representative of the employees nominated by them. The written policy must be based on the principle that non-smoking employees shall, so far as practicable, be protected from tobacco smoke in the workplace. Every written policy must prohibit smoking, at the minimum, in lifts; in office areas where more than one person works; in at least half the area of any cafeteria or lunchroom, or in the first session of any tea break or lunch break where there is more than one session; and in any part of the workplace to which the public normally has access. An employee who works in a place that is not an office may request the employer to prohibit smoking within 2 metres of his or her usual work area. Special provisions are made for certain institutions, such as hospitals, rest homes, and prisons. The approach adopted in the New Zealand Law is to treat every public place as a workplace, and it therefore does not contain the customary prohibition of smoking in specified indoor public places. Section 5(4) (a) (iii) of the Act, prohibiting smoking "in any part of the workplace to which the public normally have access", is designed to cover public places. The New Zealand Law is thus of the type mentioned earlier, in which the restriction on smoking in the workplace is designed to protect people in public places as well.

In 1988, Norway added a new section to its Law No. 14 of 9 March 1973, providing that in premises and means of transport to which the public has access, as well as in meeting rooms and work premises in which two or more persons are present, the air shall be smoke-free. This does not apply to restaurants, hotels and other establishments which serve food and/or offer overnight accommodation. Regulations of 8 July 1988 of the Ministry of Social Affairs made under the above-mentioned Law, require restaurants, hotels, etc. to introduce smoke-free environments gradually, so that not less than one-third of the seating accommodation and rooms are smoke-free by 1993. The nationwide study previously mentioned and conducted five months after the effective date of the new provisions showed that 70% of those asked to comply with the new rules stated that they had been introduced without problems, 26% stated that they had led to an improved sense of well-being, while 61% experienced no change in well-being and only 10% a lower level of well-being (Norwegian National Council on Tobacco and Health, 1990).

In Sweden, the National Board of Occupational Safety and Health and the National Board of Health and Welfare issued Recommendations in 1983 concerning smoking restrictions. As far as workplaces are concerned, the basic principle is that priority should be given in them to the desire for a smoke-free environment rather than the desire of smokers to smoke. At the time that these Recommendations were issued, they were regarded as innovative, but consideration is now being given to a stricter approach that would require all workplaces to be smoke-free, separate rooms being designated for smoking if ventilation is sufficient to prevent smoke from spreading into smoke-free areas (M. Haglund, personal communication, 1990).

A noteworthy development in the effort to achieve smoke-free worksites in the private sector has been the adoption and implementation of subnational and local legislation. The experience of

Canada and the USA illustrates this approach. In Canada, both provincial and municipal legislation controls smoking in private worksites. For example, the 1989 legislation of the Province of Ontario prohibits smoking in all areas of the workplace except in designated smoking areas, public areas, and areas used for lodging and private dwellings. As of 1988, 22 Canadian municipalities had enacted workplace by-laws that generally require workplaces to have written smoking policies which attempt to accommodate the preferences of both smokers and non-smokers. Many by-laws provide that, if the concerns of smokers and non-smokers cannot be accommodated, smoking must be banned. By-laws also impose requirements with regard to compliance, posting signs, and penalties. Enforcement in the City of Toronto was assisted by provision of a budget of more than Can$500 000 to educate the public and to hire staff for consultation and enforcement. The extensive promotion campaign undertaken included radio commercials in several languages, a television campaign, advertisements in means of mass transportation and newspapers, a direct mail package to employers, and a telephone hotline service (Calgary Health Services, 1988).

In the USA, state governments have been slower to introduce smoking restrictions for private worksites than for their own employees, but 13 states have enacted such legislation (US Department of Health and Human Services, 1989). An example of such a law is the New York State Clean Indoor Air Act of 1989, amending the public health law in relation to smoking restrictions. It provides that each employer must adopt and implement a written smoking policy that requires, at a minimum, a smoke-free work area for non-smoking employees; a work area for smoking if all employees assigned to the work area agree to the designation; and contiguous non-smoking areas in employee cafeterias, lunch rooms, and lounges sufficient to meet the demand. The policy must also prohibit smoking in auditoria, gymnasiums, restrooms, elevators, classrooms, hallways, employee medical facilities, and company vehicles occupied by more than one person. Violation is punishable by a civil penalty of up to $1000, if imposed by the state, and up to $500 if imposed by a local enforcement official.

Increasingly common in the United States are local ordinances, enacted either by popular vote or by city councils, requiring adoption of a written smoking policy in the workplace. As of 1988, 297 cities and counties require both public and private employers to adopt such a policy and, in the event of a conflict between the concerns of non-smokers and smokers, those of non-smokers must take precedence. Most of these ordinances make no exception for small workplaces and also prohibit retaliation against an employee who exercises his or her right under a smoking ordinance (Pertschuk & Shopland, 1989).

Voluntary action

The large volume of legislation enacted at all levels of government to restrict smoking in the workplace does not begin to reflect the wide coverage of antitobacco worksite policies. As non-smoking increasingly becomes the society norm, industries and businesses are taking voluntary action, either unilaterally or in conjunction with workers and their unions, to develop policies that restrict or even ban smoking in the workplace. A review of such actions in European countries — Belgium, France, Germany, Greece, Italy, the Netherlands, Portugal, and Spain — shows the ingenious strategies that companies have adopted, including prizes, bonuses, and extra holidays for non-smoking employees, equivalent to the time smokers take for smoking breaks (*BASP Newsletter*, 1990a). Employers in Mongolia offer two days' holiday or the cash equivalent to any employee who stops smoking for six months or more (J. Mackay, personal communication, 1991).

In the USA, the rapid growth of corporate smoking-control policies reflects a major change in the situation. Whereas formerly companies were faced with the problem of deciding whether such a policy should be adopted, the problem now is to decide which type of policy to adopt. Complete smoking bans are increasingly common (Fielding, 1991). One problem in the adoption of smoking-control policies has been the attitude of unions, particularly where employers have unilaterally imposed smoking restrictions, but such policies have been found to be acceptable to unions where management has a strong health and safety programme (Brown et al., 1988).

General experience

The groundswell of legislation and voluntary action to restrict smoking in the workplace that has occurred in the last decade indicates that smoke-free work environments are on the way to becoming the general rule. Lessons learned from this experience may be summarized as follows:

1. The wealth of scientific information available on the adverse effects of the interaction between smoking and hazardous materials for both smokers and non-smokers leaves no option but to ban smoking in all workplaces where such

materials are used (US Department of Health and Human Services, 1985).

2. Comprehensive legislation restricting smoking in all public and private worksites where two or more employees work has proved to be feasible and acceptable. Enforcing such legislation has been straightforward where a written smoking policy is required and provision is made for accommodating the interests of smokers and non-smokers, but giving precedence to a smoke-free environment in the event of a dispute. In the USA, a trend has been noted among management and workers in both private and public workplaces away from acceptance of smoking and the precedence of the rights of the smoker to clear discouragement of smoking (Fielding, 1991).

3. Legislation enacted at the subnational level of government in countries with a federal structure and at the local level in all countries has been successful in controlling smoking in the workplace. Involving citizens in local campaigns helps ensure the passage and enforcement of local by-laws and ordinances.

4. Enactment of legislation to restrict worksite smoking engenders voluntary action by industry, workers, and trade unions. Employers, concerned about possible liability for the effects of environmental tobacco smoke, are increasingly undertaking voluntary controls. As pointed out at the European Conference on Tobacco Policy, a workplace smoking policy benefits both non-smokers and smokers and can be an important part of a workplace health promotion programme to improve lifestyles generally (World Health Organization, 1990b).

Chapter 11

Preventing young people from smoking

> A major problem in getting people to see tobacco as harmful is the long delay between cause and effect. Youngsters may start smoking in their teenage years, but they may die from the effects of tobacco some 40 years later. Damage to the body from smoking accumulates, so those who start earliest will be at the greatest risk in middle age. This puts a particularly sinister aspect on the increase in teenage smokers over the last 10–15 years. The world population of under 20-year-olds is about 2 billion. On present smoking patterns we can expect very large numbers of them to smoke and about 10% of them to die from it. Can we accept the absurdity of 200 million of today's children dying from an avoidable cause?
>
> Richard Peto. Women and tobacco, *World health forum*, 1990, **11**(1):3–13.

Recognition that the earlier smoking is started the more dangerous it is has impelled legislative action designed to protect young people. It is now well established that those who start smoking early in life have greater difficulty in stopping, are more likely to become heavy smokers, and are at a higher risk of developing smoking-related diseases than those who begin to smoke at later ages (US Department of Health and Human Services, 1986, 1989). The difficulty that young people have in stopping smoking indicates that nicotine addiction quickly becomes established in children. A survey of 15-year-olds in the United Kingdom found that 51% of those smoking five or more cigarettes a day would like to stop, while 27% thought they would not be able to stop no matter how hard they tried (Revill & Drury, 1980). In the USA, a survey found that 47% of high school seniors who were smoking daily would like to stop, but only 17% of teenagers who smoked regularly stopped by the time they were high school seniors (Johnston et al., 1987).

These stark facts assume increased significance when viewed in the light of the marketing strategy of the tobacco industry as revealed by evidence given in the legal suit challenging the Tobacco Products Control Act of Canada:

> Young smokers represent the major opportunity group for the cigarette industry ...
>
> Imperial Tobacco Ltd 1971, Matinee Marketing Plans, Exhibit AG-204
>
> If the last ten years have taught us anything, it is that the industry is dominated by the companies who respond most effectively to the needs of younger smokers. Our efforts on these brands will remain on maintaining their relevance to smokers in these younger groups in spite of the share performance they may develop on older smokers.
>
> Overall Market Conditions — F88, an Imperial Tobacco document, Exhibit AB-214 (F88 means Fiscal 1988)

Smoking is started almost always during the teenage years. In many countries, smoking is starting at increasingly younger ages (US Department of Health and Human Services, 1989). In New Zealand, the formative years for smoking are between 10 and 13. By age 15, 33% of girls and 20% of boys (27% overall) are daily or monthly smokers. A dramatic increase in the percentage of young women taking up smoking has meant that in 1988 more than half of New Zealand women under 25 years of age were or had been smokers, and more than one-third were current smokers. Lung cancer rates in New Zealand women have tripled since 1964, the year in which the first US Surgeon General's report alerted the world to smoking as a major cause of lung cancer (New Zealand Toxic Substances Board, 1989).

In France, 250 000 young people between the ages of 15 and 16 begin smoking each year, of whom 70 000–80 000 will die of cancer between ages 45 and 50. Moreover, 65% of these smokers begin to smoke before age 13. The report presenting these facts to the French National Assembly commented that: "this situation alone justified the intervention of the legislator" (Commission des Affaires Culturelles, Familiales et Sociales, 1990).

A study in Bangladesh found that as many as 42% of smokers started smoking between the ages of 15 and 19; nearly 20% started smoking before 15 years of age. Most alarming is the finding that the age of starting smoking has decreased over time (Islam et al., 1990).

It is difficult to motivate young people to avoid a practice having harmful effects that become apparent only many years later. Rational arguments have not been sufficiently effective in discouraging young people from smoking. A combination of various strategies is called for, and legislation may play an essential role by

118

banning sales to minors, prohibiting smoking in schools and other places where young people gather, and creating a smoke-free environment.

There is nevertheless some disagreement among smoking-control advocates on the best strategies to be adopted. At the European Conference on Tobacco Policy, held in Madrid in 1988, there were more differences of opinion on the question of prohibiting tobacco sales to minors than on any other question. Advocates of a ban on sales to minors urged enactment and enforcement of such bans as a signal to children and adults that the public authorities recognize that smoking is dangerous and that children and young people should be protected against it. Opponents of sales bans feared that these measures would merely make smoking look more desirable to young people by establishing smoking as part of the adult world and giving it the aspect of a "forbidden fruit" (World Health Organization, 1990b). A number of factors tip the scales in favour of strong legislative measures to ban sales to minors and effective enforcement of such bans. These include the fact that teenagers continue to start to smoke despite information and education on the dangers of tobacco use; the evidence on the addictive nature of tobacco, among children as well as adults; the difficulty faced by the tobacco industry in opposing such legislation; and the increasing number of countries, now numbering 19, that specifically ban sales of cigarettes and tobacco products to minors.

Basic reasons for discouraging young people from smoking

Legislation on tobacco use and young people is designed to:

— decrease morbidity and mortality from diseases caused by smoking among young people, for whom the risk increases the longer they smoke;

— prevent the onset of smoking among adolescent girls, in order to avoid the special risks to women (for women using oral contraceptives, smoking increases the risk of heart attack; women who smoke are at increased risk of cervical cancer; and smoking during pregnancy increases the risk of miscarriage and has damaging effects on the fetus);

— prevent smoking by young adults who are parents, in view of the evidence that smoking by parents is detrimental to the health of children both by exposing them to tobacco smoke and by influencing their smoking habits;

119

— prevent the development of tobacco dependence in the most vulnerable group of the population — young people.

Types of legislation

Legislation aimed specifically at preventing smoking by young people takes several forms: (*a*) prohibition of sales of tobacco products to minors; (*b*) banning or restriction of sales of cigarettes from automatic vending machines; (*c*) prohibition of smoking in schools or other places frequented by young people; (*d*) prohibition of the free distribution of samples and loose cigarettes; (*e*) restrictions on smokeless tobacco products; and (*f*) prohibition of cigarette advertising and sponsorship of sports events and rock festivals, and generally at times and places where children and adolescents are likely to be influenced.

Prohibition of sales to minors

Legislation prohibiting the sale of tobacco products to minors is not new. It has been on the statute books for nearly a century in many places, but penalties have often been nominal and enforcement lax. In the United Kingdom, according to the 1977 Report of the Royal College of Physicians of London, a survey in 1975 revealed that, out of a random sample of 60 tobacconists' shops in England and Wales, 43 sold cigarettes to children who were obviously under 16 years of age (Royal College of Physicians of London, 1977). In 1985, according to a press release of the Department of Health and Social Security, the United Kingdom Secretary of State for Social Services announced that, under a new voluntary agreement between the industry and the Government, the industry would spend £1 million a year to encourage tobacco retailers to support the law prohibiting the sale of cigarettes to children, but no legislation was enacted in the United Kingdom to strengthen the ban on sales to minors.

In Canada, surveys in which children go into stores to test compliance with tobacco-control legislation have found that 75–100% of the stores will sell cigarettes to minors, even to children as young as 12 (National Clearinghouse on Tobacco and Health, 1990). In January 1989, a store in the City of Toronto was fined Can $25 for selling cigarettes to minors in a case brought by University of Toronto law students to demonstrate the inadequacy of existing laws (Hall, 1989).

120

In the USA, the Office of Inspector General, an agency created to promote efficiency and effectiveness in programmes of the United States Department of Health and Human Services, undertook to assess the enforcement of state laws prohibiting the sale of cigarettes to minors. In a report released in May 1990, the Office found that, although 44 states and the District of Columbia have legislation prohibiting the sale of cigarettes to minors, it is not enforced and children can easily buy cigarettes. A number of studies and controlled purchases or "stings" demonstrated that minors were able to purchase cigarettes illegally in about 80% of the stores tested (Office of Inspector General, 1990).

Legislation banning sales to minors differs in the age at which purchase of cigarettes is legal. Colombia, for example, prohibits sales of cigarettes to children under age 14. Most jurisdictions, e.g., all the states of Australia except Western Australia, prohibit sales to persons under 16. In a few jurisdictions, e.g., Western Australia, Uruguay, and the Canadian provinces of Manitoba and Prince Edward Island, sales to persons under age 18 are prohibited. In the USA, the age for legal purchase of tobacco products is 19 in three states, 18 in 36 states, 17 in four states, and 16 in one state and the District of Columbia (Centers for Disease Control, 1990b).

Enforcement of youth access legislation is generally weak, as noted above. Only recently has legislation been amended to require posting of signs at points of sale stating that sales to minors are illegal, that positive proof of age is required, and specifying the penalties. A few jurisdictions in Canada and the USA have also recently increased the penalties from a nominal to a substantial level. In the Province of Ontario, the fine for selling tobacco products to minors was increased from Can $25 to not less than Can $50 and not more than Can $500 for individuals; for corporations the minimum fine is Can $200 and the maximum is Can $25 000 (National Clearinghouse on Tobacco and Health, 1991).

In response to the poor enforcement of youth access laws in the USA, the US Department of Health and Human Services recommended model legislation to the states to control sales of tobacco products to minors. The Model Sale of Tobacco Products to Minors Control Act creates a licensing system similar to that used to control the sale of alcoholic beverages, under which a store may sell tobacco to adults only if it avoids making sales to minors; it also lays down a graduated schedule of penalties, including monetary fines and licence suspensions; provides separate penalties for failure to post a sign that sales to minors are illegal; places primary responsibility for investigation and enforcement on a designated state agency; relies mainly on state-administered civil penalties to avoid the delays and costs of the court system; sets the legal age of purchase at 19, although states may wish to consider age 21; and bans the use of vending machines to dispense cigarettes, as is the practice for alcohol (US Department of Health and Human Services, 1990b; Choi et al., 1992).

Restricting sales of cigarettes from automatic vending machines

Prohibiting or restricting sales from vending machines makes cigarettes, one of the most widely available products, less accessible to young people. Cyprus, under Law No. 51 of 1980, and Iceland, under Law No. 74 of 1984, prohibit all sales of tobacco from automatic vending machines. Belgium (Crown Order of 28 October 1979), Finland (Ordinance of 25 February 1977) and Ireland (Act No. 24 of 12 July 1988) restrict the places where vending machines may be installed and hold the owners of premises where machines are installed responsible for supervising them and preventing sales to minors. Both New Zealand (Smoke-free Environments Act 1990) and Spain (Crown Decree No. 192/1988 of 4 March 1988) require a health warning to be displayed on the vending machine, and the latter permits cigarette vending machines only in enclosed premises. In the USA, legislation in 17 states regulates the sale of tobacco products from vending machines (Legislative Clearinghouse, 1989). In 14 states, owners, operators, or supervisors of tobacco vending machines are required to post signs stating that minors are prohibited from buying cigarettes from such a machine. In five states, vending machines must be placed in areas kept under supervision so that minors cannot use them. The State of Wisconsin prohibits the placing of vending machines within 500 feet (157 m) of a school. The State of Utah has banned vending machines completely. Only one state, Colorado, bans the sale of smokeless tobacco products in vending machines.

A number of local communities have banned cigarette vending machines entirely; others have banned them from public places or restricted them to places licensed to sell liquor; and others require them to be under constant supervision. In the State of Minnesota, where one of the first Clean Indoor Air Acts was passed in 1975, the town of White Bear attained national and international prominence by totally banning sales of cigarettes from vending machines. Within five months, nine other Minnesota cities had totally banned such machines, and another 12 communities had enacted partial restrictions. Efforts by the tobacco industry to overturn these bans on the grounds that jobs would be lost if vending machines were banned were countered by the argument that requiring people rather than machines to sell cigarettes would hardly lead to fewer jobs (Lando, 1990).

Prohibiting smoking and sales in schools and other places frequented by young people

Restrictions on smoking in schools and bans on the sale of tobacco products in schools and other places frequented by young people are imposed both by legislation and by action of the school authorities. In some jurisdictions, as in Finland, for example, under Law No. 693 of 13 August 1976, smoking is entirely prohibited in day nurseries, primary and secondary schools, and all places intended for use by children at or below the age of compulsory school attendance and at public events arranged indoors for children and young people or to which children are admitted. In other jurisdictions, smoking is restricted to designated areas. Smoking by teachers has in the past been permitted in designated areas away from students, but recognition of the importance of teachers as role models for students and growth of workplace smoking-control policies generally have led increasingly to strengthened restrictions on smoking by students, faculty, and staff (Fielding, 1991).

While schools are included in virtually all legislation banning smoking in public places, enforcement may be weak. Even in jurisdictions where it is illegal for minors to buy, possess, or use tobacco products, the no-smoking rule in schools may not be effectively implemented.

Prohibiting free samples and sales of single or loose cigarettes

Free samples of cigarettes and smokeless tobacco are a matter of grave concern, since distribution of such samples may encourage experimentation with tobacco products by children and young people. Young people are the most price-sensitive age group, and smoking is generally initiated in these formative years (Davis & Jason, 1988). The tobacco companies have increased their expenditure on cigarette samples in the USA from $24.2 million in 1975 to $148 million in 1984 (Federal Trade Commission, 1986). The tobacco industry's voluntary code provides that persons who offer samples shall refuse to give a sample to any person known or appearing to be less than 21 years of age, but studies have shown that a substantial number of children and adolescents report that they have received free cigarette samples or have seen other children and adolescents receive such samples. Even in a state where the distribution of free tobacco products to minors is illegal, 4% of elementary school children and 20% of high school students reported having received free samples (Davis & Jason, 1988; US Department of Health and Human Services, 1989).

A few countries prohibit the distribution of free samples of cigarettes. In Ecuador, Supreme Decree No. 965 of 1973 prohibits the free distribution of cigarettes to minors. Recently enacted laws, such as those in New Zealand (the Smoke-free Environments Act 1990) and Singapore, ban all free distribution of tobacco products to the public except for persons associated with the sale or distribution of tobacco products. Canada bans all free distribution of cigarettes by manufacturers and importers, with no exceptions.

For the same reasons that free distribution of samples is unsound health policy, so permitting the sale of single or loose cigarettes is prohibited. Single cigarettes are an inducement for young people to take up smoking, and they carry no health warning. In many developing countries, the sale of single or loose cigarettes is common and provides occupation and income for young people, even for children.

Canada addresses this problem by prescribing in its Tobacco Products Control Regulations of 1988 that the sale of all tobacco products is prohibited unless required labelling is displayed on the package. New Zealand, under the Smoke-free Environments Act, similarly prohibits the sale or offering for sale of tobacco products unless the package containing the product displays the required health warning and list of harmful constituents and contains a package insert with information on the health effects of the product. The Bahamas (Health Services Act of 1976) likewise prohibits the sale of cigarettes unless they are contained in a package bearing a health warning. Uruguay (Law No. 15361 of 24 December 1982) prohibits the sale of single or loose cigarettes.

Restrictions on smokeless tobacco products

The threat to young people from smokeless tobacco products (tobacco that is chewed or left in the mouth, even overnight, or sniffed) has increased as the tobacco industry has intensified its promotion of these products. Recognizing that many young people turn to smokeless tobacco in the mistaken belief that it is a safe alternative to cigarettes, the WHO Study Group on Smokeless Tobacco Control called for a pre-emptive ban wherever the product has not yet been introduced (World Health Organization, 1988). As Annex 1 indicates, Australia, Belgium, Hong Kong, Ireland, Israel, Japan, Malta, New Zealand, Saudi Arabia, Singapore and the United Kingdom have prohibited the importation, sale, and use of smokeless tobacco (Karaoglu & Joossens, 1990). Legislation in Canada, France, Greece, Iceland, Luxembourg, Sweden, and the USA requires health warnings on smokeless tobacco products, as mentioned in Chapter 4. In Norway, snuff is not included in the ban on new nicotine products because its use is well established, but the Norwegian government is publishing a special report on the addictive, carcinogenic, and damaging effects of smokeless tobacco. It is recommending the use of health warnings and annual increases in taxes far exceeding the expected rise in prices (Norwegian National Council on Tobacco and Health, 1990).

Restricting tobacco advertising and promotion that may influence young people

Advertising is the principal weapon of the tobacco industry in recruiting new smokers. The tobacco industry in the USA loses every year an estimated 1–1.5 million smokers who stop smoking and another million who die from smoking-related diseases and other causes. To maintain its level of sales in the USA, therefore, the tobacco industry must recruit 2–2.5 million new smokers each year. As 90% of new smokers are children and teenagers, this would mean that at least 5000 children and teenagers in the United States started smoking each day (Warner, 1986a).

It is well known that young people generally start to smoke because they consider it an adult, sophisticated, attractive thing to do. Advertisements for tobacco reinforce this notion by depicting healthy, handsome young people engaged in pleasurable activities, e.g., in sports and socializing. Advertisements that associate smoking with beauty in nature, with sports, and even with sex are insidious influences that promote smoking among adolescents.

The demonstrated link between cigarette advertising and initiation or continuation of smoking led to the first total bans on tobacco advertising by Finland, Iceland and Norway, and to the strong partial bans in Belgium, Singapore and Sweden. An important factor in the total prohibition of all tobacco advertising and promotion by Canada in 1988, New Zealand in 1989, and France in 1990 was the impact of tobacco advertising and promotion on young people. Other countries have sought to protect their young people by specifying that tobacco advertising should not be directed to children and young people, but their legislation imposes only limited restrictions. A number of Latin American countries have adopted this approach by restricting the times and places where tobacco advertising may be presented and by prescribing the content of the advertising. Thus, in Argentina (Law No. 23344 of 31 July 1986), tobacco advertising is prohibited on television and radio from 08:00 to 22:00, although the brand name can be stated, and tobacco advertising is prohibited in theatres and cinemas to which persons under 18 are admitted. In Brazil, Order No. 490 of 25 August 1988 permits tobacco advertising on television only between 21:00 and 06:00. Chile and Colombia prohibit the depiction of young people smoking. Paraguay, in Section 202 of the Health Code, prohibits the use of figures or characters representing children or adolescents and the association of tobacco with sports, work, study, or the home.

General experience

In the effort to prevent children and adolescents from becoming addicted to tobacco, a number of lessons have been learned which can be summarized as follows:

1. Laws banning the sale of tobacco products to minors should specify a minimum legal age for access to tobacco that is high enough to eliminate the use of tobacco by young people in their teens. Few people start to smoke after the age of 19. The minimum age for purchase of tobacco might well be similar to that for the purchase of alcohol.

2. Tobacco access legislation should be strengthened and enforced. An important component of such legislation is a requirement for the posting of signs to the effect that the sale of tobacco products to minors is prohibited and that proof of age can be required when there is any doubt as to the age of the person wishing to buy such products. Requiring retailers to have tobacco licences permits revocation of the licence on the grounds of illegal sales to minors — a significant incentive for compliance with the law. A number of jurisdictions have increased the fines or civil financial penalties for violations of tobacco access laws — a measure that creates an economic incentive to obey the law.

3. A notable achievement in preventing young people from smoking has been the enactment of local ordinances banning the use of cigarette vending machines and citizen action impelling enforcement of tobacco access laws. These are

matters that are particularly amenable to local initiatives. Cigarette vending machines should be banned or, at least, restricted to indoor locations inaccessible to minors, such as bars.

4. All free distribution of cigarette samples and the sale of single or loose cigarettes should be prohibited. While cigarette taxation laws typically require cigarettes to be sold in sealed packages bearing the information that applicable taxes have been paid, these laws are frequently not respected. The practice of selling single cigarettes is widespread, even in many countries where it is prohibited.

5. All primary and secondary schools and all school buses and school events should be smoke-free. There can be no justification for allowing smoking on school property. Enforcement of this ban should command a high priority.

6. Smokeless tobacco products should be prohibited or, at a minimum, their dangerous health effects should be well publicized and strong health warnings should be obligatory.

7. Increasing taxes and prices of cigarettes and tobacco products is crucial for controlling smoking by young people, among whom demand is particularly responsive to changes in price (see Chapter 8).

8. All measures that promote a smoke-free environment are effective in preventing young people from smoking. The most important of these are banning all tobacco advertising and promotion, including indirect advertising and sponsorship of sports events, and restricting smoking in public places.

9. Enactment and effective enforcement of legislation are essential.

Among the various legislative strategies available, high priority should be given to banning all tobacco advertising and sponsorship so as to free young people from the pressure to take up smoking. Leading researchers in the USA have offered the following advice (DiFranza et al., 1987)

> If the decision about smoking can be delayed until adulthood, choosing to become a smoker is unusual. Given that only 10% of current smokers began as an adult, enforcement of minors' tobacco access laws presents a unique opportunity to deal a mortal blow to this fatal addiction. Efforts to enact comprehensive and enforceable laws ... should receive the full and enthusiastic support of the health care community.

Legislation has the power to make cigarettes less attractive and less available to young people. It contributes to an atmosphere in which children are allowed to grow up free from the pressure to smoke. Sweden has set itself the goal of making the next generation of children the smoke-free generation. Canada has adopted the slogan, "Here comes the breakaway generation" – the generation that can break away from the dangerous addiction to tobacco. WHO's World No-Tobacco Day each year is dedicated to this important goal.

Chapter 12

Health education

Public information and public education programmes comprise a vast range of activities and reflect the desire of governments, health agencies, and others to change knowledge, attitudes, and behaviour in the community at large, or in subgroups within the community . . . It is essential that the public in any country should be well informed on smoking and health. This will not necessarily of itself alter smoking rates but is a prerequisite for further action.

Controlling the smoking epidemic: report of the WHO Expert Committee on Smoking Control. WHO Technical Report Series No. 636. Geneva, World Health Organization, 1979.

Most countries have educational programmes on the hazards of smoking, but not all of them have enacted legislation making health education on tobacco mandatory, and even fewer have legislation that allocates funds to such programmes. While effective health education may exist in the absence of legislation, the enactment of legislation making health education on smoking compulsory expresses government policy and ensures effective implementation of educational programmes.

Basic reasons for requiring health education

Legislation requiring health education on tobacco is enacted for several reasons:

— to establish the public health policy of preventing the use of tobacco;

— to inform the public, particularly young people, about the health risks of tobacco use;

— to strengthen voluntary educational programmes;

— to reinforce the decisions of ex-smokers not to start smoking again;

— to provide resources (money and trained personnel) for health education programmes on smoking as part of comprehensive school health education curricula, and to earmark curriculum time for education in schools;

— to promote public opinion opposed to tobacco and in favour of smoke-free environments;

— to inform policy-makers, health professionals, and the media on issues concerning tobacco and health;

— to promote understanding of, support for, and enforcement of legislation to prohibit the advertising and promotion of tobacco, to restrict smoking in public places and workplaces, and to raise taxes on, and prices of, tobacco products.

Legislation and education go hand in hand. No legislation can be expected to succeed without education, and the impact of education is greatly enhanced by legislation. Legislation is itself an educational tool. In the field of tobacco control, legislation and education complement one another.

Types of legislation

Five basic types of legislation requiring health education have been enacted: (*a*) general statutory requirements for public information and health education on smoking; (*b*) requirements for health education in schools on the risks of tobacco use; (*c*) specific educational requirements for high-risk individuals; (*d*) public information on smoking cessation; and (*e*) legislation allocating funding for health education programmes on tobacco.

General statutory requirements

Health warnings on tobacco packages and indications of the tar and nicotine content of cigarettes constitute a form of health information required by statute. The innovation proposed by

Canada and New Zealand of also requiring a package insert is designed to provide more detailed information to the consumer than can be provided on the outside of a cigarette package.

Legislation requiring the provision of information to the public on the risks of tobacco use varies widely in scope and force. In Latin America, for example, the Constitution of 1979 of Ecuador recognizes the right of all Ecuadorians to welfare, including the protection of health, and requires programmes aimed at eliminating alcoholism and other addictions. Bolivia's Regulations of 15 March 1982 require the Health Authority to draw up mass education programmes to counteract the harmful effects of tobacco and to supervise the use of the media for tobacco advertising. In Chile, Decree No. 01 of 2 January 1986 makes the National Commission for the Control of Smoking responsible for designing and evaluating medium- and long-term programmes for smoking control in the fields of education, information, regulation, and evaluation.

In a number of countries, the legislation lays down the types of education to be conducted, the groups to be reached, and the mechanisms to be employed. In Finland, as early as 1976, Law No. 693 of 13 August 1976 on measures to restrict smoking defined the Government's obligations with respect to health education. It makes the National Board of Health responsible for countrywide information activities aimed at restricting smoking, supplying to other national and local agencies materials on the dangers of smoking, and issuing primarily to persons working with children and young people, to health care personnel, to public officials, and to the mass media information on the approach recommended in order to prevent and reduce tobacco smoking. In Spain, the legislation of Catalonia (Law No. 20 of 25 July 1985) directs the Executive Council to implement health information and education programmes and activities designed to inform the public of the harmful effects of substances liable to produce dependence, including tobacco. These measures are to be directed in particular towards children and young persons and the social groups concerned. In the USA, the Comprehensive Smoking Education Act of 1984 was enacted "to provide a new strategy for making Americans more aware of any adverse health effects of smoking, to assure the timely and widespread dissemination of research findings and to enable individuals to make informed decisions about smoking". To this end, the Secretary of Health and Human Services is directed, *inter alia*, to conduct and support research on the effects of cigarette smoking on human health and develop materials for informing the public of such effects; to coordinate all research and educational programmes relating to the effect of cigarette smoking on health; to maintain liaison with private

131

and public agencies; to collect, analyse, and disseminate (through publications, bibliographies, and otherwise) information, studies, and other data relating to the effect of cigarette smoking on human health; and to compile and make available information on state and local laws relating to the use and consumption of cigarettes. The Act also provides for the establishment of an Interagency Committee on Smoking and Health to assist in the coordination of these efforts.

Requirements for health education on smoking in schools

Health education curricula in schools have long included information on the hazards of smoking. As efforts to control the smoking epidemic have increased, and the crucial importance of reaching young people with this message has become clear, more effective health education programmes have been introduced in schools either by legislation or by administrative regulation. The advantage of legislation is that it may serve as a basis for providing training of teachers in health education methods and may ensure that curriculum time is set aside in the school programme for this activity (World Health Organization, 1990b).

In Mexico, the General Law on Health of 1983 provides for the education of the family, children, and adolescents both through individual methods and mass communications to prevent tobacco use by children and adolescents. Coordination agreements between the Secretariat of Health and Welfare and the states provide for implementing smoking control programmes in higher educational institutions and for preventing smoking by children and adolescents. In Uruguay, largely because of the concern about the increase in smoking among young people of both sexes, the Ministry of Public Health, with the active participation of the Ministry of Education, organizes No-Tobacco Day, involving educational councils at the primary, secondary, and teacher training levels.

In Norway, education on smoking and health is compulsory in primary schools. Finland's General Directive on health education (DNO 3113/02/78) specifies health education objectives, the organizational structure for health education, the functions of health education coordinators, and methods for evaluating health education programmes (Finland, National Board of Health, 1977, p. 43). Within this framework, health education on smoking and health is provided as part of the curriculum. In Sweden, government-funded education on tobacco and health began in 1964. Health education on tobacco is mandatory in all schools. The county councils are responsible for public health education in their areas (Ramström, 1983).

In the USA, nearly half the states have enacted laws requiring education on smoking and health in both primary and secondary schools. Information on the health effects of tobacco use may be included as part of general health education or a drugs-and-alcohol course. Educational programmes, however, rarely provide education on methods of stopping smoking for students who have already started. In 1985, 21 of the 50 states required school health education on effects of tobacco use, and three states required training programmes to educate teachers, school administrators, and other school personnel about the effects of nicotine and tobacco use or on the best methods for instructing students on these topics (US Department of Health and Human Services, 1989, p. 495).

Specific educational requirements for high-risk groups

A few examples exist of legislation requiring information on the dangers of smoking by high-risk groups. A Finnish Directive covering maternity centres, child health centres, and school health programmes calls for specific health education activities on tobacco (Finland, National Board of Health, 1977). In Greece, pursuant to a Decision of 1976, a Child Health Booklet must be issued to every expectant mother, to be kept as a health record for the child and presented when the child enters school. This booklet contains advice for the pregnant woman, including the recommendation that if she is a smoker she should stop or at least greatly reduce her smoking, as there is otherwise a risk that the child will be premature or underweight. In the USA, a package insert is required in each package of oral contraceptives warning the consumer that cigarette smoking increases the risk of serious side-effects on the heart and blood vessels from oral contraceptive use and advising women who use oral contraceptives not to smoke (*Code of federal regulations*, Title 21, sec. 310.501).

Public information on smoking cessation

While much legislation on tobacco control is directed at preventing people, and particularly young people, from starting to smoke, some is designed to assist the treatment of tobacco addiction. Legislation in Chile (Decree Law No. 2.763 of 1979 and Supreme

133

Decree No. 395 of 1979 of the Minister of Health), for example, requires promotion of cessation activities. While cessation programmes are generally run by voluntary organizations, legislation requiring public information on smoking cessation can increase access to them.

Funding for health education

It seems eminently reasonable to allocate a certain percentage of tobacco tax revenues to education on the health effects of tobacco use, but the number of countries doing so has grown only slowly. In Finland, Law No. 693 of 1976 required 0.5% of the tobacco tax revenue to be set aside each year in the national budget for the development of health-oriented tobacco policy, including health education, research, and evaluation. As discussed in Chapter 8, this amount was subsequently decreased and then progressively increased to 0.45%. In Iceland, the State Agency for Trade in Alcoholic Beverages and Tobacco must allocate 2% of gross sales to finance advertising and health education warning about the dangers of smoking (Law No. 74 of 1984). In Peru, the Law of 20 October 1982 provides that a tax increase of 9% on cigarettes made from blond tobacco is to be allocated to constructing and equipping a cancer hospital, to developing cancer detection centres throughout the country, and to research on neoplastic diseases. In French Polynesia, legislation introduced in 1982 provides that not less than 1% of the revenue from tobacco taxes is to be used for a health education campaign through the press, posters, and other means. In the State of California (USA), the legislation imposing an increase of $0.25 in the tax on each package of cigarettes, approved by the voters in 1988, provides that approximately 20% of the increased revenue is to be allocated to health education on the effects of tobacco use (Bal et al., 1990).

In Australia, the Tobacco Act 1987 of the State of Victoria banning tobacco advertising and providing for the buying out of tobacco-sponsored sports, created the Victorian Health Promotion Foundation, inter alia, to fund activities related to the promotion of good health, to increase awareness of programmes for promoting good health in the community through the sponsorship of sports, the arts, and other popular culture, to encourage healthy lifestyles in the community, and to fund research and development activities in support of these objectives. The Foundation is funded by an increase in the tax on cigarettes, which enables the Foundation to replace tobacco companies' sponsorship of sports and cultural events, as discussed earlier, and to support health education on tobacco (Raw et al., 1990). In Western Australia, the State Government began in 1984 to allocate A$2 million annually from tobacco revenues to education on tobacco use. In 1990, the passage in Western Australia of the Tobacco Control Act banning advertising and sponsorship by the tobacco companies created the Western Australian Health Promotion Foundation, which currently receives A$11 million annually for health education and health promotion, in addition to the Government's annual grant (M.M. Daube, personal communication, 1991).

General experience

The principal virtue of legislation on public information and health education on tobacco and health is that it makes these activities official policy. Thus, it supports the allocation of money and personnel for these purposes.

In Sweden, since 1963, the Government has provided funding for smoking-control activities, including health education. In 1964, Sweden established the world's first specialized agency on smoking and health — something that is now generally recognized as essential to provide leadership and coordination for smoking control (Ramström, 1983).

In explaining the remarkably advanced smoking-control policy and legislation of Finland, the Deputy Director of the Health Department of the Ministry of Social Affairs and Health emphasized in 1977 the importance of government policy for health education as follows (Finland, National Board of Health, 1977):

> In health education the main problems were lack of resources, deficiencies in organization and lack of defined responsibilities, leadership, and coordination; without those there is little chance of success, however convincing the message. The chief needs therefore were for funds and other resources and for coordinating activities among separate branches of administration . . .

In the years since the Swedish and Finnish Governments recognized the central role of health education in smoking control, many other countries have developed strong health education programmes on tobacco and health. Moreover, economists in the USA and the United Kingdom have demonstrated the cost-effectiveness of such programmes (Townsend, 1987).

In the USA, over the period 1953–70, Hamilton (1972) found that health education had a significant impact and was much more effective in deterring smoking than advertising was in encouraging it. The broadcasting of antismoking advertisements in 1968–70 reduced cigarette consumption by an estimated 14% (Hamilton, 1972). Warner (1977) estimated that the reduction resulting from these broadcasts was even greater — 17%. In the USA, over the four decades from the 1950s through the 1980s, the use of the mass media has been a key strategy in tobacco-control programmes. Although past studies of media campaigns have indicated that the effects on smoking behaviour were limited, there is increasing evidence that media campaigns can produce meaningful, if modest, behaviour change. With 25 years of public information on the health risks of smoking, media messages "have a greater chance of triggering a positive behavior change in this 'conditioned' population"(Erickson et al., 1990).

In the United Kingdom, publication of the reports of the Royal College of Physicians of London and the publicity attendant on their release led to a reduction in cigarette consumption among men of 5% in 1962, 1965, and 1971 (Atkinson & Skegg (Townsend), 1973; Townsend, 1987).

Townsend endorses these econometric studies as useful in identifying the effects of health education campaigns on a national basis, using annual or quarterly data, but recommends cost-effectiveness analysis of particular campaigns. She points out that an analysis of this type may be necessary to determine the most effective way to spend a budget for smoking-control programmes or to assess how much to allocate to smoking control as compared with other strategies (Townsend, 1987).

In view of the many competing demands for resources for health promotion and health services in all countries, legislation mandating health education is essential as a means of ensuring that cost-effective strategies in health education aimed at reducing tobacco consumption will be undertaken.

Chapter 13

Judicial action for tobacco control[1]

Litigation — the invocation of judicial action — is a flexible and powerful instrument with the potential for helping to accomplish a wide range of smoking-control goals. It has been used to address many of the problems that can also be handled by legislation as described in the previous chapters.

Thus, product liability litigation can help control cigarette advertising (Chapter 3), the adequacy of warnings (Chapter 4), and the presence of extraneous harmful substances (Chapter 5), as well as provide economic leverage to discourage sales (Chapter 7). Direct actions can sometimes be brought to prohibit deceptive advertising practices and enforce prohibitions (Chapter 3). Lawsuits against employers can result in smoke-free workplaces, through either direct injunctions or the deterrent effect of the prospect of having to pay compensation to adversely affected employees (Chapter 9). Young people can be protected by law suits against retailers who sell cigarettes to them illegally (Chapter 10).

Whether judicial, legislative, or executive action is preferable will depend on the issue, the country, and the time; frequently, the only way to be sure is to try all three.

In this chapter, we shall consider in turn the major types of judicial action for tobacco control that have been brought so far. Nearly all the judicial actions have been brought in industrialized countries where the tobacco-control movement is well established, but legal actions are also being considered in some developing countries.

---

[1] This chapter was written by Richard A. Daynard, Professor of Law, Northeastern University School of Law, Boston, MA, USA.

Product liability suits

Lawsuits are now being actively pursued in Canada, Finland, the United Kingdom and the USA seeking compensation for ailing smokers, or their surviving relatives, from cigarette manufacturers. The suits allege that the products are unreasonably dangerous in that their risks exceed any possible benefits, that the manufacturers have failed to give full and undiluted warnings, that they have lied about the dangers, and that they have failed to pursue safer product designs. Smoking-control groups in several Asian and Pacific countries, as well as elsewhere in Europe, are also considering bringing such actions.

Though each suit involves only one afflicted smoker, the fate of the entire cigarette industry hangs on each one. If any single smoker finally receives compensation from a tobacco company, every other victim becomes a potential claimant. If a single plaintiff's attorney proves that he or she can make money by suing tobacco companies, all plaintiffs' attorneys are thereby encouraged to try. If such lawsuits can succeed in one country, they can probably succeed in many countries. The wound, once opened, cannot be closed. Indeed, developments in individual cases have resulted in 5–10% increases or decreases in the value of tobacco stocks, while the spectre of litigation has depressed the companies' share values by 30% or more. For, while the companies can easily defend 100 suits or even pay out a few million dollars in damages, they would have great difficulty with thousands of suits or paying out billions of dollars.

Even more modest scenarios could wreak havoc with the industry's operations. To begin with, substantial expenses have to be passed on to consumers. In the USA, one round of price increases for both cigarettes and smokeless tobacco has been attributed to the companies' legal fees incurred in their thus-far-successful defence efforts. Any substantial number of plaintiffs' victories would surely force at least a 10% price increase. And any such increase would, if past experience is any guide, produce a 12% decrease in smoking among teenage boys (Warner, 1986b). Larger victories would produce even greater decreases. Since one million young people start smoking each year in the USA (US Department of Health and Human Services, 1989), and many times that number start smoking each year worldwide, decreases of this magnitude will eventually save tens of thousands of lives each year in the USA, and hundreds of thousands of lives if the effect is more widespread.

In addition, the very process of defending these suits has been costly to the industry's image. The so-called "discovery" process — the legal procedure by which plaintiffs' attorneys rummage through the industry's files looking for incriminating evidence — has thus far uncovered internal industry documents dating back to the 1930s demonstrating knowledge of the proven health effects of smoking. Papers from the 1950s and 1960s document the conspiracy among the companies to pretend that they cared about their customers' health, genuinely doubted the scientific evidence, and were engaged in bona fide investigations to get to the truth of the matter (*Cipollone v. Liggett Group 1988*). This evidence has received wide publicity, has helped to inform the public of the harmful effects of smoking, and has accelerated the decline in the industry's already low reputation and the willingness of legislators to proceed aggressively against it. Indeed, in the spring of 1992, the United States Attorney for the Eastern District of New York began a criminal investigation as to whether the evidence unearthed in this and a related civil case constituted mail fraud or wire fraud (*Wall Street journal*, 1992, p. A3).

The industry's legal defence has also had a public relations aspect which, while successful in the short term in swaying juries against tobacco plaintiffs, has been very costly to its long-term interests. The industry's position, vociferously urged by its lawyers in press briefings and media appearances, is that anyone who smokes bears "personal responsibility" for his or her resulting lung cancer, since any American "who hasn't lived in a cave since the 1950s" (one of their favourite ways of putting it) must have known that scientists were saying that smoking could kill you. The point is both a reminder to their current customers of the foolishness of continuing to use their products, as well as a concession that only a fool would have believed their continued protestations that the dangers of smoking had not been proven.

Indeed, although the industry has usually raised questions about the cause of the plaintiff's cancer, their principal defence has been based on the widespread publicity in the American media given to the epidemiological and laboratory studies beginning in 1950, on the front-page status of the findings of the 1964 Surgeon General's report (US Public Health Service, 1964), and on the fact that warning notices have appeared on every package of cigarettes sold in the USA since 1966.

This defence has both a technical, legal aspect and a so-called "common sense" aspect. The legal issue, known as "pre-emption", is whether Congress, when it passed the Federal Cigarette Labelling and Advertising Act in 1965, intended to prevent courts from considering whether the simple act of placing warnings on their packages completely satisfied the manufacturers' obligation to communicate to their customers and potential customers the full range and extent of the dangers from using their products. From 1986 onwards, five federal appeals courts concluded that the 1965 legislation should be read that way: some even went so far as to conclude that Congress intended to permit the companies to tell direct and deliberate lies about the safety of their products — just so long as they continued to put the mandated warnings on the packages (*Cipollone* v. *Liggett Group 1986, 1990*).

In July 1990, a high-level court finally disagreed, when the New Jersey Supreme Court concluded that Congress had intended no such thing (*Dewey* v. *R.J. Reynolds Tobacco Co. 1990*). Then, in February 1991, a Texas appellate court, also in a carefully reasoned opinion, agreed with the New Jersey court that Congress had no intention whatever to pre-empt tobacco liability suits (*Carlisle* v. *Philip Morris Inc. 1991*). In March 1991, the United States Supreme Court agreed to review the pre-emption issue in the *Cipollone* case. Briefs in support of the plaintiff's position were submitted on behalf of major health organizations and state and local governments. Oral arguments took place in October 1991.

On 24 June 1992 the United States Supreme Court issued its landmark decision concluding that the original 1965 Act had no pre-emptive effect whatsoever. When the Act was amended in 1969, Congress did pre-empt "requirement[s] or prohibition[s] . . . with respect to . . . advertising or promotion". The Court interpreted that provision to mean that plaintiffs cannot base their legal claims on the failure to include additional warnings in their product advertisements. It made clear, however, that "the concealment allegations, insofar as they rely on a state law duty to disclose material facts through channels of communication other than advertising and promotion" are not pre-empted. Since the tobacco industry had many ways to communicate the dangers of smoking to current and potential smokers other than product advertising and promotion, e.g., press releases, hotlines, spokespeople on radio and television shows, this means that failure-to-warn claims can be brought against the industry based on post-1969 as well as pre-1969 conduct (*Cipollone* v. *Liggett Group Inc., 1992*).

The most important claims against the industry will, however, be the fraud and conspiracy claims. Leaders of the tobacco industry were called to a meeting in December 1953 and confronted with a choice: to let the developing scientific evidence on the dangers of smoking take their toll on industry profits or to embark on a disinformation campaign to persuade the American public that there were "two sides" to the "controversy", and that the tobacco industry would research the issue and inform the public of the results. They chose the second course, and continue to pursue this disingenuous

140

campaign to this day. The ability of plaintiffs to demonstrate this outrageous behaviour to a jury can be expected to move the jurors' focus from the plaintiffs' fault in not stopping smoking (or not stopping earlier) to the defendants' fault in putting profits ahead of the lives and health of their customers.

Unlike the "pre-emption" defence, the so-called "common sense" objection to tobacco litigation, that every American smoker has been hearing about the public health findings on smoking and health, and reading the Surgeon General's warnings on the packages for two-and-a-half decades, cannot disappear at the stroke of a judicial pen. Answering this objection requires, instead, that jurors understand the addictive nature of tobacco use, the fact that most smokers have already become addicted by the time they reach maturity, and the role of the industry's massive disinformation campaign in encouraging youngsters to take up smoking and in discouraging smokers from making the necessary efforts to stop. Public awareness of these facts has increased dramatically in the last few years, greatly improving the prospects for favourable jury verdicts.

In any event, a case brought in most countries other than the USA would not face these objections. Most people in the world have not seen newspaper accounts, or heard radio or TV stories, about the studies carried out during the 1950s, or even about the 1964 Surgeon General's Report. Most countries have not — like the United States — had warning labels on cigarette packages for almost 25 years, and many of the warning labels in other countries are not even as strong as the tepid American labels.

While most countries do not — like the USA — have a contingent fee system, which encourages plaintiffs' attorneys to finance the cases in hope of future reward, most have legal systems that are generally much less expensive to use than the American system, and large numbers of potential cases which would be more difficult for the industry to defend than the American cases. Since, in most countries, a substantial proportion of cigarettes are manufactured by subsidiaries or licensees of the multinational tobacco cartel, the incriminating documents that have been obtained through the discovery process in the USA and Canada are available for use in evidence in any country in which their products are sold (Tobacco Products Liability Project, 1988, 1989). Furthermore, these companies can generally be castigated for using weaker warnings, and higher tar and nicotine levels, in developing countries than they do for comparable brands in the USA and western Europe (*Jardeleza* v. *R. J. Reynolds Tobacco Co. 1987*).

A case in Finland, filed in 1988 by a person with throat cancer against the Finnish affiliates of British-American Tobacco and R. J. Reynolds Tobacco Co., continues to have a favourable long-term outlook despite a negative decision by the Helsinki City Court in February 1992. The plaintiff is represented by a professor of law, who has received cooperation in information gathering from smoking-control groups worldwide. There were more than a dozen hearings at which evidence was received. Finnish smoking-control groups have published the testimony of each hearing in its own soft-cover book. These have helped to improve the regard for this test case in the Finnish legal and medical communities, and have led to the passage of the Law of 12 June 1990 on product liability, the first legislation anywhere in the world that explicitly recognizes the right of diseased smokers to sue cigarette companies. In a report of the Second Law Committee, which was accepted by the Parliament, the Committee explains why it disagrees with the Government's original motion to exclude tobacco from the scope of the legislation:

> In the Government's motion it is noted that the presumption is that anyone using the product must be aware of the risks that certainly or with great likelihood exist in the use of tobacco products. The marketing of tobacco products, however, concentrates mainly on children and young people and on groups with a lower degree of education than average, who are difficult to reach and hard to convince by health education or information about health risks of tobacco. The fact that the tobacco industry still fully denies the health risks connected to the use of its products, makes it especially difficult to get the information about the said risks through. The use of tobacco products results relatively soon in a form of strong dependence. This makes it difficult to stop later the use commenced already as a child or a youngster. . . .
>
> What is relevant in regard to the Product Liability Law is the relationship between the producer and the user of the product. For this reason, a warning about the dangers of the product given by a third party, like the National Board of Health, cannot be considered adequate to release the producer from the liability. . . .[T]aking into account the marketing customs and the target group of the same and the strong dependence created by tobacco products together with the fact that the tobacco industry denies health dangers caused by tobacco, it is the opinion of the Committee that the Law of Product Liability applies also to tobacco products (*Finnish Parliamentary Report*, 1990).

While the legislation applies only to cases filed after 1 September 1991 and is therefore not directly applicable to the above-mentioned case itself, it increases the likelihood that the Finnish Supreme Court will overrule the Helsinki City Court and decide the case for the plaintiff, probably in 1995. Also pointing in the same direction are 1989 and 1991 advisory rulings from the Helsinki Consumer Complaints Board that the plaintiff should prevail (*Aho* v. *Rettig Oy 1990*).

As the Aho case suggests, the very filing of such lawsuits produces tremendous media publicity, emphasizing the fact that disabling and fatal diseases caused by smoking affect individuals, as well as highlighting the duplicitous behaviour of the multinational defendants. Each legal development in any case can be the basis for further publicity. And a victory in any country will immeasurably strengthen the smoking-control movement in that country, as well as inform smokers of the dangers that they are running and demonstrate throughout the world the vulnerability of the multinational tobacco industry.

The possibilities for successful lawsuits against the tobacco industry may be enhanced where synergistic reactions, non-tobacco contaminants, or defective product designs can be shown. For example, an Australian asbestos manufacturer, who had been sued by a former employee who contracted lung cancer, brought a claim in 1990 against the manufacturers of the cigarettes which the employee had smoked for 40 years at the rate of 20 a day. Although the employee had worked in the asbestos mine for only seven months in 1961, the asbestos manufacturer had previously been ordered to pay full damages for the lung cancer in similar situations. If the claim against the cigarette manufacturers for contribution is successful in this or a similar case in the future, it will set a worldwide precedent for cigarette industry liability for its share of this synergistically caused disease (*Gallagher* v. *Midalco/CSR 1990, 1991*).

Several cases brought, beginning in 1990, against the manufacturers of Kent cigarettes and of their filters by people with mesothelioma, who had never worked with asbestos but who did smoke Kent cigarettes in the 1950s when their "Micronite" filter contained crocidolite asbestos, do not involve the "assumption of the risk" defence, since Kent smokers did not know that they were puffing on asbestos (*Ierardi* v. *Lorillard Inc. 1991*).

Victims of fires caused by cigarettes — whether the smokers themselves or others — have sued tobacco companies for their failure to redesign their cigarettes so that they do not start fires if dropped on bedding or upholstery. The United States Congress provided critical support for these suits when it stated, in the preamble to the Fire Safe Cigarette Act of 1990, that "it is technically feasible and may be commercially feasible to develop a cigarette that will have a significantly reduced propensity to ignite furniture and mattresses".

Product liability suits are also possible on behalf of another group — passive smokers. The compelling evidence that environmental tobacco smoke (ETS) causes lung cancer and other diseases, as well as the view increasingly being held in many countries that cigarette smoke imposes an unreasonable risk on non-smokers, make it likely that non-smokers will be able to sue tobacco companies on strict liability grounds for their ETS-induced diseases.

Workplace and domestic suits

Suits have been brought by non-smokers either to obtain recognition of their right to a smoke-free workplace, or to obtain compensation from their employers for injuries done to them by second-hand smoke.

Cases ordering employers to provide smoke-free workplaces for non-smoking employees have proceeded either as suits for injunctive relief to enforce a common law right to a safe workplace (*Shimp* v. *N. J. Telephone Co. 1976; Lee* v. *Massachusetts Department of Public Welfare 1983*), or on the basis of law protecting handicapped workers. In 1991, a California appellate court ruled that, since the law defines a handicapped individual as a person with a disability that "substantially limits one or more major life activities", and breathing is a major life activity, asthmatic employees should not be exposed to ETS. They also ruled that "good faith" efforts to accommodate handicapped non-smokers are not sufficient if they are not successful, and if more efficacious methods (such as banning smoking entirely) are reasonably available (*County of Fresno* v. *Fair Employment and Housing Comm'n of the State of California 1991*).

Litigation by adversely affected non-smokers seeking compensation from their employers has been brought on a wide variety of legal bases. These include negligence (*McCarthy* v. *Washington Department of Social and Health Services 1988*), workers' compensation statutes (*Schober* v. *Mountain Bell Telephone Co 1980; National Insurance Office* v. *Estate of Gun Palm 1985; Carroll* v. *Melbourne Metropolitan Transit Authority 1988; Appeal of Joan Clay 1990*), unemployment compensation statutes (*Alexander* v. *California Unemployment Insurance Appeals Board 1980*), and court decisions protecting people who complain about second-hand smoke from retaliation by their employers (*Hentzel* v. *Singer Co. 1982; Carroll* v. *Tennessee Valley Authority 1988*). These and similar cases have resulted in substantial money judgements or settlements for afflicted non-smokers in Australia, Sweden, the United Kingdom, and the United States. Equally importantly, the fear of such litigation has helped to induce employers to ban or limit workplace smoking (Sweda, 1991).

With increased public awareness of the harm that ETS causes to young children, the issue of whether a parent smokes (or permits smoking in the home) has begun to appear in child custody disputes. It surfaced in at least two cases in 1990. In one, the court ordered the mother not to smoke in the presence of her five-year-old son, while in the other the court took the issue into consideration in making a custody award (*De Beni Souza* v. *Kallweit 1990; Satalino* v. *Satalino 1990*).

144

This type of litigation will be greatly assisted by the landmark decision of 7 February 1991 in a case brought by the Australian Federation of Consumer Organisations (AFCO) against the Tobacco Institute of Australia (TIA) (*AFCO* v. *TIA 1991*). TIA had run an advertisement in 1986 in Australian newspapers — similar to ones that have been run in the USA and elsewhere — asserting that "there is little evidence and nothing which proves scientifically that cigarette smoke causes diseases in non-smokers". AFCO sought an injunction to prevent TIA from ever running such an advertisement again. The Federal Court of Australia heard testimony over a nine-month period, and even took testimony in London from Sir Richard Doll, Dr Nicholas Wald, Dr Dimitrios Trichopoulos, and Dr Dwight Janerich. The court granted the injunction; in a 210-page opinion, the judge carefully analysed and rejected the industry's pseudo-scientific arguments, holding instead that there was "compelling" evidence even in 1986 that passive smoking caused lung cancer, and overwhelming evidence that it caused asthma as well as respiratory diseases in children.

Suits resisting exploitation by transnational tobacco companies

A class action suit was brought in the Philippines in 1987 by five attorneys and their families, seeking to force the domestic licensees of Philip Morris and R. J. Reynolds to put the same labelling on the cigarettes in the Philippines as in the United States, and to remove their advertising from radio and television, as they have done in the United States (*Jardeleza* v. *R. J. Reynolds Tobacco Co. 1987*). The defendants have claimed that, by failing to put warning labels on Philippine cigarettes, they are not behaving in a racist or colonialist spirit since, they claim, there is evidence that Philippine lungs are hardier than American ones. This case is still pending, the trial having been delayed because the courthouse in which the papers had been filed mysteriously burned down.

Cases enforcing advertising bans

Several cases have been brought by the Australian smoking control movement against television stations that broadcast cigarette advertisements masquerading as sports events. The Australian Supreme Court upheld the prosecution of a television station on this basis, demonstrating a refreshingly subtle and accurate analysis of the techniques whereby cigarette companies subvert advertising restrictions.

Lawsuits to prevent illegal sales to minors

A realistic threat of a lawsuit may give retail stores strong incentives to obey the laws against selling tobacco products to minors. In *Kyte* v. *Philip Morris, Inc. and Store 24, Inc.*, a test case brought in Cambridge, Massachusetts, USA, two teenagers sued a chain of stores for illegally supplying them with cigarettes while they were under age, with the result that they are now addicted. In addition to seeking damages sufficient to cover the cost of monitoring their future medical condition for signs of lung cancer and other smoking-induced conditions, they sought an order requiring the stores to obtain positive identification from young people wishing to buy cigarettes, as they do with those wishing to buy alcohol. Faced with the certainty of additional adverse publicity if the case went to trial, as well as a likely order requiring them to pay the plaintiffs' attorneys' fees under the State's Consumer Protection Law, the store chain agreed in June 1991 to require young would-be purchasers to prove their age (*Kyte* v. *Philip Morris Inc., 1987*).

Lawsuits brought by the tobacco industry

Lawsuits have been brought by the tobacco industry in an effort to curb the activities of the smoking-control movement. These include: a trade infringement suit brought by Philip Morris' beer subsidiary against Alan Blum and Doctors Ought to Care (DOC) for selling T-shirts ridiculing a promotional event; an effort by the Swedish tobacco industry to get the legal ombudsman to suppress the very effective "Smart promotion" booklets distributed by Government and private agencies; an effort by the Netherlands tobacco industry to force health groups to apologize for suggesting that second-hand smoke is dangerous; and the effort of the Canadian industry to have Canada's tobacco advertising ban declared a violation of the free-speech provisions of the 1982 Canadian Charter of Rights and Freedoms (Department of the Secretary of State of Canada, 1987).

Thus far, these tactics appear generally to have backfired. Philip Morris quickly withdrew its complaint over DOC's T-shirts after the *Wall Street Journal* ridiculed its lack of humour, and *Time* magazine criticized its hypocrisy in purporting to love the First Amendment's protection of free speech, but only when it comes to tobacco advertising. The Swedish legal ombudsman refused to interfere with "Smart promotion", except to require that it not use a parody of a Camel advertisement for its front cover. The Netherlands court decided in 1990 that the health groups had behaved properly in warning of the dangers of environmental tobacco smoke. The tobacco companies thereafter withdrew all claims and agreed to compensate the health groups for their legal costs. All these cases have provided effective opportunities to publicize the dangers of tobacco use to the general public.

Even the Canadian action, which has produced a substantial preliminary victory for the industry, has also had important negative side-effects for it. It has already resulted in the release of industry documents revealing how its marketing devices have undermined smoking-control efforts (see Chapter 2, p. 10–11), while it has not deterred the Canadian Government from taking even bolder measures to rein in the industry. Yet, despite the evidence submitted on the health consequences of tobacco advertising and the revelations of the industry's marketing and promotion tactics, Mr Justice Jean-Jude Chabot of the Quebec Superior Court ruled on 26 July 1991 that the Tobacco Products Control Act banning tobacco advertising and sponsorship and providing for government-imposed health warnings was unconstitutional on two grounds: (1) the subject of the legislation is a matter not within the power of the Federal Government but within provincial jurisdiction; and (2) the Act contravenes the provisions governing commercial freedom of expression in the Canadian Charter of Rights and Freedoms (*RJR-Macdonald Inc.* v. *The Attorney General of Canada*; and *Imperial Tobacco Ltd.* v. *The Attorney General of Canada 1991*).

Commenting on the decision at a news conference in Ottawa on 1 August 1991, Victor Lachance of the Canadian Council on Smoking and Health said that:

> The health community does not agree with the freedom of a manufacturer to promote a known carcinogen. It is ludicrous to think that the government can exercise control over the advertising of such products as prescription drugs, professional services, firearms, sexual aids, heroin and other drugs for pain control, but not tobacco products (National Campaign for Action on Tobacco, 1991).

He pointed to the "world-precedent-setting" decline of 25% in tobacco consumption in Canada following the entry into force of the Tobacco Products Control Act in 1989, combined with higher taxes and control of smoking in public places and workplaces.

On 14 August 1991, the Government of Canada filed an appeal against Justice Chabot's decision to the Quebec Court of Appeal. A further appeal will be available to the Supreme Court of Canada.

Conclusions

The tobacco industry has shown an extraordinary ability to deflect, neutralize, or at least blunt the most pointed and promising public health campaigns aimed against it and its products. However, every promising avenue for reducing smoking and protecting potential victims should be explored. Tobacco litigation of the kinds described is within the financial reach of many pro-health organizations, and is worth considering as a means of ensuring health protection. If even a few of these cases are successful, they may destroy the industry's credibility, cripple its ability to misinform about the dangers of its products, and seriously impede its efforts to market cigarettes to children.

Chapter 14

The challenge to developing countries

> The facts of tobacco today are that the countries where consumption is growing fastest are the world's poorest and hungriest.
>
> Mike Muller, *Tobacco and the Third World: tomorrow's epidemic?* London, War on Want, 1978

More than a decade has passed since Mike Muller issued his grim statement, and in that time developing countries have begun to grapple with the additional burden that tobacco use imposes on their people, who are still suffering from infectious diseases and malnutrition. In Asia, China, with a population of more than a thousand million, has enacted its first tobacco-control law, the Law of 29 June 1991 on the exclusive sale of tobacco of the People's Republic of China, which came into force on 1 January 1992. Thailand is supplementing its legislation with a vigorous comprehensive tobacco-control programme. Of the 20 Latin American countries, 15 have some type of legislation restricting tobacco advertising and promotion (US Department of Health and Human Services, 1992). One-third of the countries in the African Region of WHO have enacted restrictions on smoking in public places. This trend in legislation is matched by activities in other spheres.

The developing countries offer large, mostly untapped markets for the multinational tobacco companies. As early as 1984, an article in the industry's trade journal, the *Tobacco reporter*, stated:

The Asian market — the lucrative and elusive Asian market. There are not many places left in the world that make US cigarette manufacturers wring their hands in anticipation and pat their wallets in hope.

In 1986, in another tobacco industry trade journal, the Vice-President, Philip Morris Asia, noted "the most important feature on the landscape, the China market" (Scull, 1986).

While the multinational tobacco companies have targeted the developing countries as a source of new markets, as discussed earlier in connection with trade policies, several factors favour the ability of such countries to protect their people against the scourge of tobacco use, one of them being sex differences in tobacco use. With the exception of parts of India, Nepal and Papua New Guinea, smoking — especially cigarette smoking — is generally a male habit in developing countries (Chapman & Leng, 1990, p.22 ; Waldron et al., 1988). However, rural women in India make extensive use of tobacco and betel quid mixed with lime, with devastating consequences in terms of oral cancer (Gupta, 1988, 1989).

Another factor to be taken into account is the low frequency of smoking in many developing countries. The per capita cigarette consumption in the rich countries is much higher than that in the poorer ones. However, experience indicates that when the per capita gross national product (GNP) of a developing country increases, cigarette consumption may also increase. The relationship between GNP and level of cigarette consumption is not linear; a small increase in GNP may be associated with a relatively large increase in cigarette consumption in some countries. A larger increase in GNP appears to have a much smaller effect on cigarette consumption (Chapman & Leng, 1990, p. 24; Chapman & Fahey, 1989).

Also on the side of the developing countries is the potential for the dissemination of knowledge about the increased risk of disease and premature death from the use of tobacco. Unfortunately, most people in developing countries, even many physicians, are unaware of the hazards of smoking and especially unaware of the degree of risk. While developing countries thus constitute a vulnerable market, their governments are in a much better position to act on the side of public health than they were a decade ago. And many developing countries have already done so.

Diseases caused by tobacco

In 1979, a WHO Expert Committee (World Health Organization, 1979) warned:

> smoking diseases will appear in developing countries before communicable diseases and malnutrition have been controlled and . . . the gap between rich and poor countries will thus be further expanded.

In November 1985, a report by the Director-General of WHO

(World Health Organization, 1985) stated that disease patterns in developing countries are already resembling those of industrialized countries. In China, for example, from 1978 to 1989, the annual production of cigarettes increased from 500 thousand million to more than 1600 thousand million. Case–control studies in China show large effects of prolonged smoking on lung cancer and unusually high death rates among non-smokers from emphysema and cancer of the oesophagus (*Tobacco alert*, January 1991).

Lung cancer is one of the three commonest cancers in India, Malaysia, and Pakistan and is frequent in both blacks and whites in Zimbabwe (Ball, 1986). It is estimated that 600 000 new cases of lung cancer occur each year throughout the world, most of them due to smoking (Parkin et al., 1984). Oral cancer is the commonest cancer in Bangladesh, India, Pakistan, and Sri Lanka, accounting for about one-third of all cancers. More than 100 000 new cases of oral cancer occur each year in south and south-east Asia. The most important cause is the chewing of tobacco (Ball, 1986). In India, tobacco causes the death of between 600 000 and one million people a year (Gupta & Ball, 1990).

In Latin America, where the multinational tobacco companies have introduced their products in conjunction with an aggressive advertising campaign and the take-over of local cigarette production, smoking is increasing faster than ever before. The WHO Regional Director for the Americas, Dr Carlyle Guerra de Macedo, predicts that, if current smoking patterns do not change, in the first decade of the 21st century more than 10 million Latin Americans will die from cancer, heart disease, and other smoking-induced diseases (Ball, 1989).

In October 1989, WHO convened a Consultation on the Statistical Aspects of Tobacco-Related Mortality (World Health Organization, 1989). From this Consultation and subsequent application of the recommended methodologies, estimates of current annual mortality from tobacco and projections of future mortality were derived for both developed and developing countries. In developing countries, cigarette sales have increased substantially; the prevalence among men exceeds 50% in many places, although the prevalence among women is generally low. Chronic disease mortality rates are high in many parts of Asia and Latin America. It was estimated, though reliable estimates are difficult to make, that during the 1990s the annual number of deaths from tobacco in the developing world would be about one million (Peto & Lopez, 1990; *Tobacco alert*, January 1991).

The litany of disease and premature death from tobacco affects people on all continents. Moreover, tobacco competes with food for family resources and, in the poorest families, may threaten the survival of thousands of children (Chapman & Leng, 1990).

Assault by the tobacco industry

Tobacco is important in developing countries in providing cash crops for farmers, jobs in tobacco processing, and tax revenues and hard currency from exports for governments. The link between the multinational tobacco companies and the governments of countries dependent on tobacco constitutes the "smoke ring" described by Taylor (1984) :

> In the Third World a new Smoke Ring is being forged which is even stronger than the one in the West. It is made up of the same political and economic links — employment, revenue, trade, advertising and promotion — but it is stronger because the governments of many developing countries are even more dependent on tobacco.

The penetration of Third World markets by the multinational tobacco companies accentuates the problems created by indigenous tobacco growing and consumption of local tobacco products. The drive by the multinational tobacco firms to find new markets in developing countries is associated with aggressive advertising and promotion of cigarettes, sponsorship of sports and films, giving away of cigarettes, and marketing of other products with the logos of cigarettes. It was the aggressive advertising and marketing of cigarettes by the multinational tobacco companies that caused China (Province of Taiwan), Japan, the Republic of Korea, and Thailand to resist so forcefully (but unsuccessfully) the threat of trade sanctions by the USA in response to the exclusion of foreign cigarettes, as described in Chapter 7. A study of British American Tobacco (Kenya) Ltd., a subsidiary of the London-based transnational, showed how the company creates relationships with the government, recruits farmers and assists them in growing tobacco, establishes interlocking directorates with other Kenyan firms, thus increasing the tobacco company's power and influence, and adopts distribution systems, marketing strategies, and advertising that increase tobacco consumption (Currie & Ray, 1984).

A further feature of the assault by the tobacco industry is its environmental impact in developing countries. Tobacco curing in such countries uses wood because oil and gas burners are too expensive. The Executive Director of the United Nations Environment Programme is reported to have stated in 1977 that the shortage of firewood was rapidly becoming the poor man's energy crisis (Muller, 1978). Tobacco curing in the developing world is leading to deforestation, so much so that Muller (1978) stated: "Perhaps every cigarette packet should carry a dual health warning: Smoking can seriously damage your health — and your land."

The tobacco industry also exposes people in developing countries to higher risks than those encountered elsewhere because of the high tar and nicotine contents of the cigarettes marketed in such countries. For example, in 1980, tar yields of cigarettes sold in the Philippines were twice those of the same brands sold in Australia, the United Kingdom, and the USA (Nath, 1986). It is to be hoped that developing countries that are restricting tobacco advertising and requiring strong, rotating health warnings, as Thailand has done, will also impose limits on the tar and nicotine content of all cigarettes, both domestic and imported.

Unfortunately, the tobacco industry does not publish data on the tar and nicotine content of cigarettes manufactured or marketed in developing countries — a reflection of the lack of public accountability in the industry's corporate practices, as noted by the United Nations Conference on Trade and Development (United Nations, 1978). Many tobacco-exporting countries do not require the packages containing cigarettes for export to show the tar and nicotine contents. Smokers in many developing countries do not have the benefit of the health warnings required on cigarette packages sold in the USA because cigarettes manufactured or packaged for export are exempt from the requirements of the US Federal Cigarette Labeling and Advertising Act, as mentioned in Chapter 7.

Finally, the *coup de grace* in the assault by the tobacco industry on the developing world is that, in the absence of effective legislation controlling advertising, "tobacco manufacturers have no hesitation in subjecting developing countries to many of the most cynical and discredited forms of advertising that are no longer acceptable in most Western countries" (Gray & Daube, 1980). Two examples may suffice to show the importance that the multinational companies attach to advertising. In Malaysia in 1988, cigarette and cigarette-related advertisers accounted for one-fifth of total advertising expenditure — an increase of 10% as compared with the expenditure six years earlier. By 1988, tobacco manufacturers were spending $32 million on tobacco advertising and sponsorship, and tobacco companies ranked first among the top ten advertisers by 1989 (Chapman & Leng, 1990). In Kenya, although British American Tobacco had a monopoly of foreign brands, it still spent almost $10 million annually on advertising and an even larger sum on promotions. This is an enormous amount, obviously designed to increase demand, not merely to prevent brand-switching (Chapman & Leng, 1990).

Strategies for developing countries

Developing countries face the spectre of rising rates of tobacco-related diseases. But there is still time to arrest the increase, to stop young people from taking up smoking and to prevent an epidemic among women. Many developing countries have enacted restrictive legislation against tobacco use, and their rate of response can be accelerated.

Much has been learned in the industrialized countries over the past 25 years as to the most effective strategies for combating the tobacco epidemic. The developing countries will not need to go through the steps of first enacting limited legislation and then having to strengthen it, as many industrialized countries have done. They may be able to adapt to their own needs the best of the legislation already enacted in industrialized countries.

Many strategies are needed if the struggle against addiction to tobacco is to be successful — education of the people, mobilization of health personnel, and involvement of a wide range of government agencies and voluntary organizations in antitobacco activities. Certainly, an important strategy, validated by experience in a number of countries, is to enact effective legislation to curb the activities of tobacco companies and to promote smoke-free environments. Legislation is an affordable mode of action that can be taken even in poor countries. There is no viable alternative, because legislation is crucial in establishing the official policy of government on smoking and health. No other mechanism speaks so authoritatively for government. Legislation can serve as a basis for freeing people from enticements to use this dangerous substance, for preventing smoking by young people, for disseminating health information to the people, and for achieving a non-smoking society. Legislation, in short, is the cornerstone of a comprehensive programme of smoking control.

Chapter 15

Development and implementation of a policy on tobacco control

> The detrimental effects of smoking have been unquestionably demon-
> strated, and outlines of countermeasures have been recommended by the
> World Health Organization. The persisting problem is a primarily ideo-
> logical and political one. Legislation and administrative practices, de-
> veloped over centuries to support the commercial objective, must be
> adapted in the case of tobacco consumption if they are to serve the interests
> of health. This will hardly be possible in any marketing economy without
> special legislation.
>
> M. Rimpelä, Cigarette smoking and public pol-
> icy, *Scandinavian journal of respiratory dis-
> eases*, 1978.

In societies where non-use of tobacco has become the social norm, policies on tobacco control are aimed at creating tobacco-free societies. The Scandinavian countries pioneered this idea, and the European Conference on Tobacco Policy, held in Madrid in 1988, set the goal of a smoke-free Europe. In North America, health-promotion strategies are directed to this objective. In describing the structure of a smoking-control programme, Gray & Daube (1980) set forth the following objectives:

— to change the behaviour of smokers and maintain that of non-smokers;

— to change the cultural background of society against which cigarette smoking is often viewed as a status symbol, and to establish the realistic view, which is that cigarettes are both unnecessary and hazardous;

— to change the economic and legislative climate so that cigarettes are less available, pressures promoting smoking are ceased, and education programmes are supported;

— to change the cigarette smoked so that it is less harmful;

— to establish non-smoking as the norm, and to ensure the right of the non-smoker to clean air.

Examining these objectives, we find that legislation plays a key role in each one. A springboard for changing individual behaviour and the attitudes of society is legislation to prohibit advertising, to require labelling and effective health warnings, to lower tar and nicotine levels, to make health education compulsory, to prevent smoking by young people, to raise taxes on, and prices of, tobacco products, and to restrict smoking in public places and work-places. On the foundation of legislation, other activities to combat smoking — public information, health education, cessation pro-grammes, research, and evaluation of smoking-control activities — can be built.

Essential for developing a multifaceted, comprehensive pro-gramme of tobacco control is a national focal point to stimulate support, and coordinate all tobacco-control activities. Long re-commended by WHO, a national agency on tobacco or health can facilitate cooperation between government and voluntary agencies, assure continuity and priority for activities on tobacco and health, and provide official recognition and support for effective anti-tobacco efforts (Roemer, 1982, 1986a).

In Norway and Sweden — countries that have achieved signi-ficant decreases in smoking rates — the national organization on smoking and health has played a key role. Sweden was perhaps the first country in the world to establish a specialized agency on smoking and health to serve as a focal point for work in this field (Nordgren, 1983). The National Smoking and Health Association of Sweden is a private organization, supported by government funds, that works closely with the National Board of Health and Welfare. In Norway, the National Council on Tobacco and Health was established in 1971 to coordinate and supervise the government anti-tobacco programme. Essential parts of this programme are: (1) the spread of information, including media campaigns directed to the general public and especially to opinion leaders (politicians, health personnel, teachers, parents); and (2) the passage and imple-mentation of legislation (Norwegian National Council on Tobacco and Health, 1990). Recognizing the value of national agencies on tobacco and health, in 1987 Hong Kong established its Council on

Smoking and Health, and in 1990 China established the Chinese Association on Smoking and Health and Viet Nam its National Campaigning Committee on Tobacco or Health. National agencies on tobacco and health may take various forms. They may be government bodies, organized independently or as components of the ministry of health or national health councils, or they may be voluntary agencies with substantial government support.

The basic functions of national agencies on tobacco and health are to formulate national policy on tobacco control and to develop strategies for implementing it. Among the activities such a national agency may undertake are: (1) the dissemination of information and the promotion of education on the health risks of tobacco use; (2) the drafting and support of legislation for the control of tobacco and its implementation; (3) providing leadership for, and coordinating the activities of, other government agencies; (4) supporting the work of voluntary agencies in this field; (5) enlisting the active participation of professional and citizen groups; (6) undertaking research on epidemiological and behavioural aspects of tobacco control; (7) evaluating the effectiveness of education, legislation, cessation, and other actions; and (8) liaison with international and regional agencies as well as national agencies of other countries concerning tobacco-control strategies.

Categorical or comprehensive legislation

Granted that legislation is an essential base for an effective tobacco control programme, what kind of legislation should be enacted? In the past, governments have generally started with restrictions on advertising and requirements for health warnings. Later, the control of harmful substances, restrictions on smoking in public places, and other measures have been added. By contrast, a few countries, notably Finland and Iceland, have enacted comprehensive statutes encompassing multiple strategies, including bans on advertising, requirements for health warnings, restrictions on smoking in public places, provisions to decrease smoking by young people, and the use of revenue from taxes to support education on tobacco and health.

Categorical legislation has the advantage of providing visibility and of focusing on a single aspect of an anti-tobacco campaign. It offers a platform for publicity and for rallying public support. Belgium, for example, accompanied its sweeping legislation banning smoking in public places with powerful publicity to achieve the maximum change in public attitudes and behaviour through this single-issue legislation. If necessary, further legislation may be enacted to modify or supplement the law as new needs are recognized.

Comprehensive legislation has the advantage of attacking the problem of tobacco use on many fronts. In setting forth an unequivocal, official policy, such legislation has the capacity to bind all departments of government to control use of tobacco. Comprehensive laws serve to mobilize all sectors of society in a concerted, integrated attack commensurate with the magnitude of the problem. Moreover, as Townsend (1990) has pointed out, each component of a comprehensive tobacco-control policy reduces smoking more; each component strengthens and adds to the credibility and success of the other strategies. While the advantages of comprehensive legislation are clear, it may not be politically feasible to enact all components of a tobacco-control programme at a single time.

Experience over the past decade has shown that both categorical and comprehensive laws can be effective. Perhaps more important than the scope of the legislation is its strength. A single strategy, such as the total ban on all tobacco advertising in Canada in 1989 and in France and New Zealand in 1990 (see Chapter 3), will probably have a more powerful impact in reducing smoking than a multitude of weaker strategies. Similarly, the action in 1991 of the Financial Secretary of Hong Kong in imposing a 100% increase in the tax on tobacco (see Chapter 8) will probably contribute to a significant reduction in smoking by young people.

National or subnational legislation

This publication has focused mainly on national legislation, which has the advantage of establishing a uniform, official policy affecting the entire population. National legislation sends a powerful message to all the people.

At the same time, in countries with a federal structure and even in those without, subnational legislation may be adopted that sets higher standards than the national norm. In Canada and the USA, provincial and state legislation, as well as local ordinances, have had enormous success, as discussed earlier. In the large cities of Latin America, legislation restricting smoking in public places is common. While the importance of national legislation is clear, the possibility of enacting subnational or local legislation that gives greater impetus to the movement towards a non-smoking society should not be overlooked.

Effectiveness of legislation in reducing smoking

It is difficult to evaluate the effects of specific types of legislation because so many factors are involved in tobacco use, but the evidence is increasing that specific interventions do have positive effects. Early research by Warner demonstrated the decline in smoking associated with the airing of antismoking messages in the media of the USA (Warner, 1979). The decline in smoking associated with price increases has been demonstrated by a wealth of research, as discussed in Chapter 8. Swedish research has revealed the positive effect of strong, rotating warnings (Ramström, 1984; Roemer, 1986b). An analysis by Tye et al. (1987) disproves the tobacco industry's contention that advertising is designed merely to influence the market share of the various brands. The authors found that "cigarettes enjoy one of the most tenacious brand-loyalties of any consumer product", with only about 10% of smokers switching brands. Reviewing a wealth of studies by researchers in Europe and the USA, they also show the power of advertising in increasing tobacco consumption. As discussed in Chapter 3, a study commissioned by the New Zealand Toxic Substances Board on the relationship between government tobacco-promotion policies and consumption trends in 33 countries provides even more convincing evidence of the decrease in smoking in countries with restrictive legislation (New Zealand Toxic Substances Board, 1989).

While more analyses of specific interventions may add further weight to the case, the effect of legislative restrictions generally has been clearly demonstrated. In a 1984 study, researchers in the United Kingdom analysed data obtained from 14 countries between 1962 and 1980, concluding that countries with legislative programmes made substantially more progress in containing and reducing smoking levels than those which used the approach of a voluntary agreement (Cox & Smith, 1984). In Hong Kong, in the two-year period following the introduction of restrictive legislation and a 400% tax increase on cigarettes, daily smoking rates declined by 16% (J. Mackay, personal communication, 1985). In Norway, in the five years following the enactment of the Tobacco Law of 1973, which outlawed advertising, raised tobacco taxes, and prompted strong educational programmes, cigarette sales declined by 15%, particularly among young people (Tye et al., 1987). Figs A4.1 and A4.2 in Annex 4 depict the effect of legislative measures in Norway and Finland on the consumption of tobacco products. A quantitative evaluation of the effectiveness of tobacco-control legislation in European Community countries found that "legislative measures may be effective both by affecting price levels and through other mechanisms, including health education and the formation of a more general anti-smoking ethos" (Dalla-Vorgia et al., 1990).

As mentioned earlier, a regression analysis covering 22 countries of the Organisation for Economic Co-operation and Development over 26 years showed that comprehensive legislative approaches, including tax increases, advertising bans, and strong warnings on tobacco packages, were effective in reducing consumption. The study further showed that mild control measures had no measurable effect but that, once measures extended beyond a threshold of partial advertising bans and mild health warnings, progressively stronger measures had a progressively stronger effect in discouraging tobacco consumption (Laugesen & Meads, 1990).

Weakness of the voluntary initiative

The tobacco industry asserts that cooperation between governments and the industry, rather than legislation, is the appropriate strategy to control use of tobacco. Agreements to regulate advertising and to achieve lower tar and nicotine contents still exist in a number of countries.

In recent years, countries that have long had agreements with the industry have enacted legislation. New Zealand is a notable example, and Australia and Denmark are also enacting legislation.

The United Kingdom has had the longest experience of industry agreements to control advertising and other matters. Although the industry has been forced to agree to firmer health warnings, serious criticism of the voluntary agreement has been voiced on the grounds that the industry has failed to agree to stronger restrictions on advertising, has sought to evade restrictions by placing tobacco insignia on non-tobacco products, has expanded promotion activities controlled by the agreement and, to an even greater extent, those not controlled by it. The Royal College of Physicians of London has repeatedly called for the replacement of the voluntary agreement by effective legislation. The British experience over the years confirms the statement by the Chairman of the Norwegian National Council on Smoking and Health (Bjartveit, 1978b):

> Experience in many countries has . . . shown that the tobacco industry will seek to reduce the impact of virtually all smoking control measures and will not willingly agree to any voluntary codes likely to have an adverse impact on tobacco sales. Further, legislation is a much clearer and firmer governmental signal of how serious the problem is, than some hardly visible limitations

obtained through negotiations with bodies representing the vast economic interests in this field. People will soon find out that such compromises are just window-dressing pretending that the government is genuinely concerned.

In Finland, similarly, it was found that (Rimpelä, 1978):

All efforts to achieve a solution by means of an entente between commercial and health-policy interests have proved specious, and in the long run have served only to delay more effective measures for the reduction of tobacco consumption.

National and international action

In a number of countries, the initial impetus for national legislation has been a nationwide analysis of the problem of tobacco use and a report recommending legislative action. To take a recent example, the report of the New Zealand Toxic Substances Board made the case for a legislative ban on all tobacco advertising. A subsequent analysis provided further persuasive evidence for the effectiveness of comprehensive tobacco-control legislation (Laugesen & Meads, 1990). In France, documentation on the prevalence of smoking among young people and the role of advertising in encouraging the use of tobacco impelled the enactment of a total ban on tobacco advertising (Commission des Affaires Culturelles, Familiales et Sociales, 1990). Other countries, faced with the need to control tobacco use, might well begin their legislative work with prevalence surveys and analysis and publication of information on their own conditions related to tobacco use.

Another strategy that has proved effective in advancing tobacco-control legislation on national agendas has been action at the regional level — conferences, workshops, reports, and consultancies. The International Union against Cancer (UICC) has pioneered such efforts. The European Conference on Tobacco Policy, held in Madrid in November 1988, provided a forum for the exchange of information and opinions on action to control tobacco use. It launched new legislative efforts by the 32 Member States of the European Region of WHO to control the smoking epidemic in Europe (World Health Oraganization, 1990b). The Asian Consultancy on Tobacco Control, under the leadership of Dr Judith Mackay, has stimulated action by the Asian countries that have been targeted by the tobacco industry as lucrative potential markets. Clearly, regional meetings and consultancies provide a means for exchanging scientific and technical information that strengthens political resolve to combat the tobacco epidemic.

Contributions by international agencies

The activities of international agencies on the issue of tobacco and health are critical to controlling the smoking epidemic. WHO is unequivocally committed to stopping the use of tobacco. As discussed in Chapter 1, each World Health Assembly has adopted stronger and more specific policies and strategies to prevent avoidable deaths and disability resulting from the use of tobacco (see Annex 2). In 1991, Dr H. Nakajima, Director-General of WHO, outlined to the plenary session of the Economic and Social Council of the United Nations the serious socioeconomic and health problems involved in tobacco production and consumption in developing countries. He expressed the hope that "in due course the competent agencies of the United Nations system will take up with WHO, in a spirit of multisectoral cooperation, the important issues of crop substitution, industrial and tobacco trade issues, government subsidies to tobacco growers, and import duties and taxes on tobacco products" (Nakajima, 1991).

For the past decade, the Secretariat of FAO has cooperated with WHO in drawing the attention of governments to WHO's resolutions concerning smoking and health. FAO will no longer assist countries with tobacco production, and has offered technical cooperation to any government that wishes to explore the possibilities for alternative crops (Marongiu, 1980). Unfortunately, as yet there have been few such requests. The World Bank has also announced that it will make no further loans for tobacco production.

In 1979 and 1980, the Health Ministers of the Arab States of the Gulf Area adopted a series of resolutions on smoking and health (*International digest of health legislation*, 1981). Resolution 28, "Health hazards of smoking", adopted in 1979, is designed to protect children and young people from the hazards of smoking and to safeguard the rights of non-smokers to enjoy a smoke-free environment. Resolution 24, "Public health hazards of smoking", adopted in 1980, calls on Member States that have not yet done so to prohibit the advertising of tobacco products in newspapers and magazines; requests the Member States to prevent tobacco companies from sponsoring sports events; urges Ministers of Information to reduce television programmes that show participants smoking; urges States in the region to stress the need to limit and gradually reduce the areas of land on which tobacco crops may be grown; requests ministers of health to urge Member States to increase customs duties levied on cigarettes to bring prices in all the States of the region into alignment; recommends the prohibition of the promotion or advertising of tobacco and its derivatives and accessories, through cigarette candy, ashtrays, and clothes; requests a study of the tar and nicotine contents of imported cigarettes; establishes a standard warning for cigarette and tobacco packages and all publicity ("Smoking is a leading cause of lung cancer and of pulmonary and cardiovascular disease"); requests airlines to refrain from selling cigarettes and tobacco on aircraft; and authorizes the preparation of posters and publications to promote awareness of smoking hazards.

In May 1980, at the Ninth Meeting of the Health Ministers of the Arab States of the Gulf Area, resolution 3, "Smoking control", reaffirmed previous actions by the Health Ministers. It endorsed the recommendations of the Secretariat that maximum permissible limits should be set of 15 mg of tar and 1 mg of nicotine per cigarette, and that each State should provide the necessary laboratories for monitoring these levels; approved guidelines for educational curricula on smoking hazards; and advocated raising customs duties on cigarettes, tobacco, and tobacco derivatives by at least 30% of the base price on 1 January 1980.

The European Economic Community has provided a model for cooperative action by governments at the regional level on issues of tobacco and health. In 1989, Recommendation 1101 of the Parliamentary Assembly of the Council of Europe urged Member States "to implement comprehensive, multisectoral policies on tobacco". In accordance with its "Europe against Cancer" programme, Directives of the Council of the European Communities have provided for the approximation of laws, regulations, and administrative provisions of the Member States concerning the tar content of cigarettes, the labelling of tobacco products, the prohibition of all forms of tobacco advertising on television, and the restriction of smoking in public places (see Annex 1, Tables D1, D2 and D4). Under the second action plan of the European Economic Community for 1990–1994, work is proceeding on other proposals for legislation on tobacco, including harmonizing the labelling of all tobacco products, banning the manufacture and sale of moist snuff in the European Community, regulating further advertising of tobacco products, aligning taxes on tobacco products upwards, and eliminating tax-free sales of tobacco products for travellers within the Community (A. Karaoglou, personal communication, 1991; *BASP Newsletter*, 1990a,b).

The Asia Pacific Association for the Control of Tobacco (APACT), committed to the goal of achieving a smoke-free Asia in the 21st century, was established to coordinate the tobacco-control efforts of Asian countries. In 1991, its Executive Committee adopted a resolution calling for a national tobacco-control programme in each Asian country with the following components and activities:

163

— a national tobacco-control agency;

— data collection, including data on smoking prevalence and cost analysis;

— health education and information;

— legislative and administrative measures to ban all forms of tobacco advertising, sponsorship, and promotion;

— action designed to: ensure that public places and worksites are smoke-free; reduce and disclose tar and nicotine levels in cigarettes; require strong, rotating health warnings; ban or restrict new forms of tobacco products; prohibit sales to minors; and prohibit cigarette vending machines;

— cessation programmes;

— tax and price policies based on health considerations;

— action to prevent smoking by women in Asia, few of whom currently smoke but who are being targeted by the tobacco companies.

These vigorous and specific actions by international bodies are encouraging signs that the alarm sounded by WHO is being heeded by influential groups. The leadership given by ministries of health to the efforts to control the smoking epidemic is impressive. Much remains to be done, however, if the drive of the transnational tobacco corporations to penetrate the markets of the developing countries is to be slowed and ultimately halted.

Integration with education and health services

Examination of the development and implementation of legislation around the world to control the tobacco epidemic suggests that several policies are fundamental to successful legislative action.

First, it is important to integrate legislation with a comprehensive campaign of public information, health education, and smoking cessation activities. The role of the media in such health education efforts is crucial. Experience in a number of countries indicates that information and education reinforce legislation, and that legislation lays the basis for information and education. Each complements the other.

Second, it is advisable to link implementation of anti-smoking legislation to health services, since smoking-control activities are part of preventive health. Linkage with the health services enhances the credibility and effectiveness of measures to control the use of tobacco.

Third, as discussed earlier, establishing a national agency on smoking and health helps to achieve cooperation among all government and voluntary agencies involved in smoking-control activities. Legislation establishing such an agency provides official recognition, financial support, and, most importantly, leadership for this work.

Outlook for the future

Looking back at the development of legislation to control tobacco use around the world, we see significant progress in terms of the number of countries that have enacted legislation and in the strength and effectiveness of their laws. Noteworthy are the acceptance and approval of legislative controls by the people and the success of governments in enforcing their legislation.

Looking ahead, we see that much remains to be accomplished in order to achieve smoke-free societies. A number of obstacles stand in the way of protecting the people against tobacco addiction — the power and tenacity of the tobacco industry, the competing demands of other health programmes, and the constraints on financial and personnel resources. Despite these obstacles, the question we must ask ourselves is: how many generations must die prematurely and needlessly from tobacco-related diseases before the smoking epidemic is arrested? The dire warning of Richard Peto and Alan Lopez must be heeded: that if no further change occurs in the proportion of young adults who become regular smokers, about 10 million of the world's population now living will eventually die each year from tobacco-related disease beginning in about the year 2025 (Peto & Lopez, 1990).

Fortunately, the tobacco-control forces are gaining strength. Networks of scientists, public health leaders, health professionals of various kinds, policy-makers, and consumers have been organized to bring about the transition to smoke-free societies. Scientific knowledge has been well disseminated. Information is available on experience in developing and implementing legislation to ban tobacco advertising, in raising taxes on tobacco products, in preventing young people from smoking, and in ensuring smoke-free public places and workplaces.

Governments confronting the worldwide tobacco epidemic are increasingly recognizing their ethical responsibility to exercise political will on the side of health. As they undertake effective tobacco-control programmes, they are turning more and more to legislation as an essential tool to express that political will. Legislation, well designed and fully enforced, can provide the leverage necessary for an effective, comprehensive programme to make control of tobacco not simply a goal but a reality.

References

Adriaanse H, Van Reek J (1992) Adults in the European community favour a tobacco advertising ban. *Tobacco control*, **1**: 57.

Aho v. *Rettig Oy and Suomen Tupakka Oy*, 5.1 TPLR 2.4, 5.3 TPLR 2.119 (1990).

Alexander v. *California Unemployment Insurance Appeals Bd*, 162 Cal. Rptr 411 (1980).

Amos A (1990) Women's magazines and tobacco — the preliminary findings of a survey on the tobacco policies of the top women's magazines in Europe. In: Durston B, Jamrozik K, eds, *Tobacco and health 1990. The global war. Proceedings of the Seventh World Conference on Tobacco and Health*. Perth, Health Department of Western Australia, pp. 912–916.

Appeal of Joan Clay, Case no. 2:11:1935, Comm'r's File CI/364/1989 (Social Security Comm'r, United Kingdom, 16 July 1990).

Asian advertising review 88–89 (1989) *Asian advertising and marketing*, April: 24–76.

Atkinson AB, Skegg (Townsend) JL (1973) Antismoking publicity and the demand for tobacco in the UK. *Manchester school*, **41**: 265.

Australian Federation of Consumer Organisations v. *Tobacco Institute of Australia*, 6. 1A TPLR 2.77 (Federal Court of Australia, 1991).

Bagdikian BH (1987) *The media monopoly*, 2nd ed. Boston, Beacon Press.

Bal DG et al. (1990) Reducing tobacco consumption in California. *Journal of the American Medical Association*, **264**: 1570–1574.

Ball K (1986) Smoking spells death for millions. *World health forum*, **7**: 211–216.

Ball K (1989) Tobacco: a doctor speaks. *African business*, June: 12–14.

BASP Newsletter (1990a) No. 8, March.

BASP Newsletter (1990b) Smoking prevention. No. 9, June.

BASP Newsletter (1990c) Smoking prevention. No. 11, December.

Beaglehole R (1991) Science, advocacy and health policy: lessons from the New Zealand tobacco wars. *Journal of public health policy*, **12** (2): 175–183.

Benowitz NL et al. (1983) Smokers of low-yield cigarettes do not consume less nicotine. *New England journal of medicine*, **309** (3): 139–142.

Bjartveit K (1978a) The Norwegian Tobacco Act. *Scandinavian journal of respiratory diseases* (Suppl. 102): 142–146.

167

Bjartveit K (1978b) Governmental action on smoking and health. *Bulletin of the International Union against Tuberculosis*, **53** (4): 334–339.

Bjartveit K (1990) Fifteen years of comprehensive legislation: results and conclusions. In: Durston B, Jamrozik K, eds, *Tobacco and health 1990. The global war. Proceedings of the Seventh World Conference on Tobacco and Health*, Perth, Health Department of Western Australia, pp. 71–80.

Bjartveit K, Lund KE (1987) *Smoking control in Norway*. Oslo, National Council on Smoking and Health.

British medical journal. (1980) Call for stronger government action against smoking. **2**: 1574.

Brown ER et al. (1988) Workplace smoking policies: attitudes of union members in a high-risk industry. *Journal of occupational medicine*, **30**: 312–320.

Buchholz P (1980) Legal aspects of the control of tobacco. *Legal medical quarterly*, **4**: 14–34.

Calgary Health Services (1988) *Smoking by-laws in Canada*. Calgary.

Canadian Cancer Society et al. (1988) *Tobacco taxation and public health. A submission to the Honourable Robert Nixon, Treasurer of Ontario*. Toronto.

Canadian Department of National Health and Welfare (1989) Tobacco products control regulations, *Canada gazette*, Part I, 18 January.

Canadian Department of National Health and Welfare (1990) *Health protection branch information letter #776*, 1 March.

Carlisle v. *Philip Morris, Inc.*, 6.1 TPLR 2.1 (Texas Ct. of Appeals, 3d Dist., 1991).

Carroll v. *Melbourne Metropolitan Transit Authority*, Workcare claim, Victoria Accident Compensation Tribunal, noted in 3.7 TPLR 1.92 (1988).

Carroll v. *Tennessee Valley Authority*, 697 F. Supp. 508 (D.D.C. 1988).

Centers for Disease Control (1990a) Cigarette advertising — United States — 1988. *Morbidity and mortality weekly report*, **39** (16): 261–265.

Centers for Disease Control (1990b) State laws restricting minors' access to tobacco. *Morbidity and mortality weekly report*, **39** (21).

Chapman S (1985) *Cigarette advertising and smoking: a review of the evidence*. London, British Medical Association, Professional Division.

Chapman S, Fahey P (1989) *Cigarette smoking and economic prosperity: the relationship of GNP per capita and cigarette consumption in 103 countries*. Sydney, Department of Community Medicine, University of Sydney.

Chapman S, Leng WW (1990) *Tobacco control in the Third World: a resource atlas*. Penang, International Organization of Consumers Unions.

Chapman S, Richardson J (1990) Tobacco excise and declining tobacco consumption: the case of Papua New Guinea. *American journal of public health*, **80** (5): 537–540.

Chen TTL, Winder AE (1990) The opium wars revisited as US forces tobacco exports in Asia. *American journal of public health*, **80** (6): 659–662.

Choi WS et al. (1992) Restricting minors' access to tobacco — a review of state legislation 1991. *American journal of preventive medicine*, **8** (1): 19–22.

Cipollone v. *Liggett Group Inc.*, 789 F.2d 181 (3d Cir.), cert. denied, 107 S. Ct. 907 (1986).

Cipollone v. *Liggett Group Inc.*, 683 F. Supp. 1487 (D. N. J. 1988).

168

Cipollone v. *Liggett Group Inc.*, 893 F. 2d 541 (3d Cir. 1990).

Cipollone v. *Liggett Group Inc.*, 112 S. Ct. 2608, 120 L. Ed. 2d 407, 60 U.S.L.W. 703 (24 June 1992).

Cockburn A (1989) Light up in Asia. *The Nation*, 30 October, p. 483.

Collishaw NE (1990) *Monitoring effectiveness of Canada's health-oriented tobacco policies.* Paper presented to the 1990 National Workshop on Smoking and Health. Halifax, Nova Scotia, 21 September 1990.

Collishaw NE et al. (1990) *Monitoring effectiveness of Canada's health-oriented tobacco policies.* Paper presented to the Seventh World Conference on Tobacco and Health, Perth, Western Australia.

Collishaw NE et al. (1985) An estimate of the demand for tobacco in Canada 1950–1982. In: *Proceedings of the 34th International Congress on Alcoholism and Drug Dependence, Calgary, Alberta, 4–10 August,* pp. 201–203.

Commission des Affaires Culturelles, Familiales et Sociales (1990) *Rapport fait à l'Assemblée Nationale sur le projet de loi (no 1418) relatif à la lutte contre le tabagisme et à la lutte contre l'alcoolisme. [Report to the National Assembly of France on the proposed law, No. 1418, concerning the struggle against smoking and the struggle against alcoholism.]* Document No. 1482, distributed 22 June 1990.

Connolly GN (1991) Tobacco, trade, GATT and Eastern Europe. *Tobacco on trial,* 15 July pp. 1–2.

Connolly GN (1988) *World health implications of United States tobacco trade policies.* Presentation to the US Interagency Committee on Smoking and Health, 18 February 1988.

Correa P et al. (1983) Passive smoking and lung cancer. *Lancet,* **2**: 595–597.

Council of Europe Consultative Assembly (1973) *Recommendation 716 on the control of tobacco and alcohol advertising and on measures to curb consumption of these products.*

Council of the European Communities and the representatives of the governments of the Member States (1986) *Resolution on a programme of action of the European Communities against cancer* (86/C184/05).

County of Fresno v. *Fair Employment and Housing Comm'n of the State of California,* noted in 6.1 TPLR 1.4 (1991).

Cox H, Smith R (1984) Political approaches to smoking control: a comprehensive analysis. *Applied economics,* **16**: 569–582.

Currie K, Ray L (1984) Going up in smoke: the case of British American tobacco in Kenya. *Social science and medicine,* **19** (11): 1131–1139.

Dalla-Vorgia P et al. (1990) An evaluation of the effectiveness of tobacco-control legislative policies in European Community countries. *Scandinavian journal of social medicine,* **18**: 81–89.

Daube MM (1975) Towards an advertising ban. In: *Proceedings of the 3rd World Conference on Smoking and Health,* Bethesda, MD, National Institute of Health, pp. 841–850 (DHEW publication No. (NIH) 77–1413).

Daube MM (1990) Call for cigarette chemical warning. *West Australian,* 3 July.

Davis RM, Jason LA (1988) The distribution of free cigarette samples to minors. *American journal of preventive medicine,* **4** (1): 21–24.

Davis RM et al. (1990) 'Common courtesy' and the elimination of passive smoking. *Journal of the American Medical Association,* **263** (16): 2208–2210.

Davis RM et al. (1990) Information on tar and nicotine yields on cigarette packages. *American journal of public health*, **80** (5): 551–553.

De Beni Souza v. *Kallweit*, case no. 807516 (Sacramento Cty. Calif. 1990).

De Givry Y (1984) The impact of the 1976 antismoking legislation in France. *International digest of health legislation*, **35**(2): 463–467.

Denoix P (1979) Tobacco — current French legislation. In: *Carcinogenic risks — strategies for intervention*. Lyon, International Agency for Research on Cancer, p. 14 (Scientific Publications Series, No. 25).

Department of the Secretary of State of Canada (1987) *The Charter of Rights and Freedoms: a guide for Canadians*. Ottawa.

Dewey v. *R. J. Reynolds Tobacco Co.*, 577 A. 2d 1239 (N. J. 1990).

DiFranza JR et al. (1987) Legislative efforts to protect children from tobacco. *Journal of the American Medical Association*, **257**: 3387–3389.

DiFranza JR et al. (1991) RJR Nabisco's cartoon camel promotes Camel cigarettes to children. *Journal of the American Medical Association*, **266**: 3149–3153.

Doll R, Hill AB (1950) Smoking and carcinoma of the lung. *British medical journal*, **2**: 729–748.

Doll R, Hill AB (1956) Lung cancer and other causes of death in relation to smoking. *British medical journal*, **2**: 1071–1081.

Doll R, Hill AB (1964a) Mortality in relation to smoking: ten years' observations of British doctors. *British medical journal*, **1**: 1399–1410.

Doll R, Hill AB (1964b) Mortality in relation to smoking: ten years' observations of British doctors (conclusion). *British medical journal*, **1**: 1460–1467.

Dumas A (1978) Cigarette ads — conscience versus profits. *Broadcasting and television weekly*, 10 August.

Durston B, Jamrozik K, eds. (1990) *Tobacco and health 1990. The global war. Proceedings of the Seventh World Conference on Tobacco and Health*. Perth, Health Department of Western Australia.

Economist Intelligence Unit (1983) *Tobacco and food crops in the Third World*. London (Studies in Agriculture and Commodities, No. 3).

Erickson AC et al. (1990) Past lessons and new uses of the mass media in reducing tobacco consumption. *Public health reports*, **105** (3): 239–244 (May-June).

European Bureau for Action on Smoking Prevention (1991) Smoking prevention. *BASP newsletter*, No. 12, April.

Federal Trade Commission (1986) *Report to Congress pursuant to the Federal Cigarette Labeling and Advertising Act, 1984*.

Femi-Pearse D (1983) Aspects of smoking in developing countries in Africa. *New York State journal of medicine*, **83** (13): 1312–1313.

Fielding JE (1986) Banning worksite smoking. *American journal of public health*, **76** (8): 957–959.

Fielding JE (1991) Smoking control at the workplace. *Annual review of public health*, **12**: 209–234.

Fielding JE, Phenow KJ (1988) Health effects of involuntary smoking. *New England journal of medicine*, **319**: 1452–1460.

Finland, Advisory Committee on Health Education (1985) *An evaluation of the effects of an increase in the price of tobacco and a proposal for the tobacco price policy in Finland in 1985–87.* Helsinki, National Board of Health.

Finland, National Board of Health (1977) *Legislative and administrative action for control of tobacco-smoking in Finland.* Helsinki.

Finnish Parliamentary Report, 1990 (II LaVM 4/119/1989 v. p. — Motion of the II Law Committee, *Applying the law of product liability to tobacco products,* 5.3 TPLR 7.15).

Fire Safe Cigarette Act of 1990, Public Law 101–352. August 10, 1990, 101st Congress. 5.4 TPLR 7.17 (1990).

Foote E (1981) Advertising and tobacco. *Journal of the American Medical Association,* **245** (16): 1667–1668.

Gallagher v. *Midalco/CSR* (Supreme Court, West Australia), noted in 5.4 TPLR 1.153 (1990), 6.1 TPLR 1.8 (1991).

Garfinkel L et al. (1985) Involuntary smoking and lung cancer: a case-control study. *Journal of the National Cancer Institute,* **75** (3): 463–469.

Geizerova H, Masironi R (1990) Smoking restrictions in public transport and public places. WHO survey. In: Durston B, Jamrozik K, eds, *Tobacco and health 1990. The global war. Proceedings of the Seventh World Conference on Tobacco and Health,* Perth, Health Department of Western Australia, pp. 759–762.

General Agreement on Tariffs and Trade (1990) *Thailand — restrictions on importation of and internal taxes on cigarettes. Report of the panel,* Geneva.

Glantz S, Parmley WW (1991) Passive smoking and heart disease: epidemiology, physiology, and biochemistry. *Circulation,* **83** (1): 1–12.

Globe and Mail (1991) The Canadian economy. 17 June, p. B3.

Goss J (1990) An economist's rationale for government intervention to reduce the consumption of cigarettes. In: Durston B, Jamrozik K, eds, *Tobacco and health 1990, The global war. Proceedings of the Seventh World Conference on Tobacco and Health,* Perth, Health Department of Western Australia, pp. 789–793.

Government of Victoria (1987) *Submission by the Government of Victoria to the Industries Assistance Commission Inquiry on tobacco growing and manufacturing industries.*

Gray N (1984) *Low tar cigarettes — bane or benefit.* Paper presented to the 6th International Symposium on Prevention and Detection of Cancer, Vienna, 26–29 November 1984.

Gray N, Daube M, eds (1980) *Guidelines for smoking control,* 2nd ed. Geneva, International Union against Cancer.

Gupta PC (1988) Health consequences of tobacco use in India. *World smoking and health,* 5–10.

Gupta PC (1989) An assessment of excess mortality caused by tobacco usage in India. In: Sanghvi LD, Notani P, eds, *Tobacco and health: the Indian scene.* Bombay, Tata Memorial Centre, pp. 57–62.

Gupta PC, Ball K (1990) India: tobacco tragedy. *Lancet,* **335**: 594.

Haglund M (1990) *Tobacco control in Sweden — some remarks on recent developments.* Stockholm, Department of Public Health and Epidemiology, National Board of Health and Welfare.

Hall J (1989) Law on cigarette sales to teens called outdated. *The Toronto Star,* 26 January.

Hamilton JL (1972) The demand for cigarettes: advertising, the health scare, and the cigarette advertising ban. *Review of economics and statistics*, **54**: 401.

Heise L (1988) Unhealthy alliance. With U. S. government help, tobacco firms push their goods overseas. *World-Watch*, **1** (5): 19–28.

Hentzel v *Singer Co.*, 188 Cal. Rptr 159 (1982).

Hirayama T (1981) Non-smoking wives of heavy smokers have a higher risk of lung cancer: a study from Japan. *British medical journal*, **282**: 183–185.

Hong Kong Council on Smoking and Health (1990) *Annual report*, 1989–1990.

Horovitz B (1990) 'Freedom' campaign under siege. *Los Angeles Times*, 8 May pp. D1, D7.

Humble C et al. (1990) Passive smoking and 20-year cardiovascular disease mortality among nonsmoking wives, Evans County, Georgia. *American journal of public health*, **80** (5): 599–601.

Ierardi v. *Lorillard. Inc.*, U.S.D.Ct E.D.Pa. Civ. Action No. 90–7049, 6.1 TPLR 3.11 (complaint) (1991).

Industries Assistance Commission (1981) *Manufactured tobacco*. Canberra, Australian Government Publishing Service (Report No. 256).

International Agency for Research on Cancer (1986) *Tobacco habits other than smoking*. Lyon (IARC monographs on the evaluation of the carcinogenic risk of chemicals to humans, Volume 37).

International Agency for Research on Cancer (1987a) *Tobacco smoking*. Lyon (IARC monographs on the evaluation of the carcinogenic risk of chemicals to humans. Volume 38).

International Agency for Research on Cancer (1987b) *Environmental carcinogens: methods of analysis and exposure measurement. Volume 9. Passive smoking.* Lyon (Scientific Publications Series, No. 81).

International digest of health legislation (1981) Four resolutions on smoking and health adopted by Health Ministers of the Arab States of the Gulf Area. **32** (2): 327–328.

Islam N et al. (1990) Smoking in Bangladesh — a pilot study. In: Durston B, Jamrozik K, eds, *Tobacco and health 1990. The global war. Proceedings of the Seventh World Conference on Tobacco and Health*, Perth, Health Department of Western Australia, pp. 242–244

Janerich DT et al. (1990) Lung cancer and exposure to tobacco smoke in the household. *New England journal of medicine*, **323** (10): 632–636.

Jardeleza v. *R. J. Reynolds Tobacco Co.*, Quezon Trial Ct., 2.7 TPLR 3.409 (complaint) (1987).

Johnston LD et al. (1987) *National trends in drug use and related factors among American high school students and young adults, 1975–1986.* US Department of Health and Human Services, Public Health Service, Alcohol, Drug Abuse, and Mental Health Administration, National Institute on Drug Abuse (DHHS Publication No. (ADM) 87–1535).

Joossens L, Raw M (1991) Tobacco and the European common agricultural policy. *British journal of addiction*, **86**: 1191–1202.

Karaoglu A, Joossens L, eds. (1990) *Report on a new form of smokeless tobacco: moist snuff.* Brussels, European Bureau for Action on Smoking Prevention.

Kyle KL (1990) *Tobacco advertising ban in Canada*. A brief presented to the

Subcommittee on Health and the Environment, Committee on Energy and Commerce, US House of Representatives, 12 July.

Kyte v. *Philip Morris, Inc. and Store* 24, *Inc.*, 2.9 TPLR 2.208 (Super. Ct. Mass. 1987).

Lancet (1990) Europe ~~against~~ for cancer. **336**: 1036

Lando HA (1990) The movement to restrict vending machines in Minnesota: the fight against pre-emption. In: Durston B, Jamrozik K, eds, *Tobacco and health 1990, The global war. Proceedings of the Seventh World Conference on Tobacco and Health*, Perth, Health Department of Western Australia, pp. 741–744.

Laugesen M, Meads C (1990) Do tobacco advertising bans lower consumption? Tobacco advertising restrictions, price, income and tobacco consumption in OECD countries, 1960–86. In: Durston B, Jamrozik K, eds, *Tobacco and health 1990, The global war: Proceedings of the Seventh World Conference on Tobacco and Health*, Perth, Health Department of Western Australia, pp. 126–129.

Ledwith F (1984) Does tobacco sports sponsorship on television act as advertising to children? *Health education journal*, **43** (4): 85–88.

Lee v. *Massachusetts Department of Public Welfare*, 1.2 TPLR 2.82 (Mass. Super. Ct. 1983).

Legislative Clearinghouse (1989) *State legislated actions on tobacco issues.* Washington, DC

Lenfant C (1983) Are low-yield cigarettes really safer? *New England journal of medicine*, **309** (3): 181–182.

Lev M (1991) Tobacco and alcohol lose more ground. *The New York Times*, 24 January p. C4.

Lewit EM (1989) U. S. tobacco taxes: behavioural effects and policy implications. *British journal of addiction*, **84**: 1217–1235.

Lewit EM (1990) Economics of tobacco in developing countries: telling it like it is. In: Durston B, Jamrozik K, eds, *Tobacco and health 1990. The global war. Proceedings of the Seventh World Conference on Tobacco and Health*, Perth, Health Department of Western Australia, pp. 785–787.

Lewit EM, Coate D (1982) The potential for using excise taxes to reduce smoking. *Journal of health economics*, **1**: 121–145.

Lewit EM et al. (1981) The effects of government regulation on teenage smoking. *Journal of law and economics*, **24**: 545–569.

Lokschin FL, Barros FC (1983) Smoking or health: the Brazilian option. *New York State journal of medicine*, **83** (13): 1314–1315.

The Times (1991) Tobacco aid is to end. 12 February.

McCarthy v. *State of Washington Dep't of Social and Health Serv.*, 759 p. 2d 351 (Wash. Sup. Ct. 1988).

Mackay JM (1986) The tobacco industry and tobacco advertising in Hong Kong. In: *Proceedings, Conference on Strategies for Smoking Control*, Hong Kong.

Malhotra SP (1988) The economic significance of tobacco and the future outlook. Paper presented at the First European Conference on Tobacco Policy — *Tobacco or health: the way ahead*, Copenhagen, WHO Regional Office for Europe.

Maron DJ, Fortmann SP (1987) Nicotine yield and measures of cigarette smoke exposure in a large population: are lower-yield cigarettes safer? *American journal of public health*, **77** (5): 546–549.

Marongiu P (1980) FAO activities in tobacco. In: Ramström LM, ed, *The smoking epidemic, a matter of worldwide concern.* Stockholm, Almquist & Wiksell International, pp. 320–321.

Mills PK et al. (1990) History of cigarette smoking and risk of leukemia and myeloma: results from the Adventist Health Study. *Journal of the National Cancer Institute,* **82** (23): 1823–1836.

Muller M (1978) *Tobacco and the Third World: tomorrow's epidemic?* London, War on Want.

Murphy J (1990) International trade body sends a health message on tobacco in battle over US forcing Thailand to accept US tobacco. *The nation's health,* November.

Naett C, Joossens L (1992) Steps towards a tobacco advertising ban in the European Community. *Tobacco control,* **1**: 57.

Nakajima H (1990) WHO — Part of a global strategy for a tobacco-free society. In: Durston B, Jamrozik K, eds, *Tobacco and health 1990. The global war. Proceedings of the Seventh World Conference on Tobacco and Health,* Perth, Health Department of Western Australia, pp. 9–10.

Nakajima H (1991) Presentation to Economic and Social Council, Second regular session of 1991. Geneva, 3–26 July.

Nath UR (1986) *Smoking: Third World alert.* Oxford, Oxford University Press.

National Campaign for Action on Tobacco (1991) *News release,* Ottawa, 1 August.

National Clearinghouse on Tobacco and Health (1990) *Children and tobacco. Legislation in Canada — the current status.* Ottawa (Fact Sheet Series, No. 9).

National Insurance Office v. *Estate of Gun Palm,* case no. 2722/83:8, 6.1 TPLR 2.65 (Ins. Ct of Appeal, Sweden, 1985).

New Straits Times (1991) Ban on duty-free cigarette sales. 1 January.

New Zealand Toxic Substances Board (1989) *Health or tobacco: an end to tobacco advertising and promotion,* Wellington.

Nordgren P, ed. (1983) *Smoking control in Sweden.* Stockholm, Swedish National Smoking and Health Association.

Nordic Council of Ministers (1972) *Recommendation number 12.* Helsingfors, 22 February.

Norwegian National Council on Tobacco and Health (1990) *New political initiatives 1988–90. Controlling tobacco.* Oslo.

Novello A (1991) Can we prevent the Virginia Slims woman from catching up with the Marlboro man? *World smoking and health,* **16** (2): 2.

O'Connell DL et al. (1981) Cigarette smoking and drug use in school children. II. Factors associated with smoking. *International journal of epidemiology,* **10** (3): 223–231.

O'Connor M (1990) Voluntary agreements between the government and the tobacco industry and the control of tobacco promotion in the United Kingdom. In: Durston B, Jamrozik K, eds, *Tobacco and health 1990. The global war. Proceedings of the Seventh World Conference on Tobacco and Health,* Perth, Health Department of Western Australia, pp. 739–740.

Office of Inspector General (1990) *Youth access to cigarettes.* Washington, DC, Department of Health and Human Services.

Office of Technology Assessment (1985) *Staff memo: smoking-related deaths and financial costs.* Washington, DC.

Parkin DM et al. (1984) Estimates of the worldwide frequency of twelve major cancers. *Bulletin of the World Health Organization*, **62** (2): 163–182.

Pearl R (1938) Tobacco smoking and longevity. *Science*, **87**: 216–217.

People v. *Cook.* 34 N. Y. 2d 100, 312 N. E. 2d 452 (1974) upholding Cigarette Tax Law Regulations of New York City Finance Administrator, Article 2-a.

Pertschuk M, Shopland DR, eds. (1989) *Major local smoking ordinances in the United States. A detailed matrix of the provisions of workplace, restaurant, and public places smoking ordinances.* Bethesda, MD, US Department of Health and Human Services, Public Health Service, National Institutes of Health (NIH publication No. 90–479).

Peto R (1990) Women and tobacco. *World health forum*, **11** (1): 3–13.

Peto R, Lopez AD (1990) Worldwide mortality from current smoking patterns: WHO consultative group on statistical aspects of tobacco-related mortality. In: Durston B, Jamrozik K, eds, *Tobacco and health 1990. The global war. Proceedings of the Seventh World Conference on Tobacco and Health*, Perth, Health Department of Western Australia, pp. 66–68.

Philip Morris Companies Inc. (1989) The story of a government that almost didn't happen. *The New York Times*, 3 November, p. A18.

Piha T (1990) The Finnish experience of tar regulation: "light cigarettes." *BASP newsletter*, No. 8, 3–5.

Posadas de Puerto Rico Associates, DBA Condado Holiday Inn v. *Tourism Company of Puerto Rico et al.*, 478 U.S. 328, 106 S. Ct. 2968 (1986).

Ramström L, ed. (1980) *The smoking epidemic, a matter of worldwide concern. Proceedings of the Fourth World Conference on Smoking and Health, Stockholm, 1979.* Stockholm, Almquist & Wiksell International.

Ramström L (1983) Sweden's programme to eliminate smoking — activities and success to date. In: *Smoking control in Sweden.* Stockholm, Swedish National Smoking and Health Association.

Ramström L (1984) Population scale evidence that smoking control can prevent lung cancer. In: *Proceedings of the Sixth International Symposium for Prevention and Detection of Cancer, Vienna, 26–29 November 1984.*

Raw M et al. (1990) *Clearing the air. A guide for action on tobacco.* London, British Medical Association.

Reid D, Seymour L (1987) *How two million people gave up smoking: the effects of tax increases and the U.K. national health education programme, 1980–86.* Paper contributed to the WHO European Action on Tobacco Programme, March 1987.

Revill J, Drury CG (1980) An assessment of the incidence of cigarette smoking in fourth year school children and factors leading to establishment. *Public health (London)*, **94**: 243–260.

Riding A (1990) What price tobacco ads? A countdown in France. *The New York Times*, 9 April.

Rimpelä M (1978) Cigarette smoking and public policy. *Scandinavian journal of respiratory diseases*, (Suppl. 102): 139–141.

RJR Macdonald and Imperial Tobacco Limited v. *Attorney-General of Canada*, Quebec Superior Court, Montreal, 1989.

RJR-Macdonald Inc. v. *The Attorney General of Canada*, No. 500-05-009755-833 and *Imperial Tobacco Ltd.* v. *The Attorney General of Canada*, No. 500-05-08760-883, Superior Court, Province of Quebec, District of Montreal, 26 July 1991.

Roemer R (1982) *Legislative action to combat the world smoking epidemic.* Geneva, World Health Organization.

Roemer R (1986a) *Recent developments in legislation to combat the world smoking epidemic.* Geneva, World Health Organization (unpublished WHO document WHO/SMO/HLE/86.1).

Roemer R (1986b) Legislative action to control smoking — accomplishments and challenges. In: Skirrow J, ed. *Strategies for a smoke-free world. Selected resource documents from the International Workshop on Smoking and Health.* Calgary, Alberta Alcohol and Drug Abuse Commission.

Roemer R (1988) *Legislative strategies for a smoke-free Europe.* Copenhagen, WHO Regional Office for Europe and the Commission of the European Communities.

Rothstein M (1990) Uneasy partners: arts and Philip Morris. *The New York Times,* "The Living Arts": 18 December, p.B1, 10.

Royal College of Physicians of London (1962) *Smoking and health. Summary and report of the Royal College of Physicians of London on smoking in relation to cancer of the lung and other diseases.* London, Pitman Medical Publishing.

Royal College of Physicians of London (1971) *Smoking and health now.* London, Pitman Medical Publishing.

Royal College of Physicians of London (1977) *Smoking and health (the Third Report from the Royal College of Physicians of London).* London, Pitman Medical Publishing.

Royal College of Physicians of London (1983) *Health or smoking? Follow-up report.* London, Pitman Medical.

Satalino v. *Satalino,* case no. 11440/86, 34 ATLA L. R. 16 (Nassau Cty, N. Y. 1990).

Schmeisser P (1988) Pushing cigarettes overseas. *The New York Times Magazine,* 10 July.

Schmidt F (1990) 'Light' smoking is no expedient, In: Durston B, Jamrozik K, eds, *Tobacco and health* 1990. *The global war. Proceedings of the Seventh World Conference on Tobacco and Health,* Perth, Health Department of Western Australia, pp. 428–429.

Schober v. *Mountain Bell Telephone Co.,* 630 p. 2d 1231 (N. M. Sup. Ct. 1980).

Scull R (1986) Bright future predicted for Asia Pacific. *World tobacco,* **9**: 34–41.

Shepherd PL (1985) Transnational corporations and the international cigarette industry. In: Newfarmer R, ed, *Profits, progress and poverty.* Notre Dame, Indiana, University of Notre Dame Press.

Shimp v. *N. J. Telephone Co.,* 368 A. 2d 408 (N. J. Super. Ct. 1976).

Simpson D (1988) The public health and public debate. *Health and hygiene,* **9**: 29–34.

Slattery ML et al. (1989) Cigarette smoking and exposure to passive smoke are risk factors for cervical cancer. *Journal of the American Medical Association,* **261** (11): 1593–1598.

Smith RC (1978) The magazines' smoking habit. *Columbia journalism review,* January/February: 29–31.

Smoking and health reporter (1985) Thumbs up/thumbs down. 2: 3.

South China Morning Post (1991) 7 March.

Stebbins KR (1987) Tobacco or health in the Third World: a political economy perspective with emphasis on Mexico. *International journal of health services*, **17** (3): 521–536.

Sweda E (1991) Summary of legal decisions regarding smoking in the workplace and other places, 6.2 TPLR 4.11.

Swedish Committee for Tobacco Control (1990) *Tobacco Act. Report of the Committee for Tobacco Control*. Presented to the Minister of Health and Social Affairs, Stockholm.

Taylor P (1984) *The smoke ring: the politics of tobacco*. London, The Bodley Head.

Taylor SA (1989) Tobacco and economic growth in developing nations. *Business in the contemporary world*, 55–70.

Tobacco alert (1984) **1** (2): 4, June.

Tobacco alert (1985) **2** (1): 2, March.

Tobacco alert (1986) Study confirms high tar levels in developing countries. 15/16.

Tobacco alert (1990) The European common agricultural policy in the tobacco sector: in need of review.

Tobacco alert (1991) January.

Tobacco on trial (1990) 17 December.

Tobacco on trial (1991) 15 February.

Tobacco Products Liability Project (1988). Selected exhibits from the *Cipollone* case.[1]

Tobacco Products Liability Project (1989). Selected exhibits from the *Palmer* case.[1]

Tobacco reporter (1987) **114** (8): 34.

Townsend J (1987) Economic and health consequences of reduced smoking. In: Williams A, ed, *Health and economics. Proceedings of Section F (Economics) of the British Association for the Advancement of Science, Bristol, 1986*. London, Macmillan Press, pp. 139–161.

Townsend J (1990) *Price and income elasticity of demand, taxation and the smoking epidemic*. Paper presented to the Seventh World Conference on Tobacco and Health, Perth, Western Australia.

Trichopoulos D et al. (1981) Lung cancer and passive smoking. *International journal of cancer*, **27**: 1–4.

Tye JB et al. (1987) Tobacco advertising and consumption: evidence of a causal relationship. *Journal of public health policy*, **8** (4): 492–508.

United Nations (1978) *Marketing and distribution of tobacco*. Geneva (Report No. TD/B/C.1/205).

US Department of Health, Education, and Welfare (1979) *Smoking and health: Report of the Surgeon General*. Rockville, MD, Office on Smoking and Health, Office of the Assistant Secretary for Health, Public Health Service (DHEW Publication No. (PHS) 79–50066).

---

[1] These and other documents are available from: Professor R. A. Daynard, Chairman, Tobacco Products Liability Project, Northeastern University School of Law, 400 Huntington Avenue, Boston, MA02115, USA.

US Department of Health and Human Services (1980) *The health consequences of smoking for women: a report of the Surgeon General.* Rockville, MD, Office on Smoking and Health, Office of the Assistant Secretary for Health.

US Department of Health and Human Services (1981) *The health consequences of smoking — the changing cigarette: a report of the Surgeon General.* Washington, DC, Office on Smoking and Health (DHHS Publication No. (PHS) 81-50156).

US Department of Health and Human Services (1984) *The health consequences of smoking: chronic obstructive lung disease. A report of the Surgeon General.* Office on Smoking and Health (DHHS Publication No. (PHS) 84-50205).

US Department of Health and Human Services (1985) *The health consequences of smoking. Cancer and chronic lung disease in the workplace: a report of the Surgeon General.* Public Health Service, Office on Smoking and Health (DHHS Publication (PHS) 85-50207).

US Department of Health and Human Services (1986) *The health consequences of involuntary smoking: a report of the Surgeon General.* Public Health Service, Centers for Disease Control (DHHS Publication No. (CDC) 87-8398).

US Department of Health and Human Services (1988) *The health consequences of smoking: nicotine addiction. A report of the Surgeon General, 1988.* Public Health Service, Centers for Disease Control, Center for Health Promotion and Education, Office on Smoking and Health (DHHS Publication No. (CDC) 88–8406).

US Department of Health and Human Services (1989) *Reducing the health consequences of smoking: 25 years of progress. A report of the Surgeon General.* Rockville, MD, Public Health Service, Centers for Disease Control, Center for Chronic Disease Prevention and Health Promotion, Office on Smoking and Health (DHHS Publication No. (CDC) 89–8411).

US Department of Health and Human Services (1990a) *Highlights of state tobacco and health data.* Program Services Activity, Office on Smoking and Health, Center for Chronic Disease Prevention and Health Promotion, Centers for Disease Control, Public Health Service.

US Department of Health and Human Services (1990b) *Model Sale of Tobacco Products to Minors Control Act. A model law recommended for adoption by states or localities to prevent the sale of tobacco products to minors.*

US Department of Health and Human Services (1992) *Smoking and health in the Americas. A 1992 report of the Surgeon General, in collaboration with the Pan American Health Organization.* Atlanta, GA, Public Health Service, Centers for Disease Control, National Center for Chronic Disease Prevention and Health Promotion, Office on Smoking and Health (DHHS Publication No. (CDC) 92–8419).

US Federal Trade Commission (1981) *Report of "tar", nicotine and carbon monoxide of the smoke of 187 varieties of cigarettes.* Washington, DC.

US National Research Council (1986) *Environmental tobacco smoke: measuring exposures and assessing health effects.* Washington, DC, National Academy Press.

US Public Health Service (1964) *Smoking and health: report of the Advisory Committee to the Surgeon General of the Public Health Service.* Washington, DC, US Department of Health, Education, and Welfare (PHS Publication No. 1103).

US Public Health Service (1967) *The health consequences of smoking: a Public Health Service review.* Washington, DC, US Department of Health, Education and Welfare (PHS Publication No. 1696, revised 1968a).

178

Vaithinathan BR (1990) *Measures taken to discourage smoking in Singapore.* Singapore, Ministry of Health.

Wald N et al. (1981) Trends in tar, nicotine and carbon monoxide yields of UK cigarettes manufactured since 1934. *British medical journal*, **282**: 763–765.

Waldron I et al. (1988) Gender differences in tobacco use in Africa, Asia, the Pacific and Latin America. *Social science and medicine*, **27** (11): 1269–1275.

Warner KE (1977) The effects of the anti-smoking campaign on cigarette consumption. *American journal of public health*, **67**: 645–650.

Warner KE (1979) Clearing the airwaves: the cigarette ban revisited. *Policy analysis*, **5** (4): 435–450.

Warner KE (1984) Cigarette taxation: doing good by doing well. *Journal of public health policy*, **5** (3): 312–318.

Warner KE (1986a) *Selling smoke: cigarette advertising and public health.* Washington, DC, American Public Health Association.

Warner KE (1986b) Smoking and health implications of a change in the federal cigarette excise tax. *Journal of the American Medical Association*, **255** (8): 1028–1032.

Warner KE (1988) The tobacco subsidy: does it matter? *Journal of the National Cancer Institute*, **80** (2): 81–83.

Warner KE (1990a) Tobacco taxation as health policy in the Third World. *American journal of public health*, **80** (5): 529–531.

Warner KE (1990b) Tobacco taxation and economic effects of declining tobacco consumption. In: Durston B, Jamrozik K, eds, *Tobacco and health 1990. The global war. Proceedings of the Seventh World Conference on Tobacco and Health*, Perth, Health Department of Western Australia, pp. 81–87.

Warner KE et al. (1986) Public policy on smoking and health: toward a smoke-free generation by the year 2000. A statement of a working group to the Subcommittee on Smoking of the American Heart Association. *Circulation*, **73** (2): 381A–395A.

Whelan E (1984) *A smoking gun: how the tobacco industry gets away with murder.* Philadelphia, George F. Stickley.

Wilson K (1990) Western Australia Tobacco Control Bill 1990. Second Reading Speech.

Winstanley M, ed. (1989) *Tobacco in Australia: facts and issues.* Surrey Hills, NSW, Action on Smoking and Health (ASH Australia).

World Health Organization (1975) *Smoking and its effects on health: report of a WHO Expert Committee.* Geneva (WHO Technical Report Series, No. 568).

World Health Organization (1976) *Legislative action to combat smoking around the world: a survey of existing legislation.* Geneva.

World Health Organization (1979) *Controlling the smoking epidemic: report of the WHO Expert Committee on Smoking Control.* Geneva (WHO Technical Report Series, No. 636).

World Health Organization (1982) *Prevention of coronary heart disease: report of a WHO Expert Committee.* Geneva (WHO Technical Report Series, No. 678).

World Health Organization (1983) *Smoking control strategies in developing countries: report of a WHO Expert Committee.* Geneva (WHO Technical Report Series, No. 695).

World Health Organization (1985) *Tobacco or health.* Geneva (unpublished document EB77/1986/rec/1).

World Health Organization (1986) *Community prevention and control of cardiovascular disease: report of a WHO Expert Committee.* Geneva (WHO Technical Report Series, No. 732).

World Health Organization (1988) *Smokeless tobacco control: report of a WHO Study Group.* Geneva (WHO Technical Report Series, No. 773).

World Health Organization (1989) *Report of a WHO Consultation on Statistical Aspects of Tobacco-related Mortality.* Geneva (unpublished document, WHO/ TOH/CLH/90.2).

World Health Organization (1990a) *Prevention in childhood and youth of adult cardiovascular diseases: time for action: report of a WHO Expert Committee.* Geneva (WHO Technical Report Series, No. 792).

World Health Organization (1990b) *It can be done: a smoke-free Europe. Report of the first European Conference on Tobacco Policy Madrid, 7–11 November 1988.* Copenhagen, WHO Regional Office for Europe (European Series, No. 30).

World Health Organization (1991a) *WHO Programme on Tobacco or Health: implementation of resolutions WHA42.19 and WHA43.16.* Geneva (unpublished document WHA44/1991/REC/1).

World Health Organization (1991b) *Legislative responses to the tobacco epidemic.* Amsterdam, Martinus Nijhoff.

Wynder EL, Graham EA (1950) Tobacco smoking as a possible etiological factor in bronchiogenic carcinoma. *Journal of the American Medical Association,* **143**: 329–336.

Wynder EL, Kabat GC (1988) The effect of low-yield cigarette smoking on lung cancer risk. *Cancer,* **62**: 1223–1230.

Yach D (1986) The impact of smoking in developing countries with special reference to Africa. *International journal of health services,* **16** (2): 279–292.

Annex 1

Tabular summary of legislation

Information on legislation is presented by WHO region, for each of which the following tables are given:

1. Control of tobacco advertising and promotion.
2. Health warnings and statement and control of tar and nicotine (T/N) content.
3. Restrictions on places of sale.
4. Restrictions on smoking in public places.
5. Restrictions on smoking in the workplace.
6. Preventing young people from smoking.
7. Health education on tobacco.
8. Legislation establishing a national organization for policy development and coordination.

A. African region

Table A1. Control of tobacco advertising and promotion

Country	Total ban	Restrictions on the use of mass media (television, radio, press, billboards)	Restrictions on the promotion of tobacco through sponsorship of sports and cultural events	Restrictions on the content, format, or location of advertising
Algeria	X			
Burkina Faso		X		
Gambia[1]		X		
Mozambique*	X			
Nigeria[2]			X	W
Senegal[3]		X		X
Sudan*	X		X	

* Text of legislation not available to author.
W = health warning required.

Notes to Table A1

1. Gambia. The Tobacco Products (Control of Advertisements) Act, 1985 prohibits the advertising of tobacco products on television and radio and by photographs and films, as well as by the display or distribution of notices, signs, posters, models, placards, labels, or showcards. Advertising on billboards and by lotteries or games is banned.

2. Nigeria. The Tobacco Smoking (Control) Decree 1990 provides that a health warning is required on tobacco advertising in newspapers, magazines, radio, television, cinemas, billboards, and handbills. Sponsorship or promotion of sports events by the tobacco industry is prohibited.

3. Senegal. Law No. 85-23 of 25 February 1985 prohibits the advertising of tobacco products on television. Where the promotion or advertising of tobacco products is authorized, it may be effected only under conditions specified by decree. Under Decree No. 85-1375 of 28 December 1985, advertising announcements may not employ the voice of, or depict a person under 21 years of age, and films advertising tobacco may not be projected during programmes for young persons.

Table A2. Health warnings and statement and control of tar and nicotine (T/N) content

Country	Familiar warning	Rotating/strong warnings	Smokeless tobacco warnings	Statements of T/N content	Control of T/N content
Algeria	X			X	
Burkina Faso	X			X	
Ghana*	X				
Kenya	X				
Mauritius	X				
Nigeria[1]		X		X	
Senegal	X			X	

* Text of legislation not available to author.

Notes to Table A2

1. Nigeria. The Tobacco Smoking (Control) Decree 1990 requires the following rotating warnings on cigarette packages and on advertising:

> The Federal Ministry of Health warns that tobacco smoking is dangerous to health.
> Smokers are liable to die young.

The tar and nicotine content of each unit of the product must be stated on the package.

Table A3. Restrictions on places of sale

Country	Government buildings	Health establishments	Schools and places where young people congregate	Other
		No information available		

Note: Restrictions on the use of vending machines are presented in Table A6.

Table A4. Restrictions on smoking in public places

Country	Government agencies	Health establishments	Schools and places where young people congregate	Public transport	Lifts	Indoor public places	Markets and food storage places	Restaurants
Algeria[1]								
Benin*		X		X				
Botswana*		X	X	X				
Burkina Faso		X	X					
Cape Verde*		X	X	X				
Chad*		X	X					
Central African Republic*		X	X					
Côte d'Ivoire		X	X	X	X	X		
Kenya*								
Lesotho*		X	X	X				
Madagascar*			X	X				
Mauritius[2]		X	X		X	X	X	
Mozambique*								
Niger*		X	X	X	X	X		
Nigeria[3] (Benue State)	X	X	X	X		X		
Senegal[1]								
Togo*		X	X	X				
Uganda*		X	X	X				
United Republic of Tanzania*			X					

* Text of legislation not available to author.

Notes to Table A4

1. Algeria (Law No. 85-05 of 16 February 1985) and Senegal (Law No. 85-23 of 25 February 1985) provide that the public places in which smoking is prohibited are to be specified by administrative regulations.

2. Mauritius. Under Regulations effective 1 July 1990, smoking is prohibited in any ward or room earmarked for treatment or examination of patients, including a casualty room and waiting room for patients in a public hospital, dispensary, clinic, or other health institution; in any classroom, library, and students' workshop in a preprimary, primary, secondary, or tertiary educational institution; and in any sports hall, gymnasium and swimming pool to which the public has access. No person may smoke while engaged in the preparation, serving, or sale of food in a public place.

3. Nigeria. The Tobacco Smoking (Control) Decree 1990 bans smoking in a wide variety of public places; cinemas, theatres, and stadiums; offices; public transportation; lifts; medical establishments; schools, and nursery institutions.

Table A5. Restrictions on smoking in the workplace

Country	General laws restricting smoking in the workplace	Government agencies	Health establishments	Schools	Authorization for administrative regulations or accommodation of smokers and non-smokers	Other
Algeria					X	
Mauritius[1]						X
Senegal					X	

Note to Table A5

1. Mauritius. The Public Health (Prohibition of Smoking) Regulations of 1990 prohibit smoking while engaged in the preparation, serving, or sale of foodstuffs in a public place.

Table A6. Preventing young people from smoking

Country	Prohibiting sales to minors	Restricting sales from vending machines	Prohibiting sales in schools and other places frequented by young people	Restricting advertising that influences young people	Other
Mauritius	X				
Senegal				X	

Table A7. Health education on tobacco

Country	Public education	Anti-smoking education in schools	Allocation of funds
Algeria	X		

Table A8. Legislation establishing a national organization for policy development and coordination to control tobacco use

Country	National organization
Kenya	Kenya Action on Smoking and Health (KASH) (voluntary organization)

187

B. Region of the Americas[1]

Table B1. Control of tobacco advertising and promotion

Country or territory	Total ban	Restrictions on the use of mass media (television, radio, press, billboards)	Restrictions on the promotion of tobacco through sponsorship of sports and cultural events	Restrictions on the content, format, or location of advertising
Argentina[1]		X	X	XW
Bahamas				W
Bermuda				W
Bolivia[2]		X	X	XW
Brazil[3]		X	X	XW
Canada[4]	X	X	X	W
Cayman Islands		X		
Chile[5]		X		W
Colombia[6]		X		XW
Costa Rica[7]		X		X
Cuba	X			
Ecuador[8]		X		W
El Salvador[9]		X		
Mexico[10]		X		XW
Panama[11]		X		W
Paraguay[12]		X		X
Peru[13]		X		W
Trinidad and Tobago[14]		X		XW
United States of America[15]		X		W
Uruguay[16]		X		W
Venezuela[17]		X		W

W = health warning required.

---

[1] Minor discrepancies between the tables given here and those in the 1992 report of the Surgeon General (US Department of Health and Human Services, 1992) are due mainly to differences in availability of information.

Notes to Table B1

1. Argentina. Under Law No.23344 of 31 July 1986, advertising on television and radio is prohibited from 08:00 to 22:00, except that the brand name can be stated. Advertising directed to young people is prohibited and in theatres and cinemas to which persons under 18 are admitted. The distribution and promotion of samples at colleges and universities is prohibited. Advertising associated with the practice of sports is prohibited. Featuring personalities from artistic and cultural circles whose public consists essentially of young persons is prohibited. The use of expressions or terms characteristic of young persons is prohibited. Young persons may not be shown as models in tobacco advertising, and the representation of persons smoking excessively is prohibited. Low-tar and low-nicotine cigarettes may not be represented as beneficial to health.

2. Bolivia. Under the Regulations of 15 March 1982, advertising of tobacco is restricted to the format of "tombstone" advertising in which only the name, brand, symbol, tar and nicotine contents are given. Only products directly associated with smoking may be depicted. The content of advertising is restricted to statements concerning the quality, origin, and purity of tobacco products. Persons inhaling or exhaling cigarette smoke, adolescents, pregnant women, and children may not be shown. Tobacco advertisements may not be associated with sporting, domestic, or occupational activities. Labels and advertisements for tobacco must be licensed by the Health Authority to prevent indiscriminate promotion of tobacco consumption.

3. Brazil. Under order No. 490 of 25 August 1988, advertising of tobacco products is permitted on television only between 21:00 and 06:00. Advertising in theatres before 20:00 is prohibited if persons under 18 are admitted. Tobacco advertisements must meet certain requirements: the advertisement must not incite excessive or irresponsible consumption; it must not allude to health, holidays, or say that tobacco has soothing properties; it must not associate tobacco products with sexuality, virility, or femininity; reference to children and adolescents is prohibited; and tobacco advertising may not be addressed to young people. The size and frequency of health warnings are prescribed. Announcement of sponsorship of events by tobacco companies is limited to the presentation of the name and logo of the company, and such announcement is not permitted as part of the programme of the event.

4. Canada. The Tobacco Products Control Act of 1988 prohibits the advertising of any tobacco product offered for sale in Canada. Until 1 January 1991, a tobacco manufacturer or importer may advertise the product by signs, subject to a limitation on the amount to be expended on their preparation and presentation. The Act limits the amount of a tobacco manufacturer's or importer's contributions to cultural or sporting activities or events where brand names of tobacco products are used to the value of contributions to such events in 1987. Regulations under the Act specify the health warnings that must appear on signs, the number and size of signs at a retailer's place of business, and on vending machines.

   The Act is coming into force in stages. Print media advertising was prohibited as of 1989, signs as of January 1991, and point of sale advertising will be prohibited in 1993.

   Legislation restricting sponsorship prohibits merely the use of brand names but not corporate name sponsorship. The cigarette companies have created limited companies named after the brand names to circumvent the ban on sponsorship.

5. Chile. Under Decree No. 106 of 8 April 1981, a health warning is required on advertisements for tobacco products in print media, on television and radio, and in cinemas, where the warning must remain on the screen for at least 5 seconds after the advertisement is shown. No direct or indirect reference to minors may be made, and young people may not be depicted in tobacco advertising.

6. Colombia. Tobacco advertising is restricted to the presentation of brand, quality, price, and system of marketing. Depiction of minors and the act of smoking is prohibited. Advertising of tobacco is allowed on television only after 23:00 and is limited to 30 seconds for each brand. All commercials advertising cigarettes must devote 20% of transmission time to the warning "tobacco is harmful to health". The Council of the District of Bogotá prohibits tobacco advertising at children's sports and in scientific publications; on murals, posters, or signs in sports, cultural, educational, or residential places; and in public transportation vehicles.

7. Costa Rica. All advertising or promotion of cigarettes in newspapers, radio, television, and cinemas must be approved by the Ministry of Health so as to avoid publicity detrimental to the public health. Advertising of tobacco is prohibited on radio and television programmes intended for children.

8. Ecuador. Tobacco advertising directed at or referring to minors is prohibited. Also prohibited are broadcasting tobacco advertisements before 19:30, inserting such advertisements in programmes for children, using minors as models, advertising near schools and colleges or in comics, depicting sports figures or people who have contributed to the literature and history of Ecuador.

9. El Salvador. Tobacco advertising on radio, television, and in cinemas in programmes directed to children is prohibited, but advertising in programmes not directed to children is allowed.

10. Mexico. The legislation prohibits advertising of tobacco that asserts that the product enhances social prestige, or induces consumption by asserting that it is a sedative or reduces fatigue or tension, or by attributing to it stimulant qualities leading to success, or induces persons to consume the product on health grounds, or associates tobacco with sports, domestic, or professional activities, or emphasizes femininity or virility, or suggests greater success in sexual relations, or depicts children or adolescents, or attributes an effect of well-being, or depicts persons smoking in public. Tobacco advertising is limited to information on the characteristics, quality, and techniques of preparation of these products.

11. Panama. All advertising of tobacco must be approved by the Ministry of Health. Advertising that shows people smoking is prohibited.

12. Paraguay. Under Law No. 836/80 of 15 December 1980, tobacco advertisements may refer only to the quality and origin of the tobacco and must not encourage consumption. The use of figures or characters representing children or adolescents is prohibited, as is the association of tobacco with sports, work, study, or home. No televised promotion of tobacco may occur before 19:00 except for presentations of international meetings, whether produced locally or abroad.

13. Peru. Advertising of cigarettes is prohibited before 20:00 on radio and television and in places of entertainment during shows suitable for minors.

14. Trinidad and Tobago. The Bureau of Standards, established under the Standards Act, No. 38 of 1972, has enunciated standards based on the Code of Advertising Practice, 1969 of the Advertisers' Association of Trinidad and Tobago, which was developed in cooperation with the Advertising Standards Authority and other agencies. These standards require the traditional health warning on tobacco advertisements; permit advertisements for free samples only in the trade press; prohibit the inclusion of coupons or trading stamps in cigarette packages; and forbid the directing of tobacco advertisements and promotion at audiences including children.

15. United States of America. Federal legislation prohibits the advertising of cigarettes, little cigars, and smokeless tobacco on television and radio. Health warnings are required on print advertising and on billboard advertising.

16. Uruguay. Legible health warnings are required on written tobacco advertising, and they must remain on a screen long enough to be read. Oral advertising must refer to the health warning once for every five references to tobacco products. No promotion of tobacco products, direct or indirect, may be undertaken in schools or other educational institutions, whether public or private. Legislation proposed in 1988 would lay down standards for the advertising of tobacco products, including the prohibition of directing advertising to young people, the depiction of young people, and of low-tar and low-nicotine cigarettes as beneficial to health, and the association of smoking with sports, physical strength, social prestige, virility, or femininity; advertising would be restricted to objective facts on the characteristics of the product, its price, and quality.

17. Venezuela. Under Decree No. 849 of 21 November 1980 and Decree No. 996 of 19 March 1981, all advertising of tobacco products by television or radio that directly or indirectly encourages the consumption of cigarettes and tobacco products is prohibited.

Table B2. Health warnings and statement and control of tar and nicotine (T/N) contents

Country or territory	Familiar warning	Rotating/strong warnings	Smokeless tobacco warnings	Statements of T/N content	Control of T/N content
Argentina	X				
Bahamas		X			
Barbados	X				
Bermuda		X		X	
Bolivia	X				
Brazil	X				
Canada		X	X	X	
Chile		X			
Colombia	X				
Costa Rica		X			
Ecuador	X			X	
El Salvador	X				
Mexico	X			X	
Panama	X				
Paraguay	X				
Peru	X				
Trinidad and Tobago	X				
United States of America		X	X	(X)	
Uruguay	X			X	
Venezuela	X				

(X) = statements appear on some packages, by decision of the tobacco company.

Table B3. Restrictions on places of sale

Country	Government buildings	Health establishments	Schools and places where young people congregate	Other
Brazil				
Rio Grande do Sul[1]	X			
Chile[2]		X		
Cuba		X	X	

Note: Restrictions on the use of vending machines are presented in Table B6.

Notes to Table B3

1. Brazil. Under Law No. 7813 of 21 September 1983, the State of Rio Grande do Sul prohibits the sale of cigarettes in any establishment that is administered or subsidized by the state, including buildings of the Legislative Assembly.

2. Chile. The Ministry of Health prohibits the sale of tobacco products in all establishments of the Chilean National Health Service. The Ministry of the Interior in 1989 recommended restrictions on the sale of tobacco products in kiosks and other places in all government services.

Table B4. Restrictions on smoking in public places

Country or territory	Government agencies	Health establishments	Schools and places where young people congregate	Public transport	Lifts	Indoor public places	Markets and food storage places	Restaurants
Argentina								
Province of Cordoba	X		X	X				
Province of Jujuy	X	X	X	X	X	X	X	
Province of Mendoza	X	X	X	X	X			
San Fernando del Valle de Catamarca	X			X	X			
Valle Viejo	X			X	X			
Municipality of Buenos Aires								
Bolivia[1]				X		X	X	
City of Cochabamba	X	X	X	X	X	X		
City of Oruro			X	X		X		
Brazil[2]								
Rio Grande do Sul		X	X	X		X		
São Paulo		X	X	X		X	X	

Table B4 (continued)

Country or territory	Government agencies	Health establish-ments	Schools and places where young people congregate	Public transport	Lifts	Indoor public places	Markets and food storage places	Restaurants
Brazil (continued)								
Rio de Janeiro		X	X	X	X	X		
Porto Alegre			X	X	X	X	X	X
Curitiba						X		
Florianopolis						X	X	
Canada	X	X	X	X	X			
Province of Manitoba		X	X	X		X		X
Province of Quebec	X	X	X	X		X		
Chile[3]	X	X	X	X		X		
Colombia[4]	X	X	X	X		X		
Bogotá	X			X	X	X		
Costa Rica[5]				X				
Cuba[6]		X		X				
Guatemala[7]	X	X	X	X		X		
Honduras[8]	X	X						
Mexico[9]				X				
Federal District	X	X	X	X	X	X		
Panama[10]		X						
Paraguay[11]								
Asunción				X				
Peru[12]	X	X						
Trinidad and Tobago[13]	X	X	X	X	X	X		
United States of America	X	X	X	X	X	X	X	X
Uruguay[14]								
Montevideo		X		X		X		
Venezuela[15]	X	X	X	X		X		

Notes to Table B4

1. Bolivia. Under the Regulations of 15 March 1982, smoking is prohibited in schools, health premises, indoor public places, and public transport vehicles. Separate smoking areas are to be provided in indoor public places.

2. Brazil. On 31 May 1990, the Ministry of Health of Brazil adopted Regulation No. 731 prohibiting smoking in any health institution, public or private. It recommends that the states, the Federal District, and the municipalities adopt measures restricting smoking in public premises, public transportation vehicles, elevators, auditoriums, cinemas and theatres, libraries, and premises for use by the public. Smoking is prohibited on all flights of two hours or less, and on flights exceeding two hours, space must be reserved for smokers in the rear of the aircraft.

   In 1988, Order No. 490 of 25 August 1988 recommended that Federal, State, and municipal levels of government adopt or encourage limitations on smoking in enclosed public places that lack adequate ventilation.

   In 1980 the Secretary of State for Health and the Environment prohibited cigarette smoking in places where services are provided to the public in health units, hospitals, and other agencies of the Secretariat.

   At the State level, Rio Grande do Sul (Law No. 7813 of 21 September 1983) prohibits smoking in public educational establishments, halls used for meetings, entertainment events and lectures, and museums and libraries; in public health establishments, gymnasia or other closed premises used for sports activities, either maintained or subsidized by the State; and intercity passenger transport vehicles.

   In São Paulo, smoking is prohibited on intercity buses, in schools, hospitals, health centres, and other local public health buildings. Both the smoker and the person in charge of the facility are subject to fines for violation of the legislation. Since July 1990 all restaurants of more than 100 square metres must reserve 50% of the space for non-smokers.

   In the State of Rio de Janeiro smoking is prohibited in meetings of the Federal Council on Medicine.

   At the municipal level, the city of Rio de Janeiro has enacted legislation prohibiting smoking on buses, in elevators, cinemas and theatres, stores and supermarkets, hospitals and health services, museums, schools, garages, and taxis.

   Porto Alegre prohibits smoking in businesses, cinemas, theatres, schools, elevators, buses, and places where explosives or flammable materials are processed or stored.

   The municipalities of Curitiba and Florianopolis prohibit smoking in enclosed public places and businesses.

3. Chile. The Ministry of Education in 1981 issued Circular No. 601/81 of 11 May 1981 requiring professors, whenever possible, to refrain from smoking in class and while complying with their obligations to students. The head of the institution is responsible for the enforcement of this regulation.

   In 1981 the Ministry of Health prohibited smoking by staff in the premises of the National Health System, in patients' waiting rooms, administrative offices, elevators, auditoriums, and meeting rooms.

Acting on the recommendation of WHO, the Minister of the Interior recommends that smoking be prohibited in the waiting rooms, offices, anterooms, and places of public service in government organizations.

Law No. 18290 of 1985 prohibits smoking in public transport vehicles.

4. Colombia. The District of Bogotá prohibits smoking in cinemas, theatres, public libraries, museums, and other buildings to which the public is admitted or that are devoted to cultural or sports activities; in buses and taxis; in enclosed buildings and schools; in enclosed areas of hospitals, sanatoria, and health centres; and in government offices where the public is served.

5. Costa Rica. Smoking by employees and visitors is prohibited in government buildings, with the exception of persons incarcerated in buildings of the National Penitentiary System; however in each public institution a smoking area is to be provided.

Smoking is also prohibited in places for public entertainment, cinemas and theatres throughout the country. The owners or managers of these facilities are responsible for enforcement.

Under Decree No. 18248-MOPT-S of 23 June 1988, smoking is also prohibited in all means of public transport. Drivers are responsible for enforcement and may refuse to continue the service and seek help from the authorities.

6. Cuba. Under Ministerial Resolution No. 165 of 17 August 1981, smoking by the staff, patients, and visitors of the National Health System is prohibited. Another Ministerial Resolution of 1981 prohibits smoking on all means of public transport.

7. Guatemala. Government Accord No. 681 of 3 August 1990 prohibits smoking in public transport and in public areas in government and private offices.

8. Honduras. The Law of the Honduran Institute for the Prevention of Alcoholism and Drug Addiction, Decree No. 136–89, dated 14 October 1989, prohibits smoking in public and private schools, cinemas and theatres, collective ground, air, and sea transport, public and private hospitals, government offices and workplaces, sports centres, and sessions of the National Congress.

9. Mexico. A Decree of the Secretary of Health of 17 April 1990 restricts smoking in the medical facilities of the Secretary of Health and the National Institutes of Health, including areas for preventive, curative, and rehabilitative care, auditoria and places for group meetings, lectures, teaching, and other areas.

In the Federal District of Mexico, a Regulation for the protection of non-smokers dated 5 July 1990 restricts smoking in a wide range of indoor public places, including public transport vehicles, kindergartens, primary, secondary, and high schools, hospitals, clinics, and waiting rooms of health facilities, libraries, cinemas, theatres, auditoriums, government offices, and shops and businesses providing a service to the public, such as automobile service shops, banks, and financial, industrial, and commercial offices.

10. Panama. A Decree of 1978 prohibits smoking in buses.

11. Paraguay. A Resolution of the Ministry of Public Health and Social Welfare, issued on 23 January 1990, prohibits smoking in clinics and waiting rooms as well as in other offices and buildings of the Ministry.

   In Asunción, the Municipal Council has prohibited smoking in vehicles of the public transport system.

12. Peru. A Ministerial Resolution prohibits smoking in buildings and offices of the Ministry of Health and its decentralized agencies. The text of the resolution must be posted at the entrance to, and in visible places in the buildings and offices of the Ministry of Health. Managers and staff are required to ensure strict compliance with the ban on smoking.

13. Trinidad and Tobago. Although there is no national legislation restricting smoking on aircraft, British West Indian Airways, in compliance with regulations of the International Airline Transport Association, prohibits smoking on flights of less than 1½ hours.

14. Uruguay. Since 1976 the Faculty of Medicine of the University of the Republic of Uruguay has prohibited smoking by physicians, students, staff, patients, and visitors in hospitals of the Faculty.

   Special Order of the Ministry of Public Health No. 3904 prohibits smoking in all Ministry hospitals. This ban applies to administrative personnel while on duty and in contact with patients and their visitors.

   Smoking is prohibited in plenary sessions and working committee sessions of the Chamber of Deputies.

   Legislation proposed on 16 June 1987 would prohibit smoking in public offices, health centres, public and private schools, and public transport.

   Municipal legislation in Montevideo prohibits smoking in theatres, cinemas, circuses, and in all other places where public performances are presented, although a 1979 Decree permits the sale of cigarettes in theatres. Smoking is also prohibited by personnel of companies engaged in the storage, sale, and transportation of flammable liquids; in storage places of microcontainers of "supergas"; in storage places of cylinders and equipment for respiratory therapy; and in storage places of bulk liquid petroleum gas.

   Montevideo also prohibits smoking in city buses and on short trips (less than 110 kilometres) of interdepartmental buses. A 1975 Decree prohibits smoking by drivers of school buses. On long-distance lines, including national and international tourism buses, smoking is permitted in the last three rows of seats.

15. Venezuela. Regulations of 1979 under the Law of 13 September 1978 ban smoking in public transportation vehicles, in buildings where groups of people gather, such as waiting rooms in theatres and cinemas, hospitals and other health facilities, sports arenas, and other places that may be designated. Smoking areas may be set aside in these facilities. No-smoking signs must be posted. Managers of these public places are responsible for compliance with the ban on smoking.

   In 1985, the Venezuelan Institute of Social Security prohibited smoking in all the administrative service units of the Institute, and the Ministry of Education prohibited all smoking in school buildings.

Table B5. Restrictions on smoking in the workplace

Country	General laws restricting smoking in the workplace	Government agencies	Health establishments	Schools	Authorization for administrative regulations or accommodation of smokers and non-smokers	Other
Brazil[1]		X	X			
Rio Grande do Sul		X	X	X		
Canada[2]				X		
Province of Ontario		X	X	X	X	
Chile[1]			X			
Costa Rica[3]	X					
Cuba[1]			X			
Mexico[1]			X			
Paraguay[1]		X	X			
Peru[1]		X	X			
United States of America[4]		X	X	X	X	
Uruguay[1]			X	X		
Venezuela[1]		X	X			

Notes to Table B5

1. In Brazil, Chile, Cuba, Mexico, Peru, Uruguay, and Venezuela, smoking by employees in health premises is banned.

2. Canada. The Non-smokers' Health Act of 1990, as amended, restricts smoking in all workplaces under federal jurisdiction. The Smoking in the Workplace Act of 26 July 1989 of the Province of Ontario restricts smoking in all workplaces under provincial jurisdiction and establishes minimal standards that limit exposure to tobacco smoke in the workplace. In addition to provincial legislation, municipal by-laws regulate smoking at the workplace.

3. Costa Rica. The Decree of 23 June imposes a general ban on smoking in workplaces and requires the director of the workplace, or his representative, to ensure compliance with this provision. An area may be reserved at the workplace for smokers, to the extent that this is possible.

4. United States of America. Regulatory polices of federal agencies generally restrict smoking at the workplace. At the state level, 31 states restrict smoking at public worksites, and 13 have restricted smoking at private worksites. Local ordinances provide for accommodation of the interests of smokers and non-smokers.

Table B6. Preventing young people from smoking

Country	Prohibiting sales to minors	Restricting sales from vending machines	Prohibiting sales in schools and other places frequented by young people	Restricting advertising that influences young people	Other
Argentina[1]			X	X	X
Bahamas					X
Bolivia[2]			X	X	X
Brazil[3]	X		X	X	X
Canada	X	X	X	X	X
Chile[4]			X	X	X
Colombia[5]	X		X	X	
Costa Rica[6]	X		X		
Cuba	X			X	
Ecuador[7]	X			X	X
El Salvador[8]				X	X
Mexico[9]	X				X
Panama[10]				X	X
Paraguay[11]				X	X
Peru[12]				X	X
Trinidad and Tobago				X	X
United States of America	X	X	X	X	
Uruguay[13]	X			X	X
Venezuela[14]				X	X

Notes to Table B6

1. Argentina. Law No. 23344 of 31 July 1986 prohibits tobacco advertising on radio and television from 08:00 to 22:00, except that the name of the brand may be presented. Tobacco advertising is prohibited in publications intended for young people and in theatres and cinemas to which persons under 18 are admitted. Distribution and promotion of samples of cigarettes at colleges and universities is prohibited. Young people may not be used as models in advertisements for tobacco. Advertising directed at young people or associated with sports is prohibited.

2. Bolivia. The Regulations of 1982 ban smoking in schools as "premeditated harm" because it exposes persons of low resistance to the polluting effects of tobacco and because minors are susceptible to a bad example. Tobacco advertising must not depict children or adolescents, nor may it associate tobacco with sports. In 1984 the Minister of Education and Culture prohibited students, professors, and parents of students from smoking in public and private educational institutions throughout the country.

200

3. Brazil. The order of 25 August lays down the requirements that advertising of tobacco must meet, including a specification that no reference to children may be made and that advertising must not be addressed to them. No tobacco advertising may be presented in theatres before 20:00 if persons under 18 may attend. Advertising on television is allowed only between 21:00 and 06:00. An order of the Ministry of Health of 1990 prohibits the sale of cigarettes to minors and promotion of tobacco products through the distribution of free samples at public events. The municipalities of Rio de Janeiro, São Paulo, and Porto Alegre prohibit smoking in schools.

4. Chile. Any presentation of tobacco advertising on radio or television before 21:30 is prohibited. Young people may not be depicted in tobacco advertising. Circular No. 601/81 of the Ministry of Education of 11 May 1981 prohibits smoking in schools and by teachers during classes.

5. Colombia. Sales to minors under 14 are prohibited, as is smoking in schools.

6. Costa Rica. The Decree of 4 February 1983 prohibits the sale of cigarettes to minors in all commercial establishments. It is the responsibility of the administrators or managers of the establishments to assure compliance with the decree. Violators will be sentenced under the General Health Law, which provides for a penalty of 5–30 days in jail.

7. Ecuador. The distribution of samples of cigarettes to minors is prohibited, as is tobacco advertising aimed at children or referring to them. Tobacco advertisements may not be presented on television before 19:30 or included in programmes intended exclusively for children. Tobacco may not be advertised in or near schools, on school buses, in sports centres, or in comic books. Sports stars and young artists may not be depicted using or smoking cigarettes in posters, films, or on record albums. A similar ban applies to the use of historical figures and members of the learned professions. Encouraging smoking as a means of improving concentration or performance is prohibited.

8. El Salvador. Tobacco advertising is permitted on radio, television, and in cinemas, but only in programmes not intended for children.

9. Mexico. The General Law on Health of 1983 sets forth the objectives of the Programme against Smoking, including the education of the family, children, and adolescents about the effects of tobacco on health through individual methods and mass communication. The Law contains no specific ban on advertising directed at children.

10. Panama. All advertising of tobacco must be approved by the Ministry of Health. Such advertising may not depict persons smoking.

11. Paraguay. Tobacco advertising that depicts persons representing children or adolescents or that associates tobacco with sports is prohibited.

12. Peru. Cigarette advertising may be presented on radio and television only after 20:00 It is an offence to present tobacco advertising in performances suitable for minors before 19:00.

13. Uruguay. The sale of cigarettes, cigars, and tobacco products to minors under 18 years of age is prohibited. The sale of single or loose cigarettes is prohibited. Advertising of cigarettes is allowed on radio and television only after 21:00. It is the responsibility of television stations to avoid guests smoking on programmes between 06:00 and 24:00.

14. Venezuela. Stating that tobacco advertising leads to intemperate use of tobacco, especially by young people, Decrees of 1980 and 1981 prohibit television and radio broadcasting, respectively, of commercial advertising that leads to the use of cigarettes and tobacco products. Violation of these decrees is punishable by suspension or revocation of the broadcasting permit.

Table B7. Health education on tobacco

Country	Public education	Anti-smoking education in schools	Allocation of funds
Argentina			
San Fernando del Valle de Catamarca	X		
Bolivia[1]	X	X	
Brazil[2]	X		
São Paulo	X	X	
Canada	X	X	
Chile[3]	X	X	X
Colombia[4]	X		
Costa Rica[5]	X		
Cuba[6]	X		
Ecuador[7]	X		
El Salvador[8]	X	X	
Mexico[9]	X	X	X
Peru[10]			X
United States of America	X	X	X
Uruguay[11]	X	X	

Notes to Table B7

1. Bolivia. The Regulations of 1982 require the Health Authority (the Ministry of Social Welfare and Public Health) to draw up mass education programmes to counter the harmful effects of tobacco and to supervise the use of the media for tobacco advertising. An Intersectoral Council for health training and education, created by joint action of the Ministries of Social Welfare and Public Health and of Education and Culture, is charged with analysing the educational programmes, including compulsory anti-smoking education, for systematic and programmed teaching of health education.

2. Brazil. The Law of 11 June 1986 provides for a National Anti-Smoking Day to be held each year on 29 August, with a national campaign in the preceding week to alert the people to the dangers of tobacco.

3. Chile. The National Commission for the Control of Smoking, established by a 1986 decree, is charged with designing and evaluating a programme for smoking control in the medium and long term in the fields of education, information,

regulation, and evaluation. The Commission is required to identify resources in the public and private sectors for informational, educational, and cessation activities. The functions of the Intersectoral Commission for Primary Prevention of Alcoholism in Schools, established in 1980, have been expanded to cover prevention of the use of drugs and tobacco. In 1984, the Decree on the Advisory Joint Commission on Education was modified to strengthen joint activities of the Ministries of Health and Education and their constituent bodies and to increase support to structures at the local level.

4. Colombia. A decree enacted in 1986 provides for educational programmes and preventive campaigns on tobacco use.

5. Costa Rica. A 1988 decree urges that campaigns and activities should be undertaken to mark No-Smoking Day, established by WHO, with emphasis on the injury to health caused by smoking.

6. Cuba. The Ministerial Resolution No. 165 of 17 August 1981 requires the staff of the National Health System to take advantage of all opportunities to provide information on the harmfulness of tobacco and to persuade the people of this.

7. Ecuador. The 1979 Constitution of Ecuador recognizes the right to welfare of the population, which includes the protection of health and requires programmes aimed at eliminating alcoholism and other addictions.

8. El Salvador. The Decree of 11 May 1988 requires the Ministry of Public Health and Social Welfare to draw up programmes on the effects of the consumption of drugs and tobacco and to encourage cultural and sports activity to prevent such consumption.

9. Mexico. The General Law on Health of 1983 lays down the objectives of the Programme against Smoking, which include education of the family, children, and adolescents through individual methods and mass communications, with emphasis on the education of the family to prevent tobacco use by children and adolescents. Coordination agreements between the Secretariat for Health and Welfare and the States provide for implementing smoking-control programmes in higher educational institutions and for preventing smoking by children and adolescents.

10. Peru. Under the Law of 20 October 1982, a tax increase of 9% on cigarettes made from blond tobacco is allocated to the construction and equipping of a cancer hospital, to the development of cancer detection centres throughout the country, and to research on neoplastic diseases.

11. Uruguay. Concerned about the increase in smoking among young people of both sexes, the Ministry of Public Health, with the active participation of the Ministry of Education, has organized No-Tobacco Day, involving educational councils at the primary, secondary, and teacher training levels. Legislation proposed in 1988 would authorize a Commission for the Control for Smoking to coordinate educational programmes on tobacco with the National Administration of Public Education, the University of the Republic, and other educational organizations.

Table B8. Legislation establishing a national organization for policy development and coordination to control tobacco use

Country	National organization
Bolivia	Ministry of Health and Public Welfare
Brazil	Ministry of Health
Canada	Department of National Health and Welfare
Chile	National Commission for the Control of Smoking
Ecuador	Interinstitutional Committee against Smoking
Mexico	National Council against Addictions, with support from the Secretariat for Health and Welfare in coordination with the Governments of the various States
Panama	National Commission to Study Tobacco Use in Panama
Peru	Permanent National Commission against Tobacco
United States of America	Office on Smoking and Health, Centers for Disease Control, US Department of Health and Human Services
Uruguay	Ministry of Health acting in collaboration with the Ministry of Education and Culture
Venezuela	National Council of the Ministry of Health and Welfare, composed of representatives of the Ministry of Health and the Ministries of Agriculture, Labour, Transportation and Communications, Justice, Environment and Natural Resources, Information and Tourism, Youth Affairs, the Venezuelan Institute of Social Security, the National Academy of Medicine, the Cancer Society, and the Venezuelan Medical Federation

C. Eastern Mediterranean Region

Table C1. Control of tobacco advertising and promotion

Country	Total ban	Restrictions on the use of mass media (television, radio, press, billboards)	Restrictions on the promotion of tobacco through sponsorship of sports and cultural events	Restrictions on the content, format, or location of advertising
Afghanistan*	X			
Bahrain[1]		X		X
Cyprus				W
Egypt[2]		X		W
Iraq[3]	X			
Jordan	X			
Kuwait		X		
Lebanon				W
Morocco		X		
Pakistan[4]		X		
Saudi Arabia[5]		X		
Sudan[6]		X		

*Text of legislation not available to author.
W = health warning required.

Notes to Table C1

1. Bahrain. By order of the Minister of Information, smoking is banned in television serials, plays, and other theatrical presentations.

2. Egypt. The advertising of tobacco products on radio and television is prohibited.

3. Iraq. All advertising of tobacco is banned.

4. Pakistan. In 1977, the advertising of tobacco products and smoking in schools and public places were banned.

5. Saudi Arabia. By order of the Minister of Information, smoking in television serials, plays, and other theatrical presentations is banned.

6. Sudan. The distribution and use of any form of poster, picture, or publication for the advertising of cigarettes is prohibited.

Table C2. Health warnings and statement and control of tar and nicotine (T/N) content

Country	Familiar warning	Rotating/ strong warnings	Smokeless tobacco warnings	Statements of T/N content	Control of T/N content
Bahrain[1]		X		X	X
Cyprus	X				
Egypt	X			X	X
Iraq	X				X
Jordan	X			X	
Kuwait[2]	X	X		X	X
Lebanon	X				
Oman[1]		X		X	X
Pakistan	X				
Qatar[1]		X		X	X
Saudi Arabia[3]	X		*		
Sudan	X				
United Arab Emirates[1]		X		X	X

* Total ban.

Notes to Table C2

1. Arab Gulf States. By Resolution 24 of the Health Ministers of the Arab Gulf States, the warning in all these States is: "Health warning: Smoking is a leading cause of lung cancer and of pulmonary and cardiovascular diseases."

2. Kuwait. The warning "Smoking is a leading cause of lung cancer and of pulmonary and cardiovascular disease" was required by a Ministerial Resolution in 1980. In 1988, a Ministerial Decree modified the warning and reduced the maximum permitted levels of tar and nicotine in cigarettes offered for sale on the Kuwaiti market.

3. Saudi Arabia. The Central Laboratory in Riyadh analyses samples of cigarettes sold on the market in the Arab Gulf States to determine their nicotine and tar content.

Table C3. Restrictions on places of sale

Country	Government buildings	Health establishments	Schools and places where young people congregate	Other
Iraq[1]				X

Note: Restrictions on the use of vending machines are presented in Table C6

Note to Table C3

1. In conformity with resolution 24 adopted at the Eighth Meeting of the Health Ministers of the Arab States of the Gulf Area, held in Baghdad on 20–26 January 1980, Iraq requested airlines not to sell cigarettes and tobacco on board their aircraft.

Table C4. Restrictions on smoking in public places

Country	Government agencies	Health establishments	Schools and places where young people congregate	Public transport	Lifts	Indoor public places	Markets and food storage places	Restaurants
Bahrain		X	X					
Cyprus[1]		X	X	X		X		
Egypt	X			X	X	X	X	X
Alexandria[2]						X		
Jordan				X		X		
Lebanon*								
Libyan Arab Jamahiriya*[3]								
Morocco*[4]								
Oman*[5]		X	X			X		
Pakistan[6]			X	X				
Saudi Arabia[7]	X	X	X	X				
Sudan					X			

*Text of legislation not available to author.

Notes to Table C4

1. Cyprus. Under the Regulations of 27 May 1988, the following health warning is required to be posted in cafes and restaurants: "CAUTION. Smoking is seriously harmful to your health: Ministry of Health".

2. Egypt. Under Law No. 52 of 20 June 1981, smoking is prohibited in public transport vehicles and enclosed public places defined by the Minister of Health. The Alexandria Municipal Ordinance of 20 July 1904 prohibited smoking in theatres. It was amended on 29 December 1938 and by Law No. 372 of 29 October 1956 and again in 1964 to ban smoking in public places and advertising.

3. Libyan Arab Jamahiriya. An administrative order of 1989 imposed a ban on smoking in designated public places.

4. Morocco. Legislative measures to ban smoking in public places are being reviewed by the National Parliament.

5. Oman. A decree was issued banning smoking in hospitals and health institutions except in designated places.

6. Pakistan. In 1977, the Government banned smoking in schools and public places.

7. Saudi Arabia. Smoking is prohibited in ministerial offices, government agencies, and public institutions. Domestic flights by the national airline are smoke-free.

Table C5. Restrictions on smoking in the workplace

Country	General laws restricting smoking in the workplace	Government agencies	Health establishments	Schools	Authorization for administrative regulations or accommodation of smokers and non-smokers	Other
Saudi Arabia[1]						X

Note to Table C5

1. Saudi Arabia. Smoking in public institutions is prohibited.

Table C6. Preventing young people from smoking

Country	Prohibiting sales to minors	Restricting sales from vending machines	Prohibiting sales in schools and other places frequented by young people	Restricting advertising that influences young people	Other
Bahrain		X			
Cyprus[1]		X			

Note to Table C6

1. Cyprus. The sale of cigarettes from vending machines is prohibited under Law No. 51 of 1980.

Table C7. Health education on tobacco

Country	Public education	Anti-smoking education in schools	Allocation of funds
Bahrain	X		
Iraq	X	X	
Saudi Arabia	X	X	

Table C8. Legislation establishing a national organization for policy development and coordination to control tobacco use

Country	National organization
Bahrain	Anti-Smoking Society, chaired by a laywer
Saudi Arabia	Smoking Control Society, chaired by the Minister of Health

D. European Region

Table D1. Control of tobacco advertising and promotion

Country	Total ban	Restrictions on the use of mass media (television, radio, press, billboards)	Restrictions on the promotion of tobacco through sponsorship of sports and cultural events	Restrictions on the content, format, or location of advertising
Austria		X		
Belgium[1]		X		XW
Bulgaria	X			
Czechoslovakia[2]	X			
Denmark[3]		X		
Finland[4]	X		X	
France[5]	X		X	
Germany[6]		X		W
Greece		X		
Hungary	X			
Iceland[7]	X		X	
Ireland[8]		X	X	XW
Italy	X			
Luxembourg[9]		X	X	X
Malta		X		W
Netherlands		X		
Norway[10]	X		X	
Poland[11]	X			
Portugal[12]	X		X	XW
Romania	X			
Spain[13]		X		
Sweden[14]		X		XW
Former USSR[15]	X	X		
United Kingdom[16]		(X)	(X)	(W)
Yugoslavia	X			
European Communities[17]		X		

W = health warning required.
(X) = provisions laid down by voluntary agreement.

211

Notes to Table D1

1. Belgium. The Crown Order of 10 April 1990 strengthens the controls on tobacco advertising specified in the Crown Order of 20 December 1982. Under these two orders, advertising of tobacco products on radio and television and in newspapers, reviews, and other publications aimed mainly at minors is prohibited, as is advertising:

   — by means of aircraft, boats or vehicles, except for those taking part in competitions or being used to transport tobacco, tobacco products, or similar products;

   — by using films, videotapes, slides, or other types of visual presentation;

   — by the distribution or door-to-door delivery of stickers or promotional leaflets;

   — by means of public speeches promoting tobacco products;

   — by means of free samples of tobacco, tobacco products, and other products in any form whatsoever, even under the pretext of carrying out market research, or a public opinion or consumer survey;

   — by using the brand name or symbol of tobacco, tobacco products, or similar products, or by using any other image or reference usually associated with such products, on, or close to everyday objects or by any other means other than those which are part of the personal equipment of participants in sporting competitions or of the accompanying technical team;

   — by referring to, or mentioning or representing the act of smoking or the representation of everyday products or articles linked with tobacco use;

   — by using illuminated signs, except within or at the entrance to places where tobacco, tobacco products, or similar products are available for sale.

   Where tobacco advertising is permitted, its contents are limited to the name and address of the manufacturer, importer, or distributor, the name of the product, its brand name and symbol, representations of products directly associated with smoking, tar and nicotine levels, and information on price and quality.

2. Czechoslovakia. On 28 March 1989, the Czech National Council passed Law No. 37/89 on protection against alcoholism and other addictions, which prohibits publicity, promotion, and advertising of smoking in the press and other information media. Inconsistent with this total ban on tobacco advertising is the Law of 30 October 1991 on radio and television broadcasting, adopted by the Czech and Slovak Federal Republic, which provides that advertising of tobacco products must indicate the tar and nicotine content and contain the health warning that smoking is harmful. A new Tobacco Act is in preparation.

3. Denmark. There has long been a voluntary agreement with the tobacco industry. Legislation was enacted in 1988 prohibiting the advertising on radio and television of tobacco products or goods primarily used in connection with tobacco smoking.

4. Finland. One of the first countries to enact a total ban on tobacco advertising, its Law No. 693 of 13 August 1976 banned advertising of tobacco, tobacco products and imitations, and smokers' accessories, and other sales promotion activities directed at the consumer, as well as their association with advertising for other products or services, or other sales promotion activity.

5. France. From 1976 to 1990, French legislation authorized tobacco advertising only in the "tombstone" format, in which only the name of the product, the package, and the lettering may be shown. Advertising of products using the name or emblem of tobacco products was required to conform to the same restrictions as those applying to tobacco products. Sponsorship of sports events by the tobacco industry was prohibited, with the exception of motor car racing.

   In January 1991 the National Assembly repealed the 1976 law and enacted a new statute, effective 1 January 1993, banning all advertising, direct and indirect, of tobacco and tobacco products, all free distribution of such products, and all sponsorship of tobacco that has the aim or purpose of advertising tobacco or tobacco products directly or indirectly. Indirect advertising of tobacco includes all advertising for an agency, service, activity, product or article other than tobacco or a tobacco product, when that advertising, on account of its logo, presentation, use of a trade mark, symbol, or any other distinctive sign, is suggestive of tobacco or a tobacco product.

   Until 31 December 1992 all advertising of tobacco and tobacco products, allowed under transitional provisions, must carry the health warning "Abuse is dangerous".

6. Germany. The use of advertising material is prohibited if it is likely to have an effect on physical performance or well-being, to induce adolescents to smoke, to make it appear that inhaling tobacco smoke is something to be imitated, or if it suggests that tobacco products are pure.

7. Iceland. A total ban on all advertising and promotion of tobacco products has been in force since 1971. It is reported that, overall, the ban has been closely observed, even though indirect advertising occurs on a small scale.

8. Ireland. The Tobacco (Health Promotion and Protection) Act, 1988, restricts the media that may be used for tobacco advertising. Advertising is allowed only in the print media and at points of sale. The content of advertisements is restricted to the brand name, emblem, representation of the package, and health warning. Rotating health warnings on packages and advertisements are compulsory. Expenditures on advertising and sponsorship are limited to the actual expenditures for such activities in 1985, with an increase each year to allow for inflation. Regulations under the Act restrict sponsorship of events by the tobacco industry. An event which was not sponsored prior to 1 May 1986 cannot now be sponsored. Events or activities in which the participants are aged 18 years or under cannot be sponsored. Sponsored events can be advertised only in newspapers and magazines, at the place where the event is taking place, and internally in premises which are points of retail sale. Such events cannot be advertised in comics or other publications aimed primarily at persons 18 years or under or along a public roadway. An advertisement relating to a sponsored event may contain only the name of the event, a written description of the event, the name of the sponsor, and the corporate emblem. An advertisement about a sponsored event may not appear alongside an advertisement for a tobacco product. Participants at a sponsored event or their assistants are not permitted to display the sponsor's emblem, brand name, or symbol of a tobacco product

on themselves or their equipment, such as racing cars or golf bags. The restrictions relating to participants at sponsored events were designed to defeat the industry's objective of using tobacco advertisements at such events in order to circumvent the ban on television advertising of tobacco products.

9. Luxembourg. The Law of 24 March 1989 prohibits advertising of tobacco products on television, radio, in theatres and other places open to the public, by means of boats and aircraft, by distribution of free samples of tobacco products, by using the emblem or name of the brand of tobacco products on products other than those directly related to the use of tobacco, in magazines and periodicals designed to reach minors, in stadiums and public and private sports arenas (although the name of the product on a billboard or vehicle not surrounded by text or graphic representation is allowed). The content of advertising is restricted; it may not be addressed to minors; it may not make use of arguments based on health; and it may not contain any representation of public figures. The tobacco industry is prohibited from sponsoring events for children or minors, and the organizers of such events may not accept their patronage.

10. Norway. All forms of tobacco promotion are prohibited. Tobacco products include cigarette paper, cigarette rollers, and pipes. Tobacco products may not be included in advertisements for other products, nor may a person smoking be depicted in advertisements of other products. The name or logo of a tobacco company may not be used in the sponsorship of sports or cultural events. Advertising low-price tobacco products is forbidden. Inside a sales outlet, tobacco products may be displayed only to the extent that this is necessary to serve customers in a rational way; special displays with product markers or pennants are forbidden. Window displays of tobacco products are forbidden. The secondary use of tobacco names, pictures of tobacco products, etc., on such things as playing cards, matchboxes, ashtrays, napkins, wardrobe tags, and sunshades is forbidden. The ban on tobacco advertising applies to pamphlets, catalogues, samples distributed to the consumer or other groups, whether sent through the mail, distributed at trade fairs, in shops, or in public or private places. Selling or supplying imitations of tobacco products (candy cigarettes) to persons under 16 years of age is forbidden. In order to restrict promotion of tobacco, in 1989 Norway adopted regulations (No. 1044 of 13 October 1989) prohibiting the importation, sale, and supply of new forms of products containing tobacco or nicotine. The Ministry of Social Affairs and the Directorate of Health are authorized to demand that manufacturers, importers or dealers submit representative samples of the product, or institute such investigations as are necessary to evaluate the product's characteristics and effects. The manufacturer or importer shall bear the cost of such investigations. The above-mentioned authorities are authorized to have free access to buildings, means of transport, warehouses, installation areas, etc., where products governed by these regulations are to be found.

11. Poland. Tobacco advertising on television and radio is banned. The Ordinance of 4 June 1974 also provides for a reduction in smoking on television programmes and an increase in popular scientific broadcasts on the harmful effects of smoking.

12. Portugal. Advertising is prohibited in the national media and by apposition of the name, brand, or symbol of a tobacco product to consumer goods that are not directly concerned with the use of tobacco.

214

13. Spain. Under Crown Decree No. 709/1982, informational advertising of new tobacco products with low tar or nicotine contents is permitted for two years following their introduction on the market. Legislation introduced in the Spanish Parliament would ban all tobacco advertising, except on radio from 22:00 to 08:00.

14. Sweden. Tobacco advertising is restricted to the "tombstone" format. Under the 1979 Guidelines, advertising of tobacco products in the sports pages of daily newspapers, in sports newspapers, and in publications aimed at people under 20 years of age is prohibited. Direct mail advertising and billboard advertising of tobacco products are prohibited. There is no commercial advertising on Swedish radio or television. Advertising in films, in hospitals, and in places frequented by young people is prohibited. No human figures or beautiful scenery may be shown.

In March 1990, the Committee for Tobacco Control, appointed by the Minister of Health and Social Security recommended the adoption of a comprehensive tobacco act, which would impose a total ban on tobacco advertising.

15. Former USSR. The laws in the states of the former Soviet Union are in flux. In Lithuania, for example, a draft tobacco control act would regulate cigarette production, sales, and advertising, provide for increased taxes and prices, allocate tobacco tax revenue for health education, and ban smoking in schools, health premises, and other public places.

16. United Kingdom. By voluntary agreement with the industry, all advertisements in newspapers and magazines, on posters and cinema screens, in leaflets and brochures, in consumer catalogues and circular letters must carry a reference to the government warning that appears on cigarette packets. Certain restrictions on the content of advertisements are also imposed by voluntary agreement, but much more than "tombstone" advertising is permitted. On 24 March 1986 the voluntary agreement banned advertising of cigarettes in cinemas.

17. European Communities. A Directive of 10 March 1989 prohibits tobacco advertising on television. A directive on advertising on radio is under consideration. On 12 February 1992, the European Parliament voted to support a total ban on tobacco advertising. The Council of Health Ministers will make the final decision.

215

Table D2. Health warnings and statement and control of tar and nicotine (T|N) content

Country	Familiar warning	Rotating/strong warnings	Smokeless tobacco warnings	Statements of T/N content	Control of T/N content
Austria	X				
Belgium[1]	X		X	X	X
Bulgaria	X				
Czechoslovakia	X				
Denmark[2]		X		X	X
Finland[3]		X		X	X
France[4]	X		X	X	
Germany[5]	X			X	X
Greece	X		X		
Hungary	X				
Iceland[6]		X	X		
Ireland[7]		X	*		
Israel			*		X
Luxembourg[8]		X	X	X	X
Malta[9]		X	*	X	X
Netherlands		X		X	X
Norway[10]		X	X	X	X
Portugal	X			X	X
Spain[11]		X		X	X
Sweden[12]		X	X	X	
Switzerland	X				
Former USSR	X				X
United Kingdom[13]		(X)	*		(X)
European Communities[14]		X		X	X

(X) = provisions laid down by voluntary agreement.
* Total ban.

Notes to Table D2

1. Belgium. The Crown Order of 19 January 1990 limits the tar and nicotine content of cigarettes. As of 31 December 1992, the maximum tar yield permitted is 15 mg, and the maximum nicotine yield is 1.5 mg. These limits will be lowered to 12 mg for tar and 1.2 mg for nicotine on 31 December 1997.

2. Denmark. On 28 June 1990, the Ministry of Health issued Order No. 507 requiring all packages of tobacco products to carry the general warning, "Extremely harmful to health. National Board of Health" and also a specific warning selected from a specified list. The contents of tar and nicotine, measured according to the ISO methods indicated, must be stated on the package. Law No. 426 of 13 June 1990 on the labelling of tobacco products and the tar content of cigarettes authorizes the Ministry of Health to issue provisions to implement Directives of the European Communities on the labelling of tobacco products and the tar content of cigarettes and to supervise and monitor compliance with these requirements.

3. Finland. In 1984, in Decree No. 770, the following maximum permissible levels of harmful substances were laid down for factory-manufactured cigarettes: tar (condensates) — 15 mg (previously 18 mg) per cigarette smoked; carbon monoxide — 12 mg (previously 14 mg) per cigarette smoked; nicotine — 1.2 mg (previously 1.3 mg) per cigarette smoked.

4. France. The additives (flavouring agents, texture agents, preservatives, and colouring matters) permitted to be added in the manufacture of tobacco products and the permitted levels and purity criteria for such additives are specified in an order of 16 July 1984. Under the Law of 10 January 1991, the full composition of every package of cigarettes (except filters) and the average tar and nicotine content must be indicated on the cigarette package.

5. Germany. The substances that may be used in tobacco products are subject to regulation.

6. Iceland. Under Regulations No. 499 of 28 December 1984, rotating warnings with illustrative designs are required. The warning for snuff and chewing tobacco states: "Snuff and chewing tobacco may damage the mucous membranes."

7. Ireland. The Tobacco (Health Promotion and Protection) Act, 1988, requires manufacturers of tobacco to notify the Minister of Health of constituents of tobacco products, and authorizes the Minister to control or prohibit the use of certain constituents or to prohibit the importation of tobacco products containing such constituents. Ireland bans the sale of moist snuff only.

8. Luxembourg. The Regulations of 19 June 1990 under the Law of 24 March 1989 restricting advertising of tobacco products and prohibiting smoking in certain places provide for rotating health warnings and a maximum tar yield of 15 mg per cigarette, to become effective two years after the publication of the Regulations.

217

9. Malta. Under the Tobacco (Smoking Control) Act, 1986, health warnings must be displayed in premises where tobacco products are sold so as to attract the attention of customers or other persons on the premises and to be easily seen and read by them. Under the 1987 Regulations made under the Act, rotating warnings are required on cigarette packages, in cinemas, and in advertisements.

10. Norway. The Norwegian Government has decided to strengthen the 12 rotating warnings adopted in 1984 and to add illustrative designs, as in Iceland.

11. Spain. The Crown Decree of 4 March 1988 requires rotating health warnings and the display of the tar and nicotine contents. As from 31 December 1992, the maximum tar content for cigarettes is 15 mg, and the maximum nicotine content 1.3 mg. Cigarettes classified as "low nicotine and tar", including "light", "mild", or similar designations, must have, six months after the effective date of the Decree, a tar content not exceeding 13 mg and a nicotine content not exceeding 0.9 mg. After 31 December 1992, the corresponding figures for such cigarettes are 10 mg and 0.8 mg, respectively.

12. Sweden. The legislation requires not only a declaration of the number of milligrams of tar, nicotine, and carbon monoxide but also comparison figures (the arithmetical average for all brands marketed in Sweden) determined each year by the National Board of Health and Welfare. Under an Order of 10 April 1986, one warning used for snuff and chewing tobacco states that these products contain nicotine and therefore may be as addictive as tobacco.

13. United Kingdom. On 24 March 1986, the Government reached an agreement with the tobacco industry requiring six rotating health warnings on tobacco packages, posters, and press advertisements, as follows:

— Smoking can cause fatal diseases.

— Smoking can cause heart disease.

— Smoking when pregnant can injure your baby and cause premature birth.

— Stopping smoking reduces the risk of serious diseases.

— Smoking can cause lung cancer, bronchitis and other chest diseases.

— More than 30,000 people die each year in the UK from lung cancer.

The sale of oral tobacco to children is prohibited by the Protection of Children (Tobacco) Act 1986. In 1990, the Oral Snuff (Safety) Regulations 1989 banned the sale of moist snuff in the following terms: "goods which consist mainly or wholly of tobacco in fine cut, ground or particulate form or in any combination of those forms and which are for oral use other than smoking." This is interpreted to exclude dry snuff and chewing tobacco. These regulations were overturned because of a legal technicality, and the Government has appealed against this ruling. The European Community, however, is expected to approve amendments to its Directive 89/622/EEC on the labelling of tobacco, which will impose a Community-wide ban on oral moist snuff. This will require some slight amendments to the United Kingdom Regulations and it is expected that the Government may introduce new regulations and drop the appeal against the existing ones.

14. European Communities. The Directive of 13 November 1989 requires all packages of tobacco products to carry the general warning, "Tobacco seriously damages health", and alternating specific warnings taken from those listed in the annex to the Directive (see p. 49) so as to guarantee the appearance of each warning on an equal quantity of unit packages, with a tolerance of around 5%. The Directive also requires tar and nicotine yields to be indicated on cigarette packages and such yields to be measured and their accuracy verified in accordance with the relevant ISO standards. The directive of 17 May 1990 sets the maximum tar yield of cigarettes marketed as 15 mg as from 31 December 1992 and as 12 mg from 31 December 1997.

Table D3. Restrictions on places of sale

Country	Government buildings	Health establishments	Schools and places where young people congregate	Other
Bulgaria			X	
Malta		X		
Netherlands[1]	X	X	X	X
Spain[2]		X	X	
United Kingdom			X	

Note: Restrictions on the use of vending machines are presented in Table D6.

Notes to Table D3

1. Netherlands. The sale of tobacco products in health care, social welfare, sports, sociocultural, and educational establishments administered by the State is prohibited under the Tobacco Law of 1988.

2. Spain. The sale of tobacco products in health establishments, educational establishments, and establishments primarily intended for the care of children and adolescents is prohibited under the Crown Decree of 1988.

Table D4. Restrictions on smoking in public places

Country	Government agencies	Health establishments	Schools and places where young people congregate	Public transport	Lifts	Indoor public places	Markets and food storage places	Restaurants
Austria[1]				X				
Belgium[2]	X	X	X	X	X	X	X	X
Bulgaria		X	X	X		X	X	X
Czechoslovakia[3]		X	X	X		X	X	X
Denmark[4]	X	X	X	X		X	X	
Finland[5]	X	X	X	X	X	X		
France[6]	X	X	X	X	X	X	X	X
Germany[7]		X	X	X		X	X	
Greece[8]		X		X	X	X		
Hungary[9]	X	X	X	X	X	X	X	X
Iceland[10]	X	X	X	X	X	X	X	
Ireland[11]		X	X	X		X	X	X
Israel[12]		X	X	X	X	X	X	
Italy[13]		X	X	X		X		
Luxembourg[14]	X	X	X	X		X		
Malta		X	X	X		X	X	
Netherlands[15]	X	X	X	X		X		
Norway[16]	X	X	X	X	X	X	X	X
Poland[17]	X	X	X	X		X	X	X
Portugal[18]		X	X	X		X		
Romania		X	X	X		X		
Spain[19]	X	X	X	X	X	X	X	
Sweden[20]	X	X	X	X	X	X	X	X
Turkey[21]				X				
Former USSR[22]	X	X	X	X		X		
United Kingdom[23]								
European Communities[24]	X	X	X	X		X		X

Notes to Table D4

1. Austria. Reports indicate that the control of smoking in public places and public transport is effective to some extent, but legislation on the subject is not available to the author.

2. Belgium. The Crown Order of 15 May 1990 strengthens the legislation banning smoking in public places enacted in 1987. The new legislation prohibits smoking in enclosed places used by the public which form part of premises where:

   — services are available to the public, with or without charge, including places serving food and/or drinks for public consumption;

   — ill or elderly people are admitted or treated;

   — health care for prevention or treatment is provided;

   — children or young people of school age are admitted, treated, or are in residence;

   — education and/or professional training are provided;

   — entertainment is offered;

   — exhibitions are mounted;

   — sports are practised.

An exception is made only for places specially designated for the provision and consumption of food and/or drinks (restaurants, snack-bars, cafes, etc.) which do not exceed 50 square metres in area. Clearly defined areas can be set aside for smokers, but they must be established so as to minimize the nuisance of smoke to non-smokers. Until December 1992, these special areas must measure less than two-thirds of the total area of the enclosed premises and, after that date, they cannot exceed half the total area of the enclosed premises. In places where smoking is permitted, a smoke extractor and/or smoke-reducing ventilation system must be installed.

3. Czechoslovakia. The legislation provides that, in public services, smoking is permitted only in places specially reserved for the purpose. This provision does not apply to restaurants, but a minimum of one section must be set aside for non-smokers, at least during normal meal hours. Smoking is prohibited in passenger trains (except in smoking compartments), in meetings and conferences in enclosed places, and in all health, school, cultural and enclosed sports premises.

222

4. Denmark. A Circular issued in March 1988 by the Ministry of Health bans smoking in all workplaces under its jurisdiction and in meetings of public councils, boards, and commissions unless all participants agree to permit smoking. The Circular also provides that individual Ministers shall introduce non-smoking environments on public premises under their jurisdiction. A Circular of the Ministry of Social Affairs dated 22 December 1988 bans smoking on premises frequented by children. Order No. 121 of the Ministry of the Environment dated 28 March 1980 regulates tobacco smoking and retail selling of food. A Circular of the veterinary authorities dated October 1974 forbids smoking on premises where food is being prepared for resale.

5. Finland. Smoking is prohibited in all public places unless specifically allowed.

6. France. Legislation has long prohibited smoking in places intended for use by groups of people if the premises do not meet specified ventilation requirements. Law No. 91–32 of 10 January 1991 prohibits smoking in places intended for collective use and in particular scholastic use and in collective means of transport, except in areas specifically reserved for smokers. A decree (No. 92–478 of 29 May 1992) under this Law, adopted by the Council of State in 1992, prohibits smoking in all public places, including businesses, restaurants, schools, workplaces, and public transport, with areas reserved for smokers. Smoking is totally prohibited in theatres, exhibition halls, sports arenas, places where food is prepared or presented for sale, lifts, taxis, aircraft on flights of less than two hours, and dining cars of trains.

7. Germany. As in the United Kingdom, there are voluntary restrictions by institutions, government agencies, and transport companies on smoking in public places.

8. Greece. The Ministerial Decision of 25 April 1980 prohibits smoking in all enclosed public places (public waiting-rooms, conference and meeting halls, lifts, etc.) belonging to State agencies, public or private companies and organizations, and in other establishments. Under the Ministerial Decision of 12 April 1979, smoking is also prohibited in public and private hospitals and private nursing homes; a smoking room, reserved for hospital personnel and visitors, is required on every floor of an establishment that has an area of 200 m^2 or more, and smokers may smoke only in these rooms.

9. Hungary. MALEV, the Hungarian airline, has prohibited smoking on all its short-distance flights.

10. Iceland. Smoking is prohibited under the Law of 28 May 1984 in specific institutions (primary schools, nurseries, and buildings used for leisure activities for children and adolescents) and in those parts of public and private institutions rendering service to, and accessible to, the public. Restaurants and places of entertainment are required to reserve a certain number of tables for non-smokers. In general, smoking is allowed only in places where it will not inconvenience non-smokers.

223

11. Ireland. Under the Tobacco (Health Promotion and Protection) Act, 1988, the Minister for Health may, by regulations, prohibit or restrict the consumption of tobacco products in a designated area or a designated facility, including aircraft, trains, public service vehicles or other facilities; in such parts of health premises and schools as may be specified; in such parts of buildings to which the public has access and which belong to or are occupied by the State or a body established under an Act of the Oireachtas or in any other area designated by the Minister; and in cinemas, theatres, concert halls and such other places of indoor public entertainment as may be specified. Violation of these regulations is punishable by a fine not exceeding £Ir100, and the owner, manager or other person in charge of a designated area or a designated facility who fails, neglects, or refuses to ensure compliance is subject to a fine not exceeding £Ir500 and/or imprisonment for six months unless he has taken all reasonable steps to ensure full compliance with the regulations. The Regulations under this Act, issued in 1990, set forth the following designated areas where smoking is prohibited: State and semi-State buildings, public offices, primary and secondary schools (a separate smoking facility may be provided for teachers), universities (specific smoking facilities may be provided), food preparation areas, supermarkets and grocery stores, bus and railway stations, sports centres, cinemas, theatres, concert halls, art galleries, museums, and public libraries. (In the last three areas, smoking facilities may be provided in staff rooms or restaurants.) Smoking is prohibited on all buses used by the public.

In another list of designated areas and facilities, smoking is restricted, and clearly defined no-smoking areas must be provided. These include health premises, hospitals, nursing and maternity homes, centres for the mentally and physically handicapped, restaurants, canteens, snack bars, trains, aircraft and the seating areas in the arrival and departure sections of aerodromes, harbours, ferryports, and airports (in the last two facilities, smoking is prohibited in at least one-third of the seating area).

12. Israel. A procedure has been established, under an Order of 1986, for serving "tickets" on violators of the law banning smoking in public places, similar to the tickets served on those committing traffic offences.

13. Italy. An exemption to the ban on smoking in specified premises imposed by the Law of 11 November 1975 is made under the Ministerial Decree of 18 May 1976 for premises in which an air-conditioning or ventilation system meeting prescribed conditions has been installed. Failure of such systems to operate within their prescribed limits must cause illuminated "No smoking" signs to switch on automatically.

14. Luxembourg. The Law of 24 March 1989 prohibits smoking in hospitals, waiting rooms of physicians and dentists, pharmacies, educational establishments, places that receive or house persons under 16 years of age, indoor sports halls, cinemas and theatres, museums, art galleries, libraries, and reading rooms open to the public, all halls and rooms of public buildings where a sign prohibits smoking, buses and non-smoking railroad cars, and non-smoking sections of airports.

15. Netherlands. The Law of 10 March 1988 requires the competent authorities to take measures to ensure that establishments, services, and companies administered by the State and public bodies can be used and activities carried on there without any nuisance arising out of the use of tobacco products.

16. Norway. Law No. 24 of 6 May 1988 amending Law No. 14 of 9 March 1973 restricts smoking in premises and means of transport to which the public has access, and in meeting rooms and work premises where two or more people are present. Under certain circumstances, premises or means of transport may be divided into smoke-free and smoking areas provided that it is not possible for the smoke to pass into the smoke-free area and that the smoke-free premises and areas are not smaller or of lower standard than the premises or areas where smoking is permitted.

    Restaurants, hotels and other establishments that serve food and/or offer overnight accommodation are exempted from these restrictions. In Regulations of 8 July 1988 issued pursuant to the above-mentioned Law, the Ministry of Social Affairs urges restaurants, hotels, etc., to arrange for smoke-free environments as soon as possible. As of 1993, not less than one-third of the seats in restaurants and of hotel rooms are to be smoke-free. Responsibility for enforcing this provision is shared by the Directorate of Labour Inspection and the Health and Social Affairs Board.

17. Poland. Smoking is banned in all organizational units under the jurisdiction of the health and welfare services, and it is recommended that other ministries, central agencies, and local governments should prohibit smoking in cafeterias and canteens for workers and students, at meetings and conferences, and that a separate room should be designated for non-smokers in waiting-rooms and clubs with several rooms. In addition to the Decree of the Ministry of Health and Social Welfare of 4 June 1974, banning smoking in organizational units of the Department of Health, the Decree of the Minister of Education of 17 October 1974 deals with reducing smoking at schools; the Decree of the Minister of Transport of 4 December 1974 concerns the reduction of smoking in the Department of Transport, including means of transport, railway and bus stations, and airports; and the Decision of the Minister of Internal Trade and Services of 6 July 1974 concerns the reduction of smoking in organizational units of the Department, including catering units, groceries, and trade shops (T. Gorski, personal communication, 1988).

18. Portugal. In 1988, smoking was banned in public places and, in 1989, the ban was extended to provide a partial ban on smoking in restaurants and other catering establishments, such as tea rooms, coffee houses, sandwich bars, pubs, and cake shops, where food is consumed on the premises. Managers of these establishments are authorized to designate a certain area within their establishments as smoke-free.

19. Spain. Smoking is not permitted in welfare centres for persons under age 16, health centres, teaching centres, public administration premises to which the public has access, auditoria, libraries, theatres, cinemas, enclosed premises for sports or entertainment, and enclosed commercial premises where people frequently assemble. If it is possible to delimit separate areas for smokers, such areas may be designated. In enclosed commercial establishments where considerable numbers of people are present, such areas must be

225

designated with particular clarity. Smoking is also prohibited on all urban and long-distance vehicles for collective transport, on school vehicles, and in rail and sea transport, where whole carriages or cabins may be allocated for smokers. Smoking is prohibited in premises where foodstuffs are prepared or sold (Crown Decree 192/1988 of 4 March 1988). Smoking by food handlers is prohibited by Crown Decree 2505-1983.

20. Sweden. In 1983, the General Recommendations (AFS 1983:10) concerning smoking restriction were issued by the National Board of Occupational Safety and Health and the National Board of Health and Welfare. The main aim of the Recommendations is that no one should against his will be subjected to discomfort or to health hazards caused by tobacco smoke in public places and workplaces. The intention of the Recommendations is to accommodate both smokers and non-smokers, priority being given to the rights of non-smokers. An Interdepartmental Committee for Tobacco Control appointed by the Minister of Health and Social Affairs recommended in 1990 that all indoor public places (including public transport and workplaces) should, in principle, be made smoke-free. Separate smoking rooms or areas may be designated under certain circumstances. Restaurants with seating for more than 50 people must have smoke-free sections comprising at least half the seats. In hotels and similar premises at least half the number of rooms must be smoke-free.

21. Turkey. As of 25 January 1988, the Ministry of Transport has banned smoking on domestic flights. On international flights, a section at the front of the aircraft including 60% of the entire seating capacity has been designated for non-smokers; on outward-bound flights, smoking is allowed only in the rear part of the aircraft.

22. Former USSR. In Resolution No. 706 of 12 June 1980, the Central Committee of the Communist Party and the Council of Ministers called on government agencies to restrict or prohibit smoking in official and work premises. By Regulations of the Ministry of Public Health and the Ministry of Education, smoking is banned in medical institutions and schools, respectively.

23. United Kingdom. There is no national legislation governing smoking in public places, which is controlled either by rules imposed by the owners or operators of the accommodation or transport or, in some cases, by by-laws. Smoking in health institutions and government buildings is regulated by the management of those institutions and buildings.

24. European Communities. The Resolution of 18 July 1989 of the Council and the Ministers for Health of the Member States invites Member States to ban smoking in enclosed premises open to the public that form part of public or private establishments and to extend the ban to all forms of public transport. Public places include:

— establishments where services are provided to the public, whether for a charge or free, including the sale of goods;

— hospitals and health care establishments;

— establishments where elderly persons are received;

— schools and other premises where children or young people are received or housed;

— establishments where higher education and vocational training are given;

— enclosed establishments used for entertainment (cinemas, theatres) and radio and television studios open to the public;

— enclosed establishments where exhibitions are held;

— establishments and enclosed places where sports are practised;

— enclosed premises of underground and railway stations, ports, and airports.

227

Table D5. Restrictions on smoking in the workplace

Country	General laws restricting smoking in the workplace	Government agencies	Health establishments	Schools	Authorization for administrative regulation or accommodation of smokers and non-smokers	Other
Austria	X					
Belgium[1]	X					
Bulgaria[1]	X					
Czechoslovakia	X					
Denmark[2]		X	X	X		
France[3]	X				X	
Germany	X					
Iceland	X					
Ireland	X				X	
Norway[4]	X					
Poland	X					
Romania	X					
Spain[5]	X					
Sweden[6]	X				X	

Notes to Table D5

1. Bulgaria. Under the Sanitary Rules published on 21 January 1969, smoking at workplaces where any non-smoker is employed is prohibited, except by written agreement of the non-smoker, and without exception where expectant or nursing mothers are employed, even if they agree.

2. Denmark. By the Circular of 23 March 1988 of the Ministry of Health, smoking is prohibited in workplaces under the Ministry's jurisdiction that constitute a place of work for more than one person in rooms for general occupation unless the employees having places of work on the same premises declare smoking to be acceptable or if effective measures are adopted to ensure that no employee is inconvenienced. Other ministers are required to introduce non-smoking environments in public premises and means of transport under their jurisdiction.

3. France. A 1992 decree of the Council of State restricts smoking in workplaces to areas designated by the head of the enterprise after consultation with representatives of the workers, but recreation rooms may not be chosen as places where smoking is allowed.

4. Norway. As from 1 July 1988, a new Section 6 of the Law of 9 March 1973 introduced by the Law of 6 May 1988 provides that the air shall be smoke-free in work premises where two or more persons are present.

5. Spain. Crown Decree 192/1988 prohibits smoking in any place where a greater risk to the health of workers exists through the combination of the harm caused by tobacco and the adverse effects of industrial contamination. Smoking is prohibited in any occupational area where pregnant women work. Smoking by food handlers is prohibited by Crown Decree 2505-1983.

6. Sweden. In 1983, detailed General Recommendations (AFS 1983:10) concerning smoking restrictions were issued by the National Board of Occupational Safety and Health and the National Board of Health and Welfare. The essential principle is that a smoker's desire to smoke should take second place to other people's desire for a smoke-free environment. Since 1988, 25 county councils have banned smoking on county council premises.

In 1990, an Interdepartmental Committee for Tobacco Control, appointed by the Minister of Health and Social Affairs recommended that all workplaces should, in principle, be made smoke-free. Separate smoking rooms or areas could be designated under certain circumstances. In workplaces, smoking would be permitted only in special smoking rooms and private offices if the ventilation is sufficient to prevent smoke from spreading into smoke-free rooms.

Table D6. Preventing young people from smoking

Country	Prohibiting sales to minors	Restricting sales from vending machines	Prohibiting sales in schools and other places frequented by young people	Restricting advertising that influences young people	Other
Belgium		X		X	
Czechoslovakia[1]	X				
Finland		X	X		
France[2]					X
Hungary					X
Iceland	X	X			
Ireland[3]	X	X		X	
Luxembourg				X	
Malta	X	X			
Norway	X				
Spain[4]	X	X	X		
Sweden[5]				X	
Former USSR	X		X		
United Kingdom	X				

Notes to Table D6

1. Czechoslovakia. Law No. 37/89 of the Czech National Council concerning protection against alcoholism and other addictions, dated 28 March 1989, prohibits the sale of tobacco to persons under 16 years of age.

2. France. Law No. 91-32 of 10 January 1991 on measures to combat tobacco use and alcoholism provides that, on the occasion of medical examinations, required once every two years for staff of public and private educational institutions, including all persons in regular contact with pupils and students, the staff shall be provided with information by the school physician concerning tobacco use and alcoholism.

3. Ireland. The Tobacco Products (Control of Advertising, Sponsorship and Sales Promotion) Regulations, 1986, provide that tobacco products may not be advertised in comics, comic supplements, or any other publications directed primarily to persons under 18 years of age.

4. Spain. Under Crown Decree No. 192/1988, the sale of tobacco products is prohibited in health establishments, educational establishments, and establishments primarily intended for the care of children and adolescents. An order of 7 November 1989 prohibits the sale and distribution of tobacco and alcoholic beverages at public school centres under the authority of the Ministry of Education and Science and directs the provincial departments of the Ministry of Education and Science to adopt the measures necessary to implement this order. Tobacco products may be sold from automatic vending machines only on enclosed premises, and the machine is to display a non-removable health warning of area not less than 20 cm^2. The sale or supply of tobacco products to persons under 16 years of age is prohibited. Minors under age 16 are prohibited from using automatic vending machines.

5. Sweden. Tobacco advertising aimed at people under 20 years of age is restricted. Under the proposed comprehensive tobacco act recommended by the Committee for Tobacco Control, sale of tobacco products to persons under 18 years of age or from vending machines would be prohibited.

Table D7. Health education on tobacco

Country	Public education	Anti-smoking education in schools	Allocation of funds
Belgium	X	X	
Finland	X		X
France		X	
Iceland[1]	X	X	X
Luxembourg		X	
Norway	X		
Portugal	X		
Spain		X	
Valencia	X	X	
Sweden	X	X	
Former USSR		X	

Notes to Table D7

1. Iceland. Since 1985, 0.2% of the gross sales of tobacco have been allocated to anti-smoking activities. This amounts to US $0.41 annually for each inhabitant.

2. Sweden. State-funded information and education on tobacco and health began in 1964. Health education on tobacco is mandatory in all schools. The county councils are responsible for public health education in their regions. The Committee on Tobacco Control has recommended increased funding (at least doubled) for health education on tobacco.

Table D8. Legislation establishing a national organization for policy development and coordination to control tobacco use

Country	National organization
Denmark	Council on Prevention and Council on Tobacco-induced Damage to Health
Iceland	Committee for Tobacco Use Prevention, Ministry of Health and Social Security
Malta	Committee on Smoking and Health to advise the Minister of Health on measures, including legislation, to reduce the health risks from tobacco and to coordinate activities for the prevention and control of smoking
Norway	National Council on Smoking and Health
Portugal	Smoking Prevention Council
Spain	
Valencia	Technical Commission to Reduce Tobacco Consumption, composed of citizens' groups, scientific associations, and institutions
Former USSR	Department of Sanitation and Prevention, Ministry of Public Health

E. South-East Asia Region

Table E1. Control of tobacco advertising and promotion

Country	Total ban	Restrictions on the use of mass media (television, radio, press, billboards)	Restrictions on the promotion of tobacco through sponsorship of sports and cultural events	Restrictions on the content, format, or location of advertising
Bangladesh*		X		W
India		X		W
Nepal		X		
Sri Lanka		X		
Thailand[1]	X			

* Text of legislation not available to author.
W = health warning required.

Notes to Table E1

1. Thailand. A resolution of the Thai cabinet of 26 April 1988 directed the Ministry of Finance to order the Thailand Tobacco Monopoly to refrain from advertising. Foreign cigarettes continued to be advertised, although they were not imported legally at that time. Accordingly, by cabinet resolution dated 20 December 1988, a total ban was imposed on all foreign cigarette advertising in all forms, both direct and indirect, in all media. On 13 March 1989 the Council of Ministers of Social Affairs adopted a resolution directing the Administrative Committee of Radio and Television Broadcasting to control strictly indirect advertising of tobacco in radio and television programmes, e.g., the expression of emotion portrayed by the action of smoking.

    On 13 March 1992 Thailand adopted the Tobacco Products Control Act banning tobacco advertising in the electronic and print media and on billboards. Two exceptions permit advertising in international magazines and on live television shows from abroad. "Advertising" is defined in the Thai law as any act that enables people to see or to know the wording for commercial purposes, such as logos or wording on T-shirts. Advertising of other products with the same name is prohibited. The production, import, advertising, or sale of products that imitate tobacco products, such as candy or savings banks for children, are banned. The free distribution of cigarettes for commercial purposes is prohibited, as are free samples, exchanges, and gifts of tobacco products for commercial purposes.

Table E2. Health warnings and statement and control of tar and nicotine (T/N) content

Country	Familiar warning	Rotating/strong warnings	Smokeless tobacco warnings	Statements of T/N content	Control of T/N content
Bangladesh	X				
India[1]	X		X		
Indonesia	X				
Sri Lanka	X				X
Thailand[2]		X		X	

Notes to Table E2

1. India. Legislation enacted in 1975 requires a health warning on packages of cigarettes and on advertising. The requirement does not apply to exported cigarettes unless the country to which cigarettes are exported requires the same or a similar health warning.

2. Thailand. A cabinet resolution of 11 July 1989 requires the printing of six different rotating health warnings on the front of cigarette packages as follows:

   — Smoking causes lung cancer and emphysema.

   — Smoking causes ischaemic heart disease.

   — Smoking is dangerous for babies in the womb.

   — Please respect the rights of non-smokers by refraining from smoking in public places.

   — Stopping smoking decreases the risk to health.

   — For your beloved children and grandchildren, please give up smoking.

Article 11 of the Tobacco Products Control Act of 13 March 1992 requires producers and importers of tobacco products to disclose the ingredients of their products in accordance with the standards of the Ministry of Health. The Ministry of Health has the right to determine what should be disclosed. Article 12 provides that the labelling of tobacco products shall be determined by the Ministry of Health.

Table E3. Restrictions on places of sale

Country	Government buildings	Health establishments	Schools and places where young people congregate	Other
India[1]	X			
Thailand[2]		X		

Note: Restrictions on the use of vending machines are presented in Table E6.

Notes to Table E3

1. India. As a component of its ban on smoking in public places, the Government of India in 1990 ordered the removal of all cigarette shops from government buildings or compounds where smoking is prohibited.

2. Thailand. The Ministry of Health has directed all trading units in health premises to refrain from selling cigarettes.

Table E4. Restrictions on smoking in public places

Country	Government agencies	Health establishments	Schools and places where young people congregate	Public transport	Lifts	Indoor public places	Markets and food storage places	Restaurants
India[1]	X	X	X	X				
Indonesia[2]		X		X				
Jakarta			X					
Sri Lanka[3]		X		X				
Colombo*						X		
Thailand[4]	X	X		X		X		
Bangkok				X		X		

*Text of legislation not available to author.

Notes to Table E4

1. India. On 7 May 1990, the Government of India issued an Office Memorandum, "Prohibition of tobacco smoking in public places". It was decided to prohibit tobacco smoking, to start with, in a few selected places, namely, hospitals, dispensaries and other health care establishments, educational institutions, conference rooms, domestic flights, air-conditioned chaircars and air-conditioned sleeper coaches in trains, and suburban trains and air-conditioned buses. All domestic flights of Indian Airlines have been made smoke-free.

2. Indonesia. The Minister of Internal Affairs has instructed the governors of all provinces to ban smoking in educational institutions.

3. Sri Lanka. The Transport Act prohibits smoking in buses. The Ministry of Health prohibits smoking in hospitals and prohibits doctors from smoking in front of patients. The municipality of Colombo prohibits smoking in cinemas.

4. Thailand. Smoking is prohibited at cabinet meetings and all other meetings in Government House, in the House of Representatives, in all types of air-conditioned public transport, and on flights of less than two hours. All buildings of the Ministry of Health are required to be smoke-free, with provision of designated smoking areas, if necessary. Health personnel must refrain from smoking in public, during work, or outside designated smoking areas. On 10 March 1989 the Minister of Public Health issued a circular to all Provincial Governors urging the adoption of similar smoke-free policies. The Nonsmokers' Health Protection Act of 13 March 1992 bans smoking in all public places designated by the Ministry of Health.

Table E5. Restrictions on smoking in the workplace

Country	General laws restricting smoking in the workplace	Government agencies	Health establishments	Schools	Authorization for administrative regulation or accommodation of smokers and non-smokers	Other
			No information available			

Table E6. Preventing young people from smoking

Country	Prohibiting sales to minors	Restricting sales from vending machines	Prohibiting sales in schools and other places frequented by young people	Restricting advertising that influences young people	Other
Thailand[1]	X	X		X	

Note to Table E6

1. Thailand. Under its Tobacco Products Control Act of 13 March 1992, Thailand bans sales of tobacco products to persons under 18 and bans sales of cigarettes from vending machines.

Table E7. Health education on tobacco

Country	Public education	Anti-smoking education in schools	Allocation of funds
Indonesia	X		
Thailand	X		

Table E8. Legislation establishing a national organization for policy development and coordination to control tobacco use

Country	National organization
Sri Lanka	Sri Lanka National Federation on Smoking and Health
Thailand	National Committee for the Control of Tobacco Use

F. Western Pacific Region

Table F1. Control of tobacco advertising and promotion

Country or territory	Total ban	Restrictions on the use of mass media (television, radio, press, billboards)	Restrictions on the promotion of tobacco through sponsorship of sports and cultural events	Restrictions on the content, format, or location of advertising
Australia[1]		X	X	
Australian Capital Territory		X	X	
South Australia			X	W
Victoria		X	X	
Western Australia	X		X	
China[2]	X			
French Polynesia	X		X	
Hong Kong[3]		X	X	XW
Macao		X		X
Malaysia[4]		X		X
New Zealand[5]	X		X	
Papua New Guinea	X			
Singapore[6]	X			

W = health warning required

Notes to Table F1

1. Australia. The Broadcasting and Television Act 1972 imposed restrictions on tobacco advertising on the electronic media. Because of a loophole in the law, television stations have been permitted to show billboards, banners, and other paraphernalia that advertise tobacco products during sporting events. Legislation has been introduced in the Australian Parliament to ban such incidental television advertising of tobacco. On 28 December 1989, under the Smoking and Tobacco Products Advertisements (Prohibition) Act, a total ban was introduced on tobacco advertising in the print media (newspapers and magazines). On 1 April 1992 the Federal Cabinet resolved to phase out tobacco advertising and sponsorship throughout the country. This resolution was passed by the Parliament in August 1992, and complements the legislation of the various states and territories.

    The Australian Capital Territory established in 1989 the ACT Health Promotion Fund with an additional 3% levy on the wholesale price of tobacco products. The income from this fund is expected to be A$900 000 a year, and it will be used in grants and sponsorships for events formerly sponsored by the tobacco industry.

237

The Tobacco Products (Licensing) Act 1986 of the State of South Australia provides for a licence fee to be paid by tobacco merchants as a contribution to State revenues in place of a consumption licence to be taken out by a consumer of tobacco products. The Tobacco Products Control Amendment Act 1988 provides for an increase in the tobacco tax to replace industry sponsorship of sports events.

In the State of Victoria, the Tobacco Act 1987 provides for the establishment of the Victorian Health Promotion Foundation, created by an increase in the tobacco tax, to replace industry sponsorship of sports events and to support health promotion and research.

In the State of Western Australia, the Tobacco Control Act 1990 phases in a ban on all tobacco advertising and promotion, prohibits sponsorship by a tobacco manufacturer or distributor promoting a tobacco product or brand name, and establishes the Western Australian Health Promotion Foundation to fund health promotion activities and to offer an alternative source of funds for sporting and arts activities currently supported by the tobacco industry.

2. China. On 29 July 1991, the Standing Committee of the 7th Plenary Session of the National People's Congress, China's highest legislative body, announced approval of China's first tobacco law, effective 1 January 1992. The Law regulates many aspects of the State national tobacco monopoly — growth, distribution, licensing, manufacture and sales, import and export of tobacco products and machinery, measures against smuggling, etc. It also contains several important provisions aimed at protecting the health of the people. Section 19 bans tobacco advertising on radio, television, and in newspapers and magazines.

3. Hong Kong. As of December 1990, amendments to the Television Code of Practice on Advertising Standards arising from the ban on tobacco advertising and sponsorship specify the conditions under which a sponsored event may be broadcast: the television station may not be paid for the broadcast; no undue emphasis may be given to the sponsorship; and references to the sponsor may not obtrude on the programme or entertainment. Advertising of a product containing nicotine is prohibited. Advertising of a non-tobacco product with the corporate name or image of a tobacco company is allowed only if the advertisement clearly demonstrates that it has no association with any tobacco products, e.g., by referring only to the corporation or the non-tobacco products of the corporation. Advertisements of events sponsored by tobacco companies are permitted if no reference is made to the attributes of the product or the slogan of the company, if the lettering is uniform and the sponsor's name does not stand out, and if the air time is not paid for by tobacco advertisers. Tobacco products may not be presented as prizes or gifts for television contests. Advertisements for tobacco accessories may be directed only to adult audiences.

4. Malaysia. The Ministry of Information, which controls the broadcast media, has banned advertisements of cigarettes, but cigarette brand names have been permitted on other products and services, e.g., Kent Fashion, Camel Adventure Gear, Marlboro Travel, Salem High Country Travel, and Mid Seven Fishing Tackle. The Censor Board under the Home Ministry is authorized to restrict the content of advertisements in the mass media.

5. New Zealand. The Smoke-free Environments Act of 1990 imposes a total ban on all advertising of tobacco products in New Zealand. The only exceptions are publications printed outside New Zealand and films or radio or television transmissions originating outside New Zealand unless their principal purpose is

the promotion of tobacco use or the targeting of a New Zealand audience. Retailers may display tobacco products inside their place of business provided no such product is visible from outside that place and may display inside their place of business notices identifying tobacco products for sale and their price. A tobacco product sold through an automatic vending machine and its price may be depicted on the exterior of the vending machine. The use of tobacco trade marks on goods other than tobacco products or in relation to sponsored events is prohibited. The tobacco industry is prohibited from organizing or promoting or making any financial contribution towards any organized activity (cultural, educational, sporting, or recreational) in New Zealand where the activity involves the use of a tobacco trade mark, except that the Minister of Health may grant an exception for craft participating in an international race under certain circumstances. The free distribution of tobacco products and the offering of rewards to purchasers of tobacco products are prohibited.

The Act establishes a Health Sponsorship Council to provide alternative sponsorship of sports and cultural events to persons and organizations that formerly received financial assistance from the tobacco industry and, when that assistance was provided, had a reasonable expectation of receiving future financial or other assistance. Funding for the Council shall consist of appropriations by Parliament, gifts and bequests, and interest earned on these funds.

6. Singapore. Legislation of 7 November 1989 imposes a total ban on all forms of tobacco advertising and sales promotion. All advertising of tobacco products on television and radio, in printed material, and on billboards is prohibited, except that on souvenirs or mementos given free of charge or as gifts, on vehicles of tobacco retailers and distributors, and at premises where tobacco products are sold. It is prohibited to sell or offer for sale tobacco products together with any other product as a free gift or vice versa, as is the selling or offering for sale of tobacco products packaged or labelled together with any other product. Distribution of free samples of tobacco products to the public is prohibited. Sponsorship of an event or promotion of goods unconnected with tobacco products is restricted in that these advertisements must not encourage or promote smoking and must be approved by the Minister of Health.

Penalties for offences under the Act have been increased from a fine of S$2000 for a first offence to S$10 000 and from a fine of S$4000 for each subsequent offence to S$20 000.

239

Table F2. Health warnings and statement and control of tar and nicotine (T/N) content

Country or territory	Familiar warning	Rotating/strong warnings	Smokeless tobacco warnings	Statements of T/N content	Control of T/N content
Australia[1]		X	*	(X)	(X)
Australian Capital Territory		X	*		
South Australia		X	*	X	
Tasmania		X	*		
Victoria	X	X	*	X	
Western Australia		X	*	X	
China[2]	X			X	X
French Polynesia				X	
Hong Kong[3]	X		*	X	X
Japan			*	X	
Macao	X				
Malaysia[4]	X				
New Zealand[5]		X	*	X	X
Papua New Guinea	X				
Singapore[6]		X	*	X	X

*Total ban.
(X) = provisions laid down by voluntary agreement.

Notes to Table F2

1. Australia. Under the Trade Practices Act 1974, a "Notice of Declaration of Unsafe Goods and of Reasons for Decision" dated 12 October 1989 prohibits the manufacture, import, and sale of oral snuff and chewing tobacco.

   A voluntary agreement between the Federal Government of Australia and the Australian tobacco manufacturers and importers, first entered into in 1982 and periodically renegotiated, provides for the indication of tar and nicotine levels on cigarette packages and specifies approved maximum yields. The 1988 agreement provides that the maximum yield for corrected particulate matter (tar) is 14 mg per cigarette and for nicotine 1.4 mg per cigarette (Winstanley, 1989).

The required health warnings in all the states of Australia are:

SMOKING CAUSES LUNG CANCER
Health Authority Warning

SMOKING CAUSES HEART DISEASE
Health Authority Warning

SMOKING DAMAGES YOUR LUNGS
Health Authority Warning

SMOKING REDUCES YOUR FITNESS
Health Authority Warning

The States of South Australia and Victoria have banned smokeless tobacco. The Governments of Tasmania and Western Australia have added smokeless tobacco products to Section 4 of their Poisons Lists, thus restricting advertising and making these products obtainable only on medical prescription.

2. China. Section 18 of the Law of 29 June 1991 requires the printing of the health warning, "Smoking is hazardous to health", and tar levels on cigarette packages. Section 5 requires the reduction of the levels of tar and other harmful substances in tobacco products.

3. Hong Kong. The Government Chemist is required to determine the tar group to which each brand of cigarettes belongs, and the Customs and Excise Service has the authority to take samples of cigarettes for analysis by the Government Chemist.

241

4. Malaysia. Under the Trade Descriptive Act (under the Ministry of Trade), all cigarette packages sold in Malaysia must contain the health warning in Malay "Warning from the Government of Malaysia: Smoking is dangerous to your health." Tar and nicotine levels are not controlled by legislation, but the Ministry of Health has directed cigarette manufacturers to keep the tar below 19 mg and nicotine below 2 mg.

5. New Zealand. The Smoke-free Environments Act 1990 requires that each tobacco package contain a health warning, a list of the harmful constituents of the product and, for products intended for smoking, a list of the harmful constituents, and their respective quantities, present in the smoke. In addition, a leaflet containing information relating to the effects of the use of the product on health must be placed inside the package with the product, if required by regulations under the Act.

Every manufacturer and importer of tobacco products is required to conduct annual tests for the constituents of each brand of tobacco product sold and the respective quantities of those constituents and to report the results of these tests and specified information concerning the weight of tobacco and of all additives used to the Director-General of Health, who may require further testing at the expense of the manufacturer or importer.

A manufacturer, importer, or distributor who publishes a tobacco advertisement without reasonable excuse is liable to a fine not exceeding NZ$50 000; in any other case to a fine not exceeding NZ$10 000. Similar fines are imposed for violations of other provisions of the Act.

6. Singapore. The Consumer Protection Regulations of 11 January 1989 require the following rotating warnings on tobacco product containers:

— Smoking causes heart disease.

— Smoking causes cancer.

— Smoking damages your lungs.

— Smoking harms those around us.

A statement of the tar and nicotine content is also required.

The Poisons (Amendment) (No. 2) Rules provide that any cigarette containing 1.3 mg of nicotine and/or 15 mg of tar will be classified as poison under the Poisons Act, so that the sale of cigarettes containing more than these levels is prohibited.

Table F3. Restrictions on places of sale

Country or territory	Government buildings	Health establishments	Schools and places where young people congregate	Other
No information available				

Note: Restrictions on the use of vending machines are presented in Table F6.

Table F4. Restrictions on smoking in public places

Country or territory	Government agencies	Health establishments	Schools and places where young people congregate	Public transport	Lifts	Indoor public places	Markets and food storage places	Restaurants
Australia[1]	X			X				
Australian Capital Territory					X			
Queensland				X				
South Australia				X				
Western Australia				X	X			
China[2]	X	X	X	X	X			
Hong Kong[3]	X	X	X	X	X	X	X	
Japan[4]				X		X		
Macao		X	X	X				
Malaysia[5]	X	X	X	X		X		
New Zealand[6]	X	X	X	X	X	X	X	X
Wellington		X		X		X		
Papua New Guinea[7]		X						
Republic of Korea[8]		X				X		
Singapore[9]	X	X	X	X	X	X	X	X
Viet Nam[10]		X				X		

Notes to Table F4

1. Australia. Smoking on domestic commercial flights was banned on 1 December 1987 by regulations under the Air Navigation Act. Smoking was banned on 1 September 1990 on scheduled international flights operating between cities in Australia. Administrative regulations require all Australian Government offices to be smoke-free. As of 1 July 1988, all interstate buses are smoke-free. State legislation and voluntary action restrict smoking in other public places.

   In the Australian Capital Territory, many government and private institutions have adopted voluntary smoke-free policies. Administrative orders generally ban smoking in hospitals and government schools. By decision of local management, smoking is restricted in airports, railway stations, and bus terminals.

   Information provided by Michael M. Daube of the Health Department of Western Australia indicates that there is little legislation specifically restricting smoking in public places and the workplace, but substantial occupational health, safety, and welfare legislation may be interpreted to apply to public places and workplaces, obviating the need for tobacco-specfic legislation. Moreover, several state governments have decided that all government offices and buildings shall be smoke-free.

2. China. The Law of 29 June 1991 prohibits smoking on public transport and in public places; the latter have not yet been defined.

3. Hong Kong. Regulations issued in 1983 restrict smoking in schools, hospitals, clinics, public areas of government offices, and food business premises.

4. Japan. Legislation prohibiting smoking in theatres and subway stations has been introduced for fire-prevention purposes. There is no legislation to prevent pollution of indoor areas by tobacco smoke.

5. Malaysia. Smoking is banned in cinemas, theatres, and indoor stadiums. Under the Road Transport Rules, smoking is banned in air-conditioned buses. In other buses, the driver and conductor are not allowed to smoke while on duty, and taxi drivers are not allowed to smoke while driving passengers. The Ministry of Transport has directed Malaysian Airlines to prohibit smoking on all domestic flights as well as flights to Singapore. By Government directive, smoking is banned in all government offices, schools, and vehicles except in the toilet or in special rooms allocated to smokers. By directive of the Ministry of Health, smoking is banned in all hospitals and government clinics. The Prisons Department has banned smoking in all prisons (because narcotic drugs have been smuggled in through cigarettes).

6. New Zealand. The Smoke-free Environments Act of 1990 restricts smoking in hospitals, rest homes, and prisons; prohibits smoking on internal flights of airlines; restricts smoking in passenger service vehicles, ships, and trains, in passenger lounges, and waiting rooms; and in restaurants. In restaurants with only one room, half the seating must be designated as non-smoking and must be separated, as far as practicable, from seating where smoking is permitted. Where there is more than one room in a restaurant, at least one room shall be designated as non-smoking. Area health boards are responsible for enforcement. The requirement that every employer prepare a written policy on smoking for every workplace of that employer (see Table F5, note 3) has the effect of achieving a general restriction on smoking in public places.

7. Papua New Guinea. Under the Tobacco Products (Health Control) Act 1987, the Minister of Health is authorized to limit or prohibit smoking in public places, including public transport vehicles.

8. Republic of Korea. Legislation passed by the National Assembly in January 1990 provides that persons who own, occupy, or manage facilities that are subject to the control of the Ministry of Health and Social Welfare shall designate certain places within the facility as smoking areas, and smoking shall be prohibited outside these designated areas.

9. Singapore. In 1970, under the Prohibition of Smoking in Certain Places Act, smoking was prohibited in cinemas, theatres, other specified buildings, and buses. In 1973 the prohibition was extended to lifts, in 1982 to amusement centres, in 1985 to government hospitals and clinics, in 1987 to all public buildings, in 1988, under the Smoking (Prohibition in Certain Places) Notification, to hospitals, maternity homes, medical clinics and nursing homes, fast-food restaurants, indoor roller-skating rinks and roller discotheques, and in 1989 to air-conditioned restaurants, supermarkets, mini-supermarkets, department stores, indoor stadiums, bowling alleys, billiard saloons, gymnasiums, aerobic and fitness centres, convention halls, and multipurpose halls used as meeting places.

10. Viet Nam. The Law of 30 June 1989 on the protection of public health prohibits smoking in meeting-halls, cinemas, theatres, and other stipulated places.

Table F5. Restrictions on smoking in the workplace

Country or territory	General laws restricting smoking in the workplace	Government agencies	Health establishments	Schools	Authorization for administrative regulations or accommodation of smokers and non-smokers	Other
Australia[1]						
Victoria	X					
Hong Kong		X	X	X		X
Malaysia[2]		X	X	X		X
New Zealand[3]	X	X	X	X		
Singapore[4]						X

Notes to Table F5

1. Australia. See Table F4, note 1; although Australia has little legislation specifically restricting smoking in the workplace, implementation of existing occupational health, safety, and welfare legislation will control worksite smoking.

2. Malaysia. By government directives, smoking is banned in all government offices, schools, and government vehicles, except in the toilet or in special rooms allocated for smokers.

3. New Zealand. The Smoke-free Environments Act of 1990 requires every employer to prepare a written policy on smoking for every workplace of that employer. Every written policy must, at the minimum, prohibit smoking in lifts or in offices where two or more people work in a common air space, in at least half of any workplace lunchroom, or in any part of the workplace to which the public normally has access. Special provisions are laid down for certain institutions, e.g. hospitals, rest homes, and prisons. Area health boards are responsible for enforcement. Violation of the statute by a corporation is subject to a maximum fine of NZ$4000, and violation by an individual to a maximum fine of NZ$400.

4. Singapore. Section 7 of the Environmental Public Health (Food Handlers) Regulations 1973 provides that "no person shall . . . smoke or use tobacco or snuff or any other preparation or chew tobacco or betel nuts while engaged in the preparation for sale or preparation for sale of any food."

Table F6. Preventing young people from smoking

Country or territory	Prohibiting sales to minors	Restricting sales from vending machines	Prohibiting sales in schools and other places frequented by young people	Restricting advertising that influences young people	Other
Australia					
Australian Capital Territory	X				X
New South Wales	X	X			
South Australia	X	X			
Tasmania[1]	X				
Victoria	X	X			
Western Australia	X	X			
China[2]					X
Hong Kong[3]			X	X	
New Zealand	X				
Papua New Guinea	X				
Republic of Korea				X	
Singapore[4]					X

Notes to Table F6

1. Australia. All six states of Australia prohibit sales of cigarettes to minors. In Western Australia, it is illegal to sell cigarettes to persons under age 18; in the other states to persons under 16. The Western Australia Tobacco Control Act 1990 restricts vending machines containing tobacco products to premises licensed to sell liquor or in areas set aside as staff amenities. The penalty for violation of the ban on the sale of tobacco products to minors has been raised from A $4 to A $5000.

2. China. The Law of 29 June 1991 on the exclusive sale of tobacco prohibits smoking by elementary and secondary school students.

3. Hong Kong. Tobacco products may not be sold in schools or institutions for children and young people.

4. Singapore. The distribution or giving of any free sample of cigarettes, cigars or any other form of tobacco to the public or any section of the public, other than to persons who are associated or concerned with the manufacture, distribution, or sale of tobacco products, is prohibited.

Table F7. Health education on tobacco

Country or territory	Public education	Anti-smoking education in schools	Allocation of funds
Australia			
Queensland	X		X
South Australia			X
Victoria	X	X	X
Western Australia			X
China	X	X	
French Polynesia	X		X
Singapore	X	X	

Table F8. Legislation establishing a national organization for policy development and coordination to control tobacco use

Country or territory	National organization
China	Chinese Association on Smoking and Health
Hong Kong	Hong Kong Council on Smoking and Health
Viet Nam	National Campaigning Committee on Tobacco or Health, chaired by Minister of Health

Summary Table A. Number of countries and territories with legislation to control the production, sale, and promotion of tobacco, by WHO region

Type of legislation	Number of countries and territories						
	All regions	Africa	Americas	Eastern Mediterranean	Europe	South-East Asia	Western Pacific
Total ban on tobacco advertising	27	3	2	3	13	1	5
Some restrictions on advertising	77	7	19	9	26	5	11
Restriction on sponsorship	18	2	4	—	8	—	4
Rotating/strong warnings on cigarette packages	29	1	6	6	11	1	4
Familiar warnings on cigarette packages	48	6	14	7	12	4	5
Statement of tar and nicotine content	40	4	6	8	15	—	7
Restrictions on places of sale	11	—	3	1	5	2	—

Summary Table B. Number of countries and territories with legislation to influence smoking practices, by WHO region

Type of legislation	Number of countries and territories						
	All regions	Africa	Americas	Eastern Mediterranean	Europe	South-East Asia	Western Pacific
Restrictions on smoking in public places	90	20	17	10	28	4	11
Restrictions on smoking in the workplace	34	3	11	1	14	—	5
Preventing young people from smoking	42	2	18	2	12	1	7
Controlling smokeless tobacco	19	—	2	1	11	1	4
Health education	36	1	14	3	12	2	4

Annex 2

Resolutions of the World Health Assembly

Resolution WHA23.32

The Twenty-third World Health Assembly,

Having considered the report of the Director-General;

Recalling the resolutions on this subject adopted by the Executive Board, the Directing Council of the Pan American Health Organization/Regional Committee for the Americas, and the Regional Committee for Europe;

Conscious of the serious effects of smoking in promoting the development of pulmonary and cardiac disease, including bronchopulmonary cancer, chronic bronchitis, emphysema and ischaemic heart disease;

Being aware that bronchopulmonary cancer is at present increasing in all countries of the world where records are available in a form which permits assessment;

Holding that health agencies must now demonstrate their concern for the reduction of the main causal factor in diseases related to smoking; and

Considering that smoking of tobacco during meetings may constitute a nuisance to non-smokers,

RESOLVES that:

(1) all those present at meetings of the Assembly and its committees be requested to refrain from smoking in the rooms where such meetings are held;

(2) the Director-General be requested:

(a) to consider the desirability of making the subject for World Health Day "The health consequences of smoking," on the earliest possible occasion;

(b) to call the attention of all Members and Associate Members to the report on limitation of smoking and to suggest that the advantages of applying the recommendations on pages 19 and 20 of that report[1] should be considered in all countries;

---

[1] See *WHO Chronicle*, **24**, 365.

(c) to consider convening an expert group to recommend further action that might be taken to discourage smoking;

(d) to examine to what extent and by what educational methods young people might be persuaded not to begin smoking;

(e) to bring to the attention of FAO the need for studying crop substitution in tobacco-producing countries;

(f) to report to the Executive Board at its forty-seventh session and to the Twenty-fourth World Health Assembly on the action proposed and the financial consequences for the Organization.

May 1970

Resolution WHA24.48

The Twenty-fourth World Health Assembly,

Having considered the report of the Director-General;

Recalling the resolutions on this subject adopted by the Twenty-third World Health Assembly, the Executive Board, and the respective Regional Committees;

Recognizing the relationship between smoking and the development of pulmonary and cardiac disease, including lung cancer, ischaemic heart disease, chronic bronchitis and emphysema; and

Believing that a sustained effort by health and education authorities and others is needed to reduce tobacco smoking and to prevent the extension of the habit, with special attention to young people and pregnant women,

1. THANKS the Director-General for his report;

2. ENDORSES the recommendations contained therein;

3. CALLS UPON all Member States and Associate Members to give all possible consideration to putting these recommendations into effect; and

4. REQUESTS the Director-General:

(i) to continue to assemble information on the health effects of tobacco smoking and the action being taken by countries to reduce the habit;

(ii) to place emphasis on the control and prevention of smoking as an integral part of operating programmes as and when feasible;

(iii) to continue in co-operation with the United Nations, the specialized agencies and the appropriate non-governmental organizations to foster a greater awareness of the health hazards of smoking and to take whatever action is deemed necessary to reduce them, and particularly to draw the attention of the Food and Agriculture Organization of the United Nations to the necessity of undertaking a study on crop diversification in tobacco-growing areas in view of the expected decrease in tobacco consumption;

(iv) to stimulate the strengthening of health education activities, including the production, dissemination and exchange of educational materials to discourage the habit of smoking; and

(v) to produce a code of practice that can guide governments in the formulation of legislative action relevant to the health consequences of smoking.

May 1971

Resolution WHA29.55

The Twenty-ninth World Health Assembly,

Recalling resolutions EB45.R9, WHA23.32, EB47.R42 and WHA24.48 concerning the health hazards of smoking and ways towards its limitation;

Noting with satisfaction that the recent WHO Expert Committee report on smoking and its effects on health,[1] prepared in accordance with resolution EB53.R31 and reviewed favourably by the Executive Board at its fifty-seventh session, provides a thorough and authoritative summary of current knowledge in the field and contains a number of important recommendations for WHO and the Member States;

Considering that the results of the Third World Conference on Smoking and Health, held in New York in June 1975, gave further support to the evidence and proposals presented by the WHO Expert Committee;

Recognizing the indisputable scientific evidence showing that tobacco smoking is a major cause of chronic bronchitis, emphysema and lung cancer as well as a major risk factor for myocardial infarction, certain pregnancy-related and neonatal disorders and a number of other serious health problems, and also has harmful effects on those who are involuntarily exposed to tobacco smoke;

Seriously concerned about the alarming worldwide trends in smoking-related mortality and morbidity and the rapidly increasing consumption of tobacco, especially in cigarettes, in countries in which it was not previously widespread, and about the growing number of young people and women who are now smoking;

Recognizing that an effective strategy to tackle the problem requires a concerted effort consisting of educational, restrictive and legislative measures, combined with coherent taxation and price policies, and supported by continuous research and evaluation on a multidisciplinary basis;

Noting that very few countries have thus far taken effective steps to combat smoking;

Believing that no organization devoted to the promotion of health can be indifferent in this matter, and that WHO has an important role to play in promoting effective policies against smoking, as envisaged in the Sixth General Programme of Work of WHO covering the period 1978–1983;

1. URGES governments of Member States to identify the actual or anticipated health problems associated with smoking in their countries;

---

[1]WHO Technical Report Series, No. 568, 1975.

2. RECOMMENDS governments of Member States:

(1) to create and to develop effective machinery to coordinate and supervise programmes for control and prevention of smoking on a planned, continuous and long-term basis;

(2) to strengthen health education concerning smoking, as a part of general health education and through close collaboration with health and school authorities, mass media, voluntary organizations, employers' and employees' organizations and other relevant agencies, taking into account the different needs of various target groups, laying emphasis on the positive aspects of non-smoking, and supporting individuals wishing to stop smoking;

(3) to consider steps which can be taken towards ensuring that non-smokers receive protection, to which they are entitled, from an environment polluted by tobacco smoke;

(4) to give serious consideration to the legislative and other measures suggested by the WHO Expert Committee in its recent report on smoking and its effects on health;

3. REQUESTS the Director-General:

(1) to continue, and intensify, WHO's antismoking activities;

(2) to collate and disseminate information on smoking habits, smoking-related health problems and smoking control activities in Member States;

(3) to give assistance and encouragement to research in smoking and health, with particular emphasis on studies that are directly relevant to the assessment and improvement of the effectiveness of antismoking activities;

(4) to promote the standardization of:

(a) definitions, measurement methods and statistics concerning smoking behaviour, tobacco consumption and the occurrence of smoking-related morbidity and mortality;

(b) laboratory techniques used for the quantitative analysis of the harmful substances in tobacco products;

(5) to give assistance, upon request, to governments in the formulation, implementation and evaluation of their policies and programmes to combat smoking;

(6) to continue, in cooperation with the United Nations, the specialized agencies and appropriate nongovernmental organizations, to make all efforts deemed necessary to reduce smoking; and particularly to work out with the Food and Agriculture Organization of the United Nations and with the United Nations a joint strategy for crop-diversification in tobacco-growing areas with a view to avoiding the anticipated economic consequences of reducing tobacco consumption in the world as a whole for public health reasons;

(7) to convene an expert committee in 1977 or 1978 to review and evaluate the world situation in regard to smoking control;

(8) to report to a future Health Assembly on developments in this field.

May 1976

Resolution WHA31.56

The Thirty-first World Health Assembly,

Recalling resolutions EB45.R9, WHA23.32, EB47.R42, WHA24.48, EB53.R31 and WHA29.55 concerning the health hazards of tobacco smoking and ways towards its limitation;

Recognizing the increasing and indisputable scientific evidence showing that tobacco smoking is a major cause of chronic bronchitis, emphysema and lung cancer, as well as a major risk factor for myocardial infarction, certain pregnancy-related and neonatal disorders and a number of other serious health problems, and that it also has harmful effects on those who are involuntarily exposed to tobacco smoke;

Seriously concerned at the alarming increase in production and consumption of cigarettes during the last two decades in some of the countries, particularly developing countries, in which it was previously not widespread, and at the extensive promotional drive for the sale of cigarettes being carried out on radio and television, in newspapers and other news media, and through association with sporting and cultural events, often inducing young people to smoke tobacco;

Noting that few countries have so far taken comprehensive action to effectively combat smoking through educational, restrictive and legislative measures for the control of publicity and advertisements in the news media, combined with coherent taxation and price policies for tobacco cultivation and cigarette production;

Believing that WHO has an important role in promoting effective policies against smoking, as envisaged in the Sixth General Programme of Work covering the period 1978–1983 inclusive;

1. URGES Member States:

(1) to strengthen health education programmes concerning tobacco smoking as a part of general education, through close collaboration among health and education authorities and other relevant agencies, taking into account the different needs of the various target groups;

(2) to adopt comprehensive measures to control tobacco smoking, *inter alia* by providing for increased taxation on the sale of cigarettes and restricting as far as possible all forms of publicity for promotion of smoking;

(3) to protect the rights of non-smokers to enjoy an atmosphere unpolluted by tobacco smoke;

(4) to seek economically sound alternative undertakings to replace tobacco growing and processing, where appropriate;

2. REQUESTS the Director-General:

(1) to continue to intensify WHO's activities in connexion with control of tobacco smoking;

(2) to collaborate with Member States, the United Nations, the specialized agencies and appropriate nongovernmental organizations as required, in the formulation, implementation and evaluation of programmes to combat smoking, including studying possibilities for crop diversification in tobacco-growing areas;

(3) to cooperate with Member States upon request in developing measures for the control of publicity with regard to smoking through the news media, especially newspapers, radio and television;

(4) to give urgent consideration to having non-smoking as a theme for World Health Day as soon as possible, and in this and other ways to give maximum publicity to an anti-smoking campaign;

(5) to encourage research as to the cause of tobacco smoking;

(6) to report on progress in this field not later than the Thirty-third World Health Assembly.

May 1978

Resolution WHA33.35

The Thirty-third World Health Assembly,

Recalling resolutions EB45.R9, WHA23.32, EB47.R42, WHA24.48, EB53.R31, WHA29.55, and WHA31.56 concerning the health hazards of tobacco smoking and WHO's role in the limitation of this harmful habit;

Noting the report of the WHO Expert Committee on Smoking Control;[1]

Reiterating its firm conviction that the effect of tobacco smoking is now a major public health problem in all industrialized countries and in many developing countries and that it will become so in the near future in all other developing countries unless action is taken now;

Mindful of the ill-effects of smoking, particularly on risk groups such as pregnant women, lactating mothers and children;

Seriously concerned about the aggressive promotional drives for the sale of cigarettes that occur in developing as well as developed countries, thus inducing the new generations to take up the habit of smoking;

Alarmed by the fact that advertising practices using psychological means in both industrialized and developing countries have the effect of inducing and perpetuating smoking habits, especially among youth;

Encouraged by the existence of total bans, restrictions or limitations on tobacco advertising in several countries;

Noting encouraging signs of expanded national activities and of increasing public awareness of the harmful health effects of cigarette smoking in many countries, partly as a result of WHO's efforts and of this year's World Health Day on "Smoking or health: the choice is yours";

Realizing that national and international strategies to combat the spreading of the habit of smoking must be carried out on a continuous, long-term basis;

Believing that WHO has an essential role to play in promoting effective smoking control policies;

---

[1] WHO Technical Report Series, No. 636, 1979.

1. URGES Member States:

(1) to strengthen, and to initiate where lacking, the smoking control strategies outlined in the above-mentioned resolutions, laying special emphasis on educational approaches, particularly with respect to youth, and on measures to ban, restrict or limit advertising of tobacco products;

(2) to support WHO's action in the field of smoking and health;

2. REQUESTS the Director-General:

(1) to further develop an effective WHO action programme on smoking and health, clearly defining lines of responsibility and priority areas, and taking into account the multidisciplinary and intersectoral character of the relationship between smoking and health;

(2) to ensure that WHO plays a leading role in coordinating international activities and to strengthen collaboration with other United Nations agencies and with relevant nongovernmental organizations, and, particularly, to pursue the study on crop diversification in tobacco-growing areas in collaboration with FAO;

(3) to collaborate with Member States in their efforts to reduce smoking;

(4) to consider problems caused by the marketing and consumption of tobacco, particularly in developing countries;

(5) to mobilize financial and other resources for the implementation of the programme;

(6) to report on progress of this programme to the Thirty-fifth World Health Assembly.

May 1980

Resolution WHA39.14

The Thirty-ninth World Health Assembly,

Recalling resolutions WHA31.56 and WHA33.35 on the health hazards of tobacco smoking and the WHO action programme on smoking and health;

Deeply concerned by the current pandemic of smoking and other forms of tobacco use, which results in the loss of the lives of at least one million human beings every year and in illness and suffering for many more;

Believing that the battle between health and tobacco must and can be won for the sake of human health;

Encouraged by the existence of total bans, restrictions or limitations on tobacco advertising in several countries;

1. AFFIRMS:

(1) that tobacco smoking and the use of tobacco in all its forms is incompatible with the attainment of health for all by the year 2000;

(2) that the presence of carcinogens and other toxic substances in tobacco smoke and other tobacco products is a known fact; and that the causal link between tobacco and a range of fatal and disabling diseases has been scientifically proven;

(3) that passive, enforced or involuntary smoking violates the right to health of non-smokers, who must be protected against this noxious form of environmental pollution;

2. CALLS for a global public health approach and action *now* to combat the tobacco pandemic;

3. DEPLORES all direct and indirect practices the aim of which is to promote the use of tobacco, as this product is addictive and dangerous even when used as promoted;

4. URGES those Member States which have not yet done so to implement smoking control strategies; these, as a minimum, should contain the following:

(1) measures to ensure that non-smokers receive effective protection, to which they are entitled, from involuntary exposure to tobacco smoke, in enclosed public places, restaurants, transport, and places of work and entertainment;

(2) measures to promote abstention from the use of tobacco so as to protect children and young people from becoming addicted;

(3) measures to ensure that a good example is set in all health-related premises and by all health personnel;

(4) measures leading to the progressive elimination of those socioeconomic, behavioural, and other incentives which maintain and promote the use of tobacco;

(5) prominent health warnings, which might include the statement that tobacco is addictive, on cigarette packets, and containers of all types of tobacco products;

(6) the establishment of programmes of education and public information on tobacco and health issues, including smoking cessation programmes, with active involvement of the health professions and the media;

(7) monitoring of trends in smoking and other forms of tobacco use, tobacco-related diseases, and effectiveness of national smoking control action;

(8) the promotion of viable economic alternatives to tobacco production, trade and taxation;

(9) the establishment of a national focal point to stimulate, support, and coordinate all the above activities;

5. APPEALS to other organizations of the United Nations system:

(1) to support WHO in all ways possible within their fields of competence;

(2) to show solidarity with WHO's efforts to stem the spread of tobacco-induced diseases by protecting the health of non-smokers on their premises, as this action would have a major exemplar role;

(3) to help Member States in identifying and implementing economic alternatives to tobacco cultivation, production and trade;

6. REQUESTS the Director-General:

(1) to strengthen the present programme on smoking and health without waiting for its official introduction in the Eighth General Programme of Work, as a visible

and resolute attitude on the part of WHO would provide Member States with encouragement and support, which are necessary prerequisites to abating the smoking pandemic before the year 2000;

(2) to mobilize support for the present programme on smoking and health in terms of funds and manpower which would ensure adequate programme continuity on a long-term basis;

(3) to coordinate activities in support of WHO's action on smoking and health with other organizations of the United Nations system at the highest executive level;

(4) to continue and strengthen collaboration with nongovernmental organizations as appropriate;

(5) to ensure that WHO plays an effective global advocacy role in tobacco and health issues and that, in common with other health institutions, it plays an exemplar role in non-smoking practices;

(6) to provide support to national smoking control efforts;

(7) to report on progress to the Executive Board at its eighty-first session and to the Forty-first World Health Assembly.

May 1986

Resolution WHA40.38

The Fortieth World Health Assembly,

Bearing in mind the objective of the World Health Organization contained in Article 1 of the Constitution, "the attainment by all peoples of the highest possible level of health";

Recalling resolution WHA39.14 on "Tobacco or health";

Expressing its satisfaction at the measures increasingly being taken by Member States to reduce smoking;

Gratified at the decision taken by the Director-General to declare the WHO premises a smoking-free area;

Aware that the consumption and use of tobacco result in serious health consequences, as well as economic and social problems, notably in developing countries;

Noting that on 7 April 1988 the World Health Organization will celebrate its fortieth anniversary;

1. CALLS UPON all Member States, as part of their continuing efforts to reduce the smoking pandemic, through all appropriate means including, where applicable, legislative and regulatory measures:

(1) to celebrate 7 April 1988 as a world no-smoking day;

(2) to encourage the population, by all appropriate means, to desist from smoking and from using tobacco in all other forms on that day;

(3) in conjunction with governmental and nongovernmental organizations, to use the occasion to launch, or strengthen existing, anti-smoking campaigns and health-promoting initiatives;

(4) to encourage vendors to refrain voluntarily from selling all forms of tobacco on that day;

(5) to inform the Director-General on actions taken in response to this resolution;

2. APPEALS to all manufacturers of tobacco and those who promote its consumption, in the spirit of this resolution and of resolution WHA39.14, to refrain voluntarily from all publicity activities in all countries, especially in developing countries, and calls upon the press and the other media in each country voluntarily to do likewise;

3. REQUESTS the Director-General to report to a subsequent Health Assembly on the action taken in this regard.

May 1987

Resolution WHA42.19

The Forty-second World Health Assembly,

Recalling resolution WHA39.14 and resolution WHA41.25 requesting the Director-General to draw up a plan of action on tobacco or health for submission through the Programme Committee to the eighty-third session of the Executive Board;

Recognizing that the use of tobacco is responsible worldwide for more than two million premature deaths annually;

Recalling that active efforts are needed to resolve the economic issues involved in reducing tobacco production;

Concerned at the fact that, while tobacco consumption is decreasing in developed countries as a result of effective health promotion supported by appropriate legislation and regulations, the developing countries are registering increases in tobacco consumption;

Reaffirming that the health services should clearly and unequivocally publicize the health risks connected with the use of tobacco and actively support all efforts to prevent the associated diseases;

1. THANKS the Director-General for having already accelerated implementation of the WHO programme on tobacco or health;

2. APPROVES the plan of action for the WHO programme on tobacco or health for 1988–1995 as proposed by the Director-General and endorsed by the Executive Board;

3. REQUESTS the Director-General:

(1) to continue to support this programme as outlined in the plan of action and to mobilize extrabudgetary funds for its implementation;

(2) to support national authorities, at their request, in taking measures to disseminate information on the health risks of tobacco, to promote life-styles without tobacco, and to control the promotion of tobacco consumption;

(3) to work, in close collaboration with national health authorities, with organizations of the United Nations system, and with relevant nongovernmental organizations in official relations with those organizations, to ensure that both health and economic aspects are fully taken into account;

(4) to review the impact of tobacco production on the economy, environment and health of the populations in developing countries which depend upon tobacco production as a major source of income, and to report on this issue to the Forty-third World Health Assembly;

(5) to collaborate actively with FAO and other relevant United Nations agencies with a view to developing agricultural projects that demonstrate how crop substitution programmes can be implemented in countries whose economies depend heavily upon tobacco production and to encouraging such countries to implement these programmes;

4. RESOLVES that each year 31 May shall be World No-Tobacco Day.

May 1989

Resolution WHA43.16

The Forty-third World Health Assembly,

Recalling the strong statement on the issue of smoking and health made by the President in opening the Forty-third World Health Assembly;

Recalling resolutions WHA33.35, WHA39.14, WHA41.25 and WHA42.19 on the health hazards of tobacco smoking and the WHO programme on tobacco or health;

Recalling the requirement contained in resolution WHA42.19 concerning a review of crop substitution and the health and economic aspects of tobacco production and consumption;

Recalling further that resolution WHA39.14 urged Member States to implement a comprehensive nine-point smoking control strategy;

Encouraged by:

(a) the significant progress made by many Member States in the implementation of this strategy;

(b) the continuing decline in tobacco consumption in Member States that have adopted comprehensive smoking control policies;

(c) recent information demonstrating the effectiveness of tobacco control strategies, and in particular:

— legislation or other measures to provide protection from involuntary exposure to tobacco smoke in workplaces, public places and public transport;

— policies to achieve progressive increases in the real price of tobacco;

— comprehensive bans and other legislative restrictive measures to control effectively direct and indirect advertising, promotion and sponsorship concerning tobacco;

Deeply concerned by increasing evidence of the dangers to health of passive smoking and by a new WHO estimate that, unless current smoking rates decrease, there will be 3 million tobacco-related deaths per year during the 1990s, and that this figure will rise sharply to 10 million deaths per year by the 2020s;

Believing that millions of future premature deaths can be avoided if current smoking rates are quickly and substantially reduced;

1. URGES all Member States:

(1) to implement multisectoral comprehensive tobacco strategies which, at a minimum, contain the nine elements outlined in resolution WHA39.14;

(2) to consider including in their tobacco control strategies plans for legislation or other effective measures at the appropriate government level providing for:

(a) effective protection from involuntary exposure to tobacco smoke in indoor workplaces, enclosed public places and public transport, with special attention to risk groups such as pregnant women and children;

(b) progressive financial measures aimed at discouraging the use of tobacco;

(c) progressive restrictions and concerted action to eliminate eventually all direct and indirect advertising, promotion and sponsorship concerning tobacco;

2. NOTES that, in countries where more than one level of government exists, national authorities may not have complete jurisdiction over these issues;

3. REQUESTS the Director-General:

(1) to intensify support for the 1988–1995 plan of action for the WHO programme on tobacco or health;

(2) to ensure the provision of sufficient budgetary resources to assist Member States in implementing comprehensive tobacco control programmes;

(3) to ensure that the report requested in resolution WHA42.19 is presented to the Forty-fourth World Health Assembly;

(4) to monitor and report biennially to the Health Assembly on the progress and effectiveness of Member States' comprehensive tobacco control programmes;

(5) to report to the Forty-fourth World Health Assembly on the progress made in assistance to countries that depend on tobacco production as a major source of financial resources for health and development, with emphasis on measurement of efficacy of such assistance.

May 1990

Resolution WHA44.26

The Forty-fourth World Health Assembly,

Recalling resolutions WHA33.35, WHA39.14, WHA41.25 and WHA42.19 on the health consequences of tobacco consumption and the WHO "tobacco or health" programme, formerly the action programme on smoking and health;

Recalling in particular resolution WHA43.16, which urges all Member States to adopt effective measures to prevent involuntary exposure to tobacco smoke in enclosed public places and public transport;

Recognizing that there is no safe level of exposure to tobacco smoke;

Aware of the technical problems of ensuring a smoke-free environment in many public conveyances, especially trains and aircraft;

Congratulating the transport authorities and companies that have adopted measures to offer their passengers a smoke-free environment and encouraging all those responsible for public transport to do likewise;

Deeply concerned about the dangers to the health, and the violation of the right to health, of non-smokers caused by enforced, or passive, smoking and about the WHO-approved estimates that the annual number of deaths in the world attributable to smoking will be about three million in the 1990s,

1. URGES all Member States:

(1) to adopt appropriate measures for effective protection from involuntary exposure to tobacco smoke in public transport;

(2) to ban smoking in public conveyances where protection against involuntary exposure to tobacco smoke cannot be ensured, and to adopt effective measures of protection wherever possible;

(3) to promote educational activities necessary to make people aware of the importance of protecting themselves and their families, especially children, against passive smoking, for example, while travelling in private cars;

2. REQUESTS the Director-General:

(1) to collaborate with the International Civil Aviation Organization and all competent international and national agencies in developing guidelines and recommendations for a smoke-free travel environment in all types of public conveyances;

(2) to support Member States at their request in implementing effective measures to protect people against involuntary exposure to tobacco smoke in public transport;

(3) to keep the Executive Board and the Health Assembly informed of the progress made in implementing this resolution as an element of the WHO "tobacco or health" programme.

May 1991

Annex 3

List of legislation reviewed[1]

AFGHANISTAN

Order of the Cabinet of 28 December 1971 (prohibiting all advertising of cigarettes)*

ALGERIA

Law No. 85-05 of 16 February 1985 on health protection and promotion (Sections 63–66) (IDHL, 1985, **36**(4): 909, 916)

ARGENTINA

Law No. 18604 of 1970 (prohibiting certain forms of advertising of cigarettes)*

Order No. 33.266 prohibiting drivers of school buses from smoking and prohibiting smoking on vehicles transporting dangerous substances

Order No. 22.900 prohibiting smoking on public transport vehicles

Order No. 09-12-910 prohibiting smoking in theatres including interior vestibules and corridors

Law No. 23344 of 31 July 1986 on restrictions on the advertising of tobacco, cigars, cigarettes, and other products intended for smoking and their packaging (IDHL, 1986, **37**(4): 796–797)

Parliamentary Decree No. 226 of 27 April 1988 requiring health warnings that smoking is prejudicial to health in all advertising and promotion of tobacco

Argentine Food Code, Article 18 (prohibiting use of tobacco in food establishments and places where food products are handled)

ARGENTINA (BUENOS AIRES)

Order No. 6762-DOC5-84 of 5 December 1984 concerning smoking in public transport, stations of the underground, school buses, vehicles transporting dangerous substances, theatres, and food establishments

---

[1] Texts marked with an asterisk were not available to the author. Texts marked with two asterisks are due to be published in forthcoming issues of the *International digest of health legislation* (abbreviated to IDHL in the list).

Law No. 10.600 of 12 November 1987 prohibiting smoking in public transport vehicles

ARGENTINA (CORDOBA)

Order No. 8425 of 11 October 1988 prohibiting smoking in the offices of the municipal government that serve the public

Law No. 7827 of 20 September 1989 prohibiting smoking in enclosed places of the executive, legislative, and judicial branches of the government

ARGENTINA (JUJUY)

Law No. 4292 of 17 June 1987 prohibiting smoking in public buildings, school rooms of all levels, hospitals, and means of urban and suburban transport

ARGENTINA (MENDOZA)

Law of 3 December 1988 prohibiting smoking in indoor public places, elevators, and public offices, in hospitals and health centres, in official banks and educational establishments of all levels

ARGENTINA (SAN FERNANDO DEL VALLE DE CATAMARCA)

Order No. 565-C-89 prohibiting smoking in enclosed places of the municipal government and ordering a campaign against smoking with the objective of extending the prohibition to all public and private places

ARGENTINA (VALLE VIEJO)

Order of 25 October 1988 prohibiting smoking in government offices, indoor public places, and means of transport

AUSTRALIA

The Broadcasting and Television Act 1972 (IDHL, 1973, **24**(3): 453)

Notice of Declaration of Unsafe Goods and of Reasons for Decision of 12 October 1989 under the Trade Practices Act of 1974 prohibiting the manufacture, import, and sale of oral snuff and chewing tobacco.

Air Navigation Regulations (Amendment) 25 November 1987

Air Navigation Regulations (Amendment) 13 September 1990

The Smoking and Tobacco Products Advertisements (Prohibition) Act 1989, 28 December 1989 (IDHL, 1991, **42**(1): 48)

AUSTRALIA (CAPITAL TERRITORY)

The Tobacco Products (Health Warnings) Ordinance 1986 requiring the printing of health warnings on containers in which tobacco products are packaged (IDHL, 1987, **38**(3): 541–542)

AUSTRALIA (NEW SOUTH WALES)

The Cigarettes (Labelling) Act, 1972 (IDHL, 1973, **24**(3): 459)

AUSTRALIA (SOUTH AUSTRALIA)

The Cigarettes (Labelling) Act, 1971–1972 (IDHL, 1973, **24**(3): 468)

The Cigarettes (Labelling) Regulations. Dated 3 May 1973 (IDHL, 1974, **25**(4):714–715)

An Act to prohibit the sale or supply of certain tobacco products to children, dated 15 November 1984 (IDHL, 1986, **37**(1): 45) (repealed by the Tobacco Products Control Act, 1986).

The Tobacco Products Control Act, 1986 (IDHL, 1988, **39**(2): 392–394)
The Tobacco Products (Licensing) Act 1986 (IDHL, 1988, **39**(2): 394–395)
The Tobacco Products Control Amendment Act 1988

AUSTRALIA (TASMANIA)

The Cigarettes (Labelling) Act, 1972 (IDHL, 1974, **25**(4): 721)
The Cigarettes (Labelling) Regulations 1973 (IDHL 1976, **27**(1): 20–21)
The Tobacco Products (Labelling) Act 1987 to prohibit the sale of tobacco products except in packages marked with health warnings (IDHL, 1988, **39**(2): 395)

AUSTRALIA (VICTORIA)

The Health (Amendment) Act 1969 (IDHL, 1972, **23**(1): 22–23)
The Tobacco Act 1987 creating a State-wide programme to reduce the prevalence of smoking in Victoria, restricting various forms of advertising, prohibiting the supply of tobacco to persons under 16 years of age and restricting the siting of vending machines, and establishing the Victorian Health Promotion Foundation (IDHL, 1988, **39**(3): 652–653)

AUSTRALIA (WESTERN AUSTRALIA)

The Tobacco (Warning Labels) Regulations, 1987 (IDHL, 1988, **39**(2): 395–396)
The Tobacco Control Act 1990 (IDHL, 1991, **42**(2): 273–275)

AUSTRIA

Decree of 15 February 1979 of the Federal Ministry of Health and Environmental Protection on smoking in hospitals (IDHL, 1980, **31**(1): 19)
The Employees' Protection Law of 1972, as amended by the Federal Law of 20 October 1982 (IDHL, 1986, **37**(1): 114–115)

BAHAMAS

The Health Services (Amendment) Act of 1976, cited as the Health Services Rules, requiring a health warning on tobacco advertising and cigarette packages.

BELGIUM

Crown Order of 28 December 1979 on the manufacture and marketing of tobacco, tobacco products, and similar products (IDHL, 1981, **32**(1): 85–86) as amended by the Crown Order of 30 March 1981 (IDHL, 1982, **33**(1):32–33)
Crown Order of 5 March 1980 on advertising for tobacco, tobacco products, and similar products (IDHL, 1981, **32** (1):86–87), as amended by Crown Order of 22 September 1980 (IDHL, 1982, **33**(1): 32)
Crown Order of 21 January 1982 amending the Crown Order of 5 March 1980 on advertising for tobacco, tobacco products, and similar products (IDHL, 1983, **34**(4): 767–768)
Decree of 2 December 1982 on the control of smoking and tobacco consumption (IDHL, 1986, **37**(1): 45–48)
Crown Order of 20 December 1982 on the advertising of tobacco, tobacco products, and similar products (IDHL, 1985, **36**(1): 62–63)

Crown Order of 20 December 1982 amending the Crown Order of 28 December 1979 on the manufacture and marketing of tobacco, tobacco products and similar products (IDHL, 1985, **36**(1): 63)

Crown Order of 31 March 1987 prohibiting smoking in certain public places (IDHL, 1987, **38**(3): 542–543)

Crown Order of 19 January 1990 modifying the Crown Order of 29 December 1979 on the manufacture and marketing of tobacco and tobacco products**

Crown Order of 10 April 1990 modifying the Crown Order of 20 December 1982 on advertising of tobacco and tobacco products**

Crown Order of 15 May 1990 prohibiting smoking in certain public places**

BERMUDA

The Tobacco Products (Public Health) Act 1987 requiring warnings on packages and advertisements for tobacco products (IDHL, 1989, **40**(1): 100)

The Tobacco Products (Public Health) Regulations 1988 requiring health warnings on cigarette packages (IDHL, 1989, **40**(1): 100–101)

BOLIVIA

Decree-Law No. 15629 of 18 July 1978 promulgating the Health Code (including Chapter IX, Tobacco) (IDHL, 1983, **34**(2): 232)

Ministerial Resolution (Ministry of Social Welfare and Public Health) of 7 April 1980 (establishing a health warning on cigarette packets)

Regulations of 15 March 1982 on the use of tobacco (IDHL, 1983, **34**(3): 538–539)

Ministerial Resolution No. 883 of 12 October 1984 prohibiting smoking in any educational establishment, private or public, throughout Bolivia

BRAZIL

Law No. 7488 of 11 June 1986 establishing a National Anti-Smoking Day (IDHL, 1989, **40**(2): 406)

Order No. 490 of 25 August 1988 restricting smoking in public places, requiring health warnings on tobacco packages, restricting advertising (IDHL, 1989, **40**(2): 406)

Regulation No. 731 of the Ministry of Health dated 31 May 1990 restricting advertising of tobacco products, requiring a health warning on packages and advertising, regulating smoking in health institutions and on airline flights, encouraging federal districts and municipalities to restrict smoking in public places, and forbidding sale of tobacco products to persons under 18 years of age (Resolution No. 490 of 25 August 1988 is repealed)

BRAZIL (RIO GRANDE DO SUL)

Order No. 1/80-SSMA of 8 April 1980 concerning smoking in the workplace, smoking in health institutions, restrictions on sales in health institutions (IDHL, 1981, **32**(1): 87)

Law No. 7813 of 21 September 1983 laying down provisions on smoking, and other provisions (IDHL, 1983, **34**(4): 768)

BRAZIL (SÃO PAULO)

Law No. 3.938 of 8 September 1950 prohibiting smoking on public transportation vehicles, in elevators, and in places of public entertainment

Law No. 8.421, of 14 July 1976 prohibiting smoking in indoor supermarkets and other stores

Law No. 9.032 of 27 March 1980 concerning educational programmes in the schools on the harmful consequences of tobacco and alcohol consumption

Law No. 9.120 of 8 October 1980 prohibiting smoking in public places, health establishments, elementary and secondary schools, and public urban transportation vehicles.

Law No. 2.845 of 20 May 1981 prohibiting smoking on school premises, sports grounds, and public health establishments

Decree No. 17.451 of 22 July 1981 regulating Law No. 9.120 of 8 October 1980 prohibiting smoking in public places, hospitals, elementary and secondary schools

BULGARIA

Sanitary Rules approved by the Chief State Sanitary Inspector to restrict smoking in working premises and workplaces (IDHL, 1970, **21**(3): 536)

Decree No. 2431 of 2 November 1973 embodying the Law on public health (Section 58) (IDHL, 1974, **25**(3): 502, 512–513)

Ordinance No. 2 on health requirements in connection with smoking (IDHL, 1980, **31**(4): 752–755)

BURKINA FASO

Order No. AN V-81 FP. SAN CAPRO.DP of 29 February 1988 containing measures aimed at the control of smoking (IDHL, 1990, **41**(2): 273–274)

CANADA

The Tobacco Restraint Act (Chapter 266 of the Revised Statutes of Canada)

Aeronautics Act: Air Regulations, amendment, SOR/87-554, dated 10 September 1987 (IDHL, 1988, **39**(1): 86)

The Tobacco Products Control Act. An Act (C-51) to prohibit the advertising and promotion and respecting the labelling and manufacturing of tobacco products, dated 31 May 1988 (IDHL, 1988, **39**(4): 858–859)

The Non-smokers' Health Act. An Act (C-204) to regulate smoking in the federal workplace and on common carriers and to amend the Hazardous Products Act in relation to cigarette advertising, dated 31 May 1988 (IDHL, 1988, **39**(4): 859–860)

The Non-smokers' Health Act, 1988, Chapter 21, Revised Statutes of Canada, as amended by Chapter 7, Revised Statutes of Canada, 1988 (IDHL, 1990, **41**(1): 83–84)

Tobacco Products Control Regulations, Statutes of Canada 1988, Chapter 20

The Non-smokers' Health Regulations. Dated 14 December 1989 (IDHL, 1990, **41**(1): 84–85)

CANADA (BRITISH COLUMBIA)

The Tobacco Products Act. Dated 27 October 1972 (IDHL, 1975, **26**(2): 268)

The Tobacco Products Regulations. British Columbia Regulation 258/72. Regulation made by Order in Council 3941, approved 2 November 1972 (IDHL, 1974, **25**(1): 52)

CANADA (MANITOBA)

An Act to Protect the Health of Non-Smokers. 15 March 1990

CANADA (NOVA SCOTIA)

The Drug Dependency Act. Dated 30 March 1972 (IDHL, 1973, **24**(1): 66)

CANADA (ONTARIO)

The Smoking in the Workplace Act, dated 26 July 1989 (IDHL, 1990, **41**(3): 450–451)

CANADA (QUEBEC)

An Act respecting the protection of non-smokers in certain public places, dated 18 June 1986 (IDHL, 1987, **38**(1): 65–66)

CAYMAN ISLANDS

The Tobacco Product and Intoxicating Liquor Advertising Law 1986, making provision for the display of a health warning in connnection with the advertisement of tobacco products and providing for the control of advertising of tobacco products and intoxicating liquor (IDHL, 1989, **40**(3): 602)

CHILE

Decree Law No. 2763 of 11 July 1979 (IDHL, 1982, **33**(4): 671) and Supreme Decree No. 395 of the Ministry of Health creating a National Commission for the Control of Smoking

Decree No. 106 of 8 April 1981 prescribing a warning in connection with the marketing and advertising of tobacco (IDHL, 1982, **33**(4): 732)

Circular No. 601/81 of the Ministry of Education, dated 11 May 1981, restricting smoking by teachers and in the schools

Circular No. 3H/95 of 23 June 1982 of the Ministry of Health prohibiting smoking by professionals, officials, and the general public in hospital rooms, clinics, waiting rooms, administrative offices serving the public, elevators, auditoriums and waiting rooms of the National Health Service

Law No. 18290 of February 1985 concerning the public transport of passengers and prohibiting smoking in the interior of public vehicles

Decree No. 1 of 2 January 1986 establishing the National Commission for the Control of Smoking (IDHL, 1987, **38**(4): 797–798)

Decree No. 164 of 4 June 1986 prescribing a new warning for use in the marketing and advertising of tobacco (IDHL, 1987, **38**(4): 787)

Circular No. 3F/123 of 13 August 1986 of the Ministry of Health restricting smoking in the health facilities of the National Health Service

Circular No. 1-27 of the Ministry of Health of July 1989 concerning promotion of the anti-tobacco campaign in the community and in the schools of the municipal education system.

Circular No. 27 of 4 July 1989 of the Ministry of the Interior recommending restrictions on smoking in government services and on the sale of tobacco products in kiosks and other places of the government services

CHINA

Law of 29 June 1991 on the exclusive sale of tobacco of the People's Republic of China (IDHL, 1991, **42**(4): 666)

272

COLOMBIA

Decree No. 1188 of 25 June 1974 promulgating the National Statute on Narcotics in which Section 20 restricts tobacco advertising in cinemas and the broadcast media (IDHL, 1978, **29**: 23–26)

Resolution No. 001974 of 7 May 1975 prescribing Regulations for the implementation of Sections 10 and 20 of Decree No. 1188 of 1974

Decree No. 3430 of 26 November 1982 concerning restrictions on advertising of tobacco

Resolution No. 4063 of 1982 regulating Decree No. 3430 of 26 November concerning restrictions on advertising

Resolution No. 07559 of 12 June 1984 creating the National Board on Tobacco and Health

Decree No. 3788 of 1986 concerning educational campaigns against tobacco

COLOMBIA (BOGOTÁ)

Accord No. 3 of 1983 concerning smoking in public places, public vehicles, schools, health establishments, and government offices

COSTA RICA

Decree No. 1520-SPPS of 24 February 1971 requiring warnings on cigarette packages (IDHL, 1974, **24**: 61)

Decree No. 17377-S of 13 January 1987 concerning health warnings on packages (IDHL, 1987, **38**(4): 787)

Decree No. 17967-S of 4 February 1988 concerning restrictions on sales to minors (IDHL, 1989, **40**(1): 101)

Decree No. 17969-S of 4 February 1988 concerning information programmes (IDHL, 1989, **40**(1): 101)

Decree No. 18216-S-TSS of 23 June 1988 concerning smoking in the workplace (IDHL, 1989, **40**(1): 101)

Decree No. 18248-MOPT-S of 23 June 1988 concerning smoking on public transport vehicles (IDHL, 1989, **40**(1): 101–102)

CÔTE D'IVOIRE

Decree No. 79-477 of 6 June 1979 prohibiting smoking in certain public places (IDHL, 1981, **32**(2): 258)

CUBA

Ministerial Resolution No. 165 of 17 August 1981 concerning smoking in health institutions, smoking in the workplace (IDHL, 1989, **40**(2): 407)

CYPRUS

The Health Protection (Smoking Control) Law of 1980 (IDHL, 1981, **32**(4): 731–732)

The Health Protection (Smoking Control) Regulations of 1988 (IDHL, 1989, **40**(1): 102)

CZECHOSLOVAKIA[1]

Order No. 45 of 13 June 1966 of the Ministry of Health concerning the establishment and protection of healthy living conditions (Section 22) (IDHL, 1967, **18**(2): 327)

---

[1] There are a number of other items of legislation in Czechoslovakia restricting smoking in public transport vehicles, etc.

273

Instructions No. 12 of 1972 of the Ministry of Health of the Czech Socialist Republic (subsection 3 of Section 21)*

Instructions No. 13 of 1973 of the Ministry of Education of the Czech Socialist Republic (subsection 2 of Section 3)*

Regulations of the Slovak Ministry of Health of 1 September 1976 (prohibiting smoking in all health establishments)

Standard CSN 56 9560. Dated 1 November 1979

Law No. 37/89 of 28 March 1989 of the Czech National Council on protection against alcoholism and other addictions

DENMARK

Law No. 398 of 10 June 1987 on the Council on Prevention and the Council on Tobacco-induced Damage to Health (IDHL, 1988, **39**(2): 396)

Order No. 416 of the Ministry of Culture prohibiting advertising of tobacco on television. Dated 18 June 1987

Circular of 23 March 1988 of the Ministry of Health on the provision of nonsmoking environments in public premises, means of transport, etc. (IDHL, 1989, **40**(2): 407–408)

Order No. 441 of 26 July 1988 on advertisements through local radio services (IDHL, 1989, **40**(1): 603)

Law No. 426 of 13 June 1990 on the labelling of tobacco products and the tar content of cigarettes (IDHL, 1991, **42**(1): 49–50)

Order No. 507 of 28 June 1990 on the labelling of tobacco products and the tar content of cigarettes (IDHL, 1991, **42**(1): 50)

ECUADOR

Supreme Decree No. 965 of 24 August 1973 promulgating Regulations governing manufacturing, sales, and advertising activities associated with the use and consumption of cigarettes and alcoholic beverages (IDHL, 1978, **29**(1): 64–65)

EGYPT

Order No. 386 of 1977 of the Ministry of Communications and Culture prohibiting the advertising of cigarettes on radio and television

Law No. 52 of 20 June 1981 on protection against the harmful effects of smoking (IDHL, 1981, **32**(3): 459)

EGYPT (ALEXANDRIA)

Alexandria Municipal Ordinance of 20 July 1904 prohibiting smoking in theatres, amended on 29 December 1938 and by Law No. 372 of 29 October 1956 and again in 1964 to ban smoking in public places and advertising

EL SALVADOR

Decree No. 955 of 11 May 1988 promulgating the Health Code (IDHL, 1990, **41**(1): 1–15)

EUROPEAN COMMUNITIES

Council Directive No. 77/805/EEC of 19 December 1977 amending Directive 72/464/EEC on taxes, other than turnover taxes, which affect the consumption of manufactured tobacco (IDHL, 1978, **29**(2): 330–331)

Resolution of 18 July 1989 of the Council and the Ministers of Health of the Member States, meeting within the Council, inviting the Member

274

States to ban smoking in enclosed premises open to the public which form part of public or private establishments and to extend the ban on smoking to all forms of public transport (IDHL, 1989, **40**(4): 890–891)

Council Directive 89/552/EEC of 3 October 1989 on the coordination of certain provisions laid down by law, regulation or administrative action in Member States concerning the pursuit of television broadcasting activities

Council Directive 89/622/EEC of 13 November 1989 on the approximation of the laws, regulations and administrative provisions of the Member States concerning the labelling of tobacco products, and requiring statements of tar and nicotine yields in specified form and health warnings on tobacco packages (IDHL, 1990, **41**(1): 85–88)

Council Directive 90/239/EEC of 17 May 1990 on the approximation of the laws, regulations and administrative provisions of the Member States concerning the maximum tar yield of cigarettes (IDHL, 1990, **41**(3): 451–452)

FINLAND

Law No. 693 of 13 August 1976 on measures to restrict smoking (IDHL, 1977, **28**(3): 486–489)

Law No. 1147 of 31 December 1976 concerning allocation of revenue from tobacco taxes to anti-smoking activities.

Ordinance No. 225 of 25 February 1977 on measures to restrict smoking (IDHL, 1977, **28**(3): 489–491)

Decree No. 227 of 25 February 1977 of the Council of State on the maximum permitted limits for substances dangerous or harmful to health that are contained in tobacco products approved for sale or that are released when such products are smoked (IDHL, 1977, **28**(3): 491)

Decree No. 254 of 25 February 1977 of the Ministry of Social Affairs and Health on smokers' accessories (IDHL, 1977, **28**(3): 491–492)

General Directive on Health Education (1978) DNO 3113/02/78

Decree No. 747 of 26 September 1979 of the Council of State on the maximum levels of harmful substances in tobacco products approved for sale and the classification of self-burning factory-manufactured cigarettes (IDHL, 1980, **31**(2): 307–308)

Ordinance No. 125 of 22 February 1980 amending the Ordinance on measures to restrict smoking (IDHL, 1980, **31**(2): 308)

Decree No. 770 of 15 November 1984 of the Council of State on the maximum levels of harmful substances in tobacco products approved for sale and the classification of factory-manufactured cigarettes (IDHL, 1985, **36**(4): 992–993)

Law No. 914 of 12 December 1986 on product safety (IDHL, 1991, **42**(1): 100–101)

Law No. 1037 of 11 December 1987 concerning allocation of revenue from tobacco taxes to anti-smoking activities

FRANCE

Law No. 76-616 of 9 July 1976 concerning measures to combat smoking (IDHL, 1976, **27**(4): 732–734)

Decree No. 77-1042 of 12 September 1977 prohibiting smoking in certain places intended for use by groups of people where this practice may have harmful effects upon health (IDHL, 1978, **29**(2): 352–353)

Decree No. 77-1273 of 17 November 1977 for the implementation of Law No. 76-616 of 9 July 1976 concerning measures to combat smoking (IDHL, 1978, **29**(2): 361)

Order of 30 January 1978 establishing the list of substances which must be indicated on cigarette packaging units and the conditions for determining the presence of such substances (IDHL, 1979, **30**(1): 44)

Order of 1 March 1978 on the limits of the space devoted to advertising of tobacco in the printed press (IDHL, 1979, **30**(1): 44)

Circular No. 519 of 1 March 1978 on the opening of tobacconists' shops in hospital establishments (IDHL, 1979, **30**(1): 44)

Order of 9 March 1978 for the implementation of the third and fourth paragraphs of Section 10 of Law No. 76-616 of 9 July 1976 concerning measures to combat smoking (IDHL, 1979, **30**(1): 44)

Order of 2 October 1978 concerning conditions for the implementation of the prohibition of smoking in aircraft (IDHL, 1979, **30**(1): 45)

Decree No. 78-1108 of 23 November 1978 for the implementation of the Law of 1 August 1905 on fraudulent practices and misbranding with regard to products or services in respect of tobacco, tobacco products, and tobacco substitutes (IDHL, 1979, **30**(4): 785–786)

Order of 5 June 1979 on the additives permitted in the manufacture of tobacco and tobacco products and their substitutes (IDHL, 1979, **30**(4): 786)

Law No. 83-25 of 19 January 1983 prescribing various measures relating to social security (IDHL, 1983, **34**(4): 767)

Order of 4 March 1983 determining the form to be taken by the distinctive mark to be apposed to the packaging of alcoholic beverages and tobacco (IDHL, 1983, **34**(4): 767)

Order of 16 July 1984 on the additives permitted in the manufacture of tobacco products and their substitutes (IDHL, 1985, **36**(3): 648)

Circular No. 231 of 13 January 1988 on the control of tobacco consumption in hospital establishments (IDHL, 1989, **40**(1): 102)

Law No. 89-18 of 13 January 1989 amending the law of 9 July 1976 concerning the fight against smoking by requiring advertising of products bearing the name or emblem of tobacco products to comply with the restrictions on advertising of tobacco

Law No. 91-32 of 10 January 1991 on measures to combat tobacco use and alcoholism (IDHL, 1991, **42**(1): 44–47)

Decree of 26 April 1991 laying down the maximum tar content of cigarettes

Decree of 26 April 1991 on the methods of analysis of the content of nicotine and tar and the methods of checking the accuracy of the information given on packages, as well as the modalities for showing health messages and the obligatory statements on packs of tobacco and tobacco products

Decree No. 92-478 of 29 May 1992 establishing the conditions for application of the prohibition of smoking in premises assigned for community use and modifying the Public Health Code.

FRENCH POLYNESIA

Deliberation No. 82-11 of 18 February 1982 of the Territorial Assembly of French Polynesia on the organization of the control of tobacco abuse and tobacco dependence in the Territory (IDHL, 1982, **33**(2): 283)

GAMBIA

The Tobacco Products (Control of Advertisements) Act, 1985 (IDHL, 1986, **37**(3): 570–571)

GERMANY[1]

Law on the protection of juveniles in public (version dated 27 July 1957)
Law of 15 August 1974 for the overall reform of foodstuffs law (IDHL, 1975, **26**(3): 524–526)
Workplace Ordinance of 20 March 1975 (Section 5)
The Tobacco Ordinance. Dated 20 December 1977 (IDHL, 1978, **29**(4): 737)

GREECE

Decision No. A2a/5648 of 20 November 1976 introducing the Child Health Booklet (IDHL, 1978, **29**(2): 379–380)
Ministerial Decision No. A2g/Ec 1989 of 2 April 1979 prohibiting smoking in hospital establishments and private nursing homes (IDHL, 1981, **32**(3): 459–460)
Ministerial Decision No. A2g/EC 3051 of 25 April 1980 prohibiting smoking in enclosed public places (IDHL, 1981, **32**(3): 460)
Ministerial Decision No. A2/ik. 6139 of 23 December 1988 on the labelling of tobacco products with regard to the harmful effect of tobacco on health (IDHL, 1989, **40**(4): 844–845)

GUATEMALA

Decree No. 80-74 of 13 September 1974 establishing a health warning on cigarette packets
Government Accord No. 681 of 3 August 1990, prohibiting smoking in public transportation vehicles and in public places in government and private offices

HONDURAS

Law of the Honduran Institute for the Prevention of Alcoholism and Drug Addiction, Decree No. 136-89 of 14 October 1989 providing for control of smoking in public places

HONG KONG

The Smoking (Public Health) (Notices) (Amendment) Order 1983 (IDHL, 1983, **34**(4): 768–769)
The Smoking (Public Health) (Amendment) Ordinance 1984 (IDHL, 1984, **35**(4): 771–772)
The Smoking (Public Health) (Amendment) Regulations 1984 (IDHL, 1984, **35**(4): 772)
The Smoking (Public Health) (Specification of Newspaper Circulation) Notice 1984 (IDHL, 1984, **35**(4): 772)
The Public Health and Municipal Services (Amendment) (No. 2) Ordinance 1986 containing a definition of "smokeless tobacco products" (IDHL, 1987, **38**(1): 66–67)

---

[1] The German Democratic Republic had a number of statutes restricting smoking and access to cigarettes. The terms of the unification of the two Germanys provide that the laws of the Federal Republic of Germany shall prevail.

The Smokeless Tobacco Products (Prohibition) Regulations 1987 (IDHL, 1987, **38**(1): 67)

The Hong Kong Council on Smoking and Health Ordinance 1987 (IDHL, 1988, **39**(1): 86–87)

HUNGARY

Regulations No. 118244 of 1972 of the Minister of Posts and Transport concerning the transportation of passengers, baggage, and urgent goods, taking into account all subsequent amendments and regulations (Sections 7 and 8)

Policy Statement No. 127128 of 1973 of the Minister of Culture concerning the internal regulations of schools

Policy Statement No. 4 of 1976 of the Ministry of Internal Trade concerning smoking in commercial and hotel establishments

Instructions No. 500551 of 1976 introducing provisions intended to restrict smoking in buses

Instructions No. 10 of 1977 of the Minister of Agriculture and Food concerning the warning notices that must appear on confectionery products and on tobacco products

Ordinance No. 10 of 14 May 1977 of the Minister of Internal Trade amending Ordinance No. 13 of 12 March 1968 concerning the marketing of tobacco products for purposes of consumption

Recommendation of the Ministry of Internal Trade of 1979 concerning abstention from smoking during children's mealtimes

Policy Statement No. 31 of 1980 of the Ministry of Health on measures to control smoking (IDHL, 1980, **31**(4): 839)

ICELAND

Law No. 59 of 18 April 1971 amending Law No. 63 of 28 May 1969 on State trade in alcoholic beverages, tobacco, and medicaments (IDHL, 1978, **29**(3): 581)

Law No. 27 of 11 May 1977 prescribing measures to reduce smoking (IDHL, 1979, **30**(3): 570)

Law No. 74 of 28 May 1984 on the prevention of the use of tobacco (IDHL, 1984, **35**(4): 772)

Regulations No. 499 of 28 December 1984 concerning warnings on tobacco products (IDHL, 1986, **37**(1): 47–48)

INDIA

The Cigarettes (Regulation of Production, Supply and Distribution) Act, 1975 (IDHL, 1977, **28**(4): 996–999)

The Cigarettes (Regulation of Production, Supply and Distribution) Rules, 1976 (IDHL, 1977, **28**(4): 999)

Prohibition of tobacco smoking in public places. Office Memorandum No. 27/1/3/90 Cab. Government of India, Cabinet Secretariat, New Delhi, 7 May 1990

INDIA (STATE OF NEW DELHI)

The Delhi (Place of Public Entertainment) Prohibition of Smoking Act, 1953

IRELAND

The Tobacco Products (Control of Advertising, Sponsorship and Sales Promotion) Act, 1978 (IDHL, 1979, **30**(4): 806–807)

The Tobacco Products (Control of Advertising, Sponsorship and Sales Promotion) Regulations, 1979 (IDHL, 1980, **31**(3): 537–538)

The Health (Restricted Article) Order, 1985 (IDHL, 1986, **37**(1): 48)

The Tobacco Products (Control of Advertising, Sponsorship and Sales Promotion) Regulations, 1986 (IDHL, 1986, **37**: 48–49, 571)

The Tobacco (Health Promotion and Protection) Act, 1988 (IDHL, 1989, **40**(1): 103–104)

The Tobacco (Health Promotion and Protection) Regulations, 1990. Dated 23 February 1990 (IDHL, 1990, **41**(3): 452)

ISRAEL

The Restriction of Smoking (Public Places) Law, 1983 (IDHL, 1984, **35**(3): 617)

The Aircraft (Operation of Aircraft and Flight Rules) (Amendment) Regulations, 1987 (IDHL, 1988, **39**(4): 861)

The Criminal Procedure (Violations Subject to a Fine — Smoking Restrictions in Public Places) Order, 1986 (IDHL, 1988, **39**(4): 861)

Order restricting smoking in public places (change in Appendix to the Law of 1983), 1988

ITALY

Law No. 165 of 10 April 1962 prohibiting advertisements for tobacco products

Law No. 584 of 11 November 1975 prohibiting smoking in specified premises and on means of public transport (IDHL, 1977, **28**(3): 621)

Ministerial Decree of 18 May 1976 laying down provisions governing air-conditioning or ventilation systems as referred to in Law No. 584 of 11 November 1975 prohibiting smoking in specified premises and in means of public transport (IDHL, 1977, **28**(4): 1018)

JAPAN

Law No. 33 of 7 March 1900 prohibiting smoking by minors, as amended by Law No. 251 of 18 December 1948

JORDAN

Law No. 64 of 1977 for the protection of public health against health hazards caused by smoking (IDHL, 1983, **34**(2): 283)

Decision No. 1 of 1980 of the Ministry of Health establishing a health warning on cigarette packets (IDHL, 1985, **36**(4): 993)

KENYA

The Public Health (Warning on Cigarette Smoking) Rules, 1984 (IDHL, 1985, **36**(4): 993)

KUWAIT

Ministerial Resolution No. 25 of 1980 on the particulars to be stated on cigarette packages (IDHL, 1981, **32**(2): 258)

Ministerial Decree No. 180 of 28 April 1988 laying down detailed provisions on the analysis of the components of imported cigarettes (IDHL, 1988, **39**(4): 861)

KUWAIT (MUNICIPALITY OF KUWAIT)

Resolution No. 981 of 1980 of the Mayor of the Municipality of Kuwait (cancelling licences for advertisements for tobacco products within the municipality) (IDHL, 1981, **32**(2): 258)

LEBANON

Decree-Law No. 101 of 16 September 1983 on the warning of citizens of the harmful effects of tobacco (IDHL, 1985, **36**(1): 63–64)

LUXEMBOURG

Law of 24 March 1989 relating to the restriction of advertising of tobacco products and prohibiting smoking in certain places (IDHL, 1990, **40**(4): 845)

Law of 19 June 1990 implementing the Law of 24 march 1989 restricting advertising of tobacco products and prohibiting smoking in certain places (IDHL, 1990, **41**(4): 636)

MACAO

Law No. 3/83/M of 11 June 1983 on the prevention and control of smoking (IDHL, 1985, **36**(3): 648–649)

MALTA

The Tobacco (Control of Advertisement) Act, 1970 (IDHL, 1973, **24**(1): 183)

The Prohibition of Advertisement of Tobacco on Television and in Cinemas Regulations, 1970 (IDHL, 1973, **24**(1): 183)

The Tobacco (Smoking Control) Act, 1986 (IDHL, 1987, **38**(3): 544–547)

The Health Warnings (On Smoking) Regulations, 1987 (IDHL, 1989, **40**(2): 408)

Smokeless Tobacco (Ban) Regulations 1988, to prohibit the importation, manufacture, preparation, storage, sale or supply of smokeless tobacco

MAURITIUS

Public Health (Prohibition of Smoking) Regulations 1990, requiring health warnings, prohibiting sales of cigarettes to minors, and restricting smoking in public places

MEXICO

Decree of 26 February 1973 promulgating the Health Code of the United Mexican States (Sections 249–252) (IDHL, 1974, **25**(1): 123–141)

Regulations of 16 December 1974 on advertising for foodstuffs, beverages, and medicaments (IDHL, 1976, **27**(1): 163–168)

The General Law on Health, dated 26 December 1983, including Chapter II, Programme Against Smoking, Chapter XI, Tobacco, and Title 13, Advertising (IDHL, 1986, **37**(3): 493, 498, 501)

Coordination Agreement of 10 November 1986 between the Federal Executive and the Executive of the State of Tabasco, for the purpose of supporting the Smoking Control Programme (IDHL, 1987, **38**(4): 787–788)

Decree of the Secretary of Health of 17 April 1990 restricting smoking in medical facilities of the Secretary of Health and in the National Institutes of Health

MEXICO (FEDERAL DISTRICT)

Regulation for the protection of non-smokers dated 5 July 1990 prohibiting smoking in indoor public places, public transport vehicles, public and private schools, hospitals and clinics, government offices, cinemas, theatres, and shops and business places where the public is being served

NETHERLANDS

The Cigarette and Cigarette Tobacco Labelling Decree (Commodities Law) of 29 April 1981 (IDHL, 1982, **33**(1): 33)

Decree of 9 December 1986 amending the Cigarette and Cigarette Tobacco Labelling Decree (IDHL, 1988, **39**(1): 87–88)

Law of 10 March 1988 prescribing measures for the restriction of tobacco use, and in particular for the protection of non-smokers (IDHL, 1989, **40**(2): 408–410)

NEW ZEALAND

The Police Offences Act 1927 (reprint as of 1 January 1974) (IDHL, 1975, **26**(2): 398–399)

The Toxic Substances Act 1979 (Sections 72–74) (IDHL, 1980, **31**(4): 855–856)

The Toxic Substances Regulations 1988. Amendment No. 2. Dated 21 March 1988

The Smoke-free Environments Act 1990 (IDHL, 1990, **41**(4): 636–640)

The Smoke-free Environments Regulations 1990

NICARAGUA

Decree of 30 June 1976 (establishing a health warning on cigarette packets)*

NIGERIA

The Tobacco Smoking (Control) Decree 1990, Decree No. 20. Dated 25 June 1990 (IDHL, 1990, **41**(4): 640–641)

NORWAY

Law of 19 April 1899 for the protection of children against the use of tobacco

Law No. 14 of 9 March 1973 on restrictive measures in trade in tobacco products, etc. (IDHL, 1975, **26**(3): 571–572)

Regulations of 25 October 1974 on the labelling of packets of cigarettes, packets of smoking tobacco, and packets of cigarette paper (IDHL, 1975, **26**(3): 572), as amended on 5 June 1975 (IDHL, 1976, **27**(3): 593–594)

Regulations of 25 October 1974 on the prohibition of tobacco advertising (IDHL, 1975, **26**(3): 572)

Regulations of 29 November 1977 on conditions governing exemptions from the prohibition on advertising in the Law on restrictive measures in trade in tobacco products, etc. (IDHL, 1979, **30**(1): 125–126)

Regulations No. 830 of 25 March 1983 on the labelling of packets of cigarettes, packets of smoking tobacco, and packets of cigarette paper (IDHL, 1984, **35**(2): 344–345)

Regulations No. 2145 of 14 December 1984 on asbestos (IDHL, 1985, **36**(4): 1060)

Law No. 24 of 6 May 1988 amending Law No. 14 of 9 March 1973 on restrictive measures in trade in tobacco products (IDHL, 1988, **39**(4): 862)

Regulations No. 563 of 8 July 1988 on protection against tobacco-induced injury (IDHL, 1988, **39**(4): 862–863)

Regulations No. 925 of 4 September 1989 amending the Regulations concerning exceptions to the ban on advertising contained in Section 2 of the Law on protection against tobacco-induced injury (IDHL, 1990, **41**(2): 274)

Regulations No. 1044 of 13 October 1989 on the prohibition of new products containing tobacco and nicotine (IDHL, 1990, **41**(2): 275)

PAKISTAN

The Cigarettes (Printing of Warning) Ordinance, 1979 (IDHL, 1984, **35**(1): 74–75)

The Cigarettes (Printing of Warning) Rules, 1982 (IDHL, 1984, **35**(1): 75)

PANAMA[1]

Cabinet Decree No. 56 of 17 March 1970 prescribing measures against cigarettes (IDHL, 1973, **24**(3): 581)

Decree No. 129 of 19 June 1978 prescribing measures on the advertising of alcoholic beverages, non-alcoholic beverages, cigarettes, and tobacco

PAPUA NEW GUINEA

The Tobacco Products (Health Control) Act 1987 (IDHL, 1988, **39**(4): 863–865)

PARAGUAY

Law No. 836/80 promulgating the Health Code, 15 December 1980 in which Sec. 202 restricts advertising of tobacco and authorizing the Ministry of Health to require a health warning on tobacco products (IDHL, 1981, **32**(4): 624–634)

Resolution S.G. No. 20 of the Ministry of Public Health and Social Welfare, 23 January 1990, prohibiting smoking in the facilities of the Ministry of Public Health and Social Welfare and setting forth means of control

Decree-Law No. 4012 regulating Articles 202–205 of the Sanitary Code on Advertising of Tobacco and Alcohol

PARAGUAY (ASUNCIÓN)

Capital Municipality Transit Rule 298 of August 1981 prohibiting smoking in urban passenger vehicles

Capital Municipality Ordinance 15,381 dated 2 February 1984 prohibiting smoking in cinemas, theatres, and other similar public places

Order of the Municipal Council, Article 298 in relation to World No-Tobacco Day, 1991 prohibiting smoking in collective public transportation vehicles

PERU

Supreme Decree No. DS-0079-70-SA of April 1970 requiring health warnings on cigarette packages and advertising and restricting advertising (IDHL 1977, **28**(3): 689)

Law No. 23482 of 20 October 1982 on the selective consumption tax on cigarettes made from blond tobacco (IDHL, 1987, **38**(1): 67)

---

[1] There are a number of other provisions in Panama restricting smoking in buses, cinemas, etc.

POLAND

Ordinance of 4 June 1974 of the Minister of Health and Social Welfare concerning restrictions on smoking based on health grounds (IDHL, 1975, **26**(1): 200–201)

PORTUGAL[1]

Order No. 212 of 18 April 1978 prohibiting smoking in urban public transport as well as in inter-urban public transport on journeys lasting up to one hour (IDHL, 1979, **30**(3): 638–639)

Order No. 375/78 of 11 July 1978 prescribing Regulations for the implementation of Order No. 212/78 of 18 April 1978 concerning the prohibition of smoking in public transport, prescribing the manner in which the prohibition and, in certain cases, permission to smoke are to be indicated, and determining the right to carry out inspection and collect fines and the manner in which this is to be done (IDHL, 1979, **30**(3): 639)

Decree-Law No. 421/80 of 30 September 1980 prescribing rules governing advertising (IDHL, 1981, **32**(3): 481–482)

Law No. 22/82 of 17 August 1982 on the control of smoking (IDHL, 1985, **36**(1): 64)

Decree-Law No. 226/83 of 27 May 1983 for the implementation of Law No. 22/82 of 17 August 1982 on the control of smoking, and establishing the Smoking Control Council (CPT) (IDHL, 1985, **36**(1): 64–65)

ROMANIA

Law of 6 July 1978 on the safeguarding of the health of the population (Section 84) (IDHL, 1979, **30**(2): 263)

SAUDI ARABIA

Royal Decree M/10 dated 1392 (H)-03-03 (1982) requiring health warnings in Arabic and English on cigarette packages as well as tar and nicotine contents, and specifying maximum tar and nicotine contents

Circular of 18 October 1983 prohibiting smoking in ministerial offices, Government agencies, and public institutions (IDHL, 1986, **37**(1): 49)

SENEGAL

Law No. 81-58 of 9 November 1981 prohibiting advertising for tobacco and smoking in certain public places (IDHL, 1983, **34**(1): 90)

Ministerial Order No. 8236 M.S.P.-D.PH. of 30 July 1982 prescribing the substances that must be indicated on the packaging units of tobacco or tobacco products and the conditions for determining the presence of such substances (IDHL, 1983, **34**(1): 90)

Law No. 85-23 of 25 February 1985 amending Law No. 81-58 of 9 December 1981 prohibiting the advertising of tobacco and smoking in certain public places (IDHL, 1986, **37**(4): 798)

Decree No. 85-1375 of 28 December 1985 specifying the conditions governing the promotion or advertising of tobacco or tobacco products (IDHL, 1986, **37**(4): 798–799)

---

[1] According to a report in the *Daily Telegraph* (London) of 11 June 1981, the Portuguese Parliament has approved a ban on smoking by children under 16 years of age.

SINGAPORE

The Prohibition of Smoking in Certain Places Act, 1970 (IDHL, 1973, **24**(1): 217)

The Prohibition of Advertisements relating to Smoking Act, 1970 (IDHL, 1973, **24**(1): 218)

The Environmental Public Health (Food Handlers) Regulations 1973

The Consumer Protection (Warning Against Danger of Smoking) Regulations, 1980 (IDHL, 1981, **32**(3): 460)

The Smoking (Prohibition in Certain Places) Notification 1988. Dated 15 June 1988 (IDHL, 1990, **41**(2): 276)

The Consumer Protection (Labelling of Tobacco Product Containers) Regulations 1989. Dated 11 January 1989 (IDHL, 1990, **41**(2): 276)

An Act to amend the Smoking (Prohibition of Advertisements) Act 1989. Dated 7 November 1989

SPAIN

Crown Decree No. 1100 of 12 May 1978 regulating advertising for tobacco and alcoholic beverages by State broadcasting media (IDHL, 1978, **29**(4): 817)

Crown Decree No. 1259 of 4 April 1979 on the designation of cigarette products as "low-nicotine" and "low-tar" (IDHL, 1981, **32**(4): 732)

Order of 23 May 1980 approving the technological standards necessary in order to perform the chemical analysis of cigarette products as referred to in Crown Decree No. 1259 of 4 April 1979 (IDHL, 1981, **32**(4): 732)

Crown Decree No. 709/1982 of 5 March 1982 regulating the advertising and use of tobacco (IDHL, 1985, **36**(2): 403–404)

Crown Decree No. 192/1988 of 4 March 1988 laying down restrictions on the sale of tobacco, for the protection of the health of the population (IDHL, 1988, **39**(3): 653–656)

Order of 8 June 1988 for the implementation of Crown Decree No. 192/1988 laying down restrictions on the sale of tobacco, for the protection of the health of the population (IDHL, 1989, **40**(3): 603)

Order of 7 November 1989 prohibiting the sale and distribution of tobacco and alcoholic beverages at public school centres under the authority of the Ministry of Education and Science (IDHL, 1991, **42**(3): 479–480)

SPAIN (CATALONIA)

Law No. 20 of 25 July 1985 on prevention and care in regard to potentially dependence-producing substances

SPAIN (VALENCIA)

Order of 20 June 1988 of the Council on Health and Consumer Affairs approving the Programme on the Reduction of Tobacco Consumption (IDHL, 1989, **40**(3): 603–605)

SRI LANKA[1]

Direction 14 under Section 6(1)(c) of the Consumer Protection Act, No. 1 of 1979 (IDHL, 1980, **31**(2): 383–384)

---

[1] There are also a number of other provisions in Sri Lanka restricting smoking in public transport vehicles.

SUDAN

The Regulation of Cigarette Smoking Act, 1982. Dated 12 April 1983 (IDHL, 1983, **34**(4): 769)

Regulation No. 16 of 1983 on the control of smoking (IDHL, 1986, **37**(1): 49)

SWEDEN

Law of 11 December 1975 concerning the warning notices and declarations of content to be displayed on tobacco products (IDHL, 1976, **27**(4): 868–869)

Order No. 32 of 31 May 1976 of the National Board of Health and Welfare concerning the warning notices and declaration of content to be displayed on tobacco products (IDHL, 1976, **27**(4): 869–870) as amended by Order No. 13 of 24 February 1978 (IDHL, 1979, **30**(2): 320–321) and Order No. 17 of 26 February 1981 (IDHL, 1981, **32**(3): 460–461)

Law No. 764 of 30 November 1978 prescribing certain provisions concerning the marketing of tobacco products (IDHL, 1980, **31**(3): 556)

Guidelines No. 7 of the National Board for Consumer Policies on the marketing of tobacco products (IDHL, 1980, **31**(3): 556–558)

Order No. 18 of 26 February 1980 of the National Board of Health and Welfare on the mean values determined in 1980 for the content of cigarette smoke in accordance with Annex B to Order No. 32 of 31 May 1976 of the National Board of Health and Welfare concerning the warning notices and declaration of content to be displayed on tobacco products (IDHL, 1980, **31**(3): 558–559)

Order No. 17 of 26 February 1981 of the National Board of Health and Welfare amending Order No. 32 of 31 May 1976 concerning the warning notices and the declaration of content to be displayed on tobacco products (IDHL, 1981, **32**(3): 460–461)

General Recommendations (AFS 1893: 10) concerning smoking restrictions, issued by the National Board of Occupational Safety and Health and the National Board of Health and Welfare (IDHL, 1988, **39**(1): 88)

Order No. 10 of 10 April 1986 of the National Board of Health and Welfare amending Order No. 32 of 1976 of the National Board of Health and Welfare concerning the warning notices and declarations of contents to be displayed on tobacco products (IDHL, 1988, **39**(1): 88–89)

Order No. 6 of 5 February 1988 of the National Board of Health and Welfare concerning the warning notice and declaration of contents on tobacco products (IDHL, 1989, **40**(1): 104)

SWITZERLAND

Ordinance on foodstuffs. Amendments of 18 October 1978 (IDHL, 1979, **30**(2): 327–328)

SWITZERLAND (CANTON OF VAUD)

Law of 29 May 1985 on public health (Sections 52–54) (IDHL, 1985, **36**(4): 942)

THAILAND

Order of the Commission on Advertisement of the Consumer Protection Board providing for a total ban on tobacco advertising in accordance with Cabinet resolutions of 26 April 1989 and 20 December 1989 approving the principles of tobacco control. *Royal Gazette*, Vol. 106, Section 25, 10 February 1989

Tobacco Products Control Act 1992. *Royal Gazette*, Vol. 109, Section 38, 5 April 1992

Nonsmokers' Health Protection Act 1992. *Royal Gazette*, Vol. 109, Section 40, 7 April 1992

TRINIDAD AND TOBAGO

An Act relating to the protection of children and young persons, industrial schools, and orphanages, and juvenile offenders (the Children Act), Chap. 46: 01, Laws of Trinidad and Tobago, 17 March 1925

Compulsory standard. Requirements for labelling: Part II — Labelling of retail packages of cigarettes. TTS 2110500 Part II, 10 March 1989

(FORMER) UNION OF SOVIET SOCIALIST REPUBLICS

Resolution No. 706 of 12 June 1980 of the Central Committee of the Communist Party of the Soviet Union and the USSR Council of Ministers on measures to intensify the campaign against smoking (IDHL, 1981, **32**(1): 87–90)

UNITED KINGDOM

The Children and Young Persons Act 1933 (Section 7)

The Television Act 1964*

The Finance Act 1978 (IDHL, 1979, **30**(3): 653)

The Tobacco Products (Higher Tar Cigarettes) Regulations 1978 (IDHL, 1979, **30**(3): 653)

An Act (Chapter 34) to amend the Children and Young Persons Act 1933, and the Children and Young Persons (Scotland) Act 1937, to make it an offence to sell any tobacco product to persons under the age of sixteen, and for connected purposes (IDHL, 1986, **37**(4): 799–800)

The Oral Snuff (Safety) Regulations 1989. Dated 13 December 1989 (IDHL, 1990, **41**(3): 452–453)

UNITED STATES OF AMERICA[1]

The Federal Cigarette Labeling and Advertising Act, 1965, as amended by the Public Health Cigarette Smoking Act, 1969 and the Comprehensive Smoking Education Act, 1984 (IDHL, 1971, **22**: 998; IDHL, 1985, **36**(3): 649)

The Comprehensive Smoking Education Act concerning information programmes, warnings on packages, evaluation of smoking control programmes, advertising restrictions (IDHL, 1985, **36**(3): 649–652)

The Comprehensive Smokeless Tobacco Health Education Act of 1986 concerning information programmes, smokeless tobacco, restrictions on sales to minors, health warnings on packages, advertising restrictions, levels of toxic constituents, evaluation of smoking control programmes (IDHL, 1987, **38**(1): 67–70)

Regulations under the Comprehensive Smokeless Tobacco Health Education Act of 1986 (IDHL, 1987, **38**(3): 547)

---

[1] There are many other items of legislation relating to smoking control at the State, county, and municipal levels.

Smoking Regulations. Part 101-20 (Management of Buildings and Grounds) of Title 41 (Public Contracts and Property Management) of the US Code of Federal Regulations (IDHL, 1987, **38**(3): 547–548)

The Department of Transportation and Related Agencies Appropriations Act 1988 concerning smoking on board aircraft (IDHL, 1988, **39**(4): 865)

Smoking aboard aircraft. Parts 121 and 135 of Title 14 (Aeronautics and Space) of the US Code of Federal Regulations (IDHL, 1989, **40**(1): 104)

An Act (Public Law 101-164) making appropriations for the Department of Transportation and related agencies for the fiscal year ending 30 September 1990 and concerning the permanent prohibition against smoking on scheduled airline flights. Dated 21 November 1989 (IDHL, 1990, **41**(3): 453)

Prohibition against smoking; final rule. Parts 121, 129, and 135 of Title 14 (Aeronautics and Space) of the US Code of Federal Regulations. Dated 28 February 1990 (IDHL, 1990, **41**(3): 453)

UNITED STATES OF AMERICA (CALIFORNIA)

Chapter 139 of the Laws of 1980 . . . relating to smoking (IDHL, 1981, **32**(1): 90)

UNITED STATES OF AMERICA (KENTUCKY)

Chapter 438 of the Human Resources Law of Kentucky, 1976 Supplement (IDHL, 1977, **28**(2): 394–395)

UNITED STATES OF AMERICA (MINNESOTA)

The Minnesota Clean Indoor Air Act. Approved 2 June 1975 (IDHL, 1976, **27**(3): 704–705)

UNITED STATES OF AMERICA (NEW YORK)

An Act to amend the penal law, in relation to a label upon cigarette packages. Approved 24 June 1965 (IDHL, 1967, **18**(2): 442)

An Act to amend chapter seven hundred eighty-seven of the laws of nineteen hundred sixty-seven, entitled "An Act directing the commissioner of education to establish a five year program for critical health problems, and making an appropriation therefore", in relation to the continuing of such program. Approved 8 May 1970 (IDHL, 1974, **25**(2): 458)

An Act to amend the public health law, in relation to smoking restrictions and to repeal article 13-E of such law relating thereto. Approved by the Governor: 5 July 1989 (IDHL, 1990, **41**(1): 88)

UNITED STATES OF AMERICA (UTAH)

Chapter 10 of the Laws of 1976 (IDHL, 1979, **30**: 146)

URUGUAY

Resolution No. 1150/970 of 21 July 1970 assigning the Ministry of Health the task of studying the effects of smoking and disseminating information thereon through a special commission (IDHL, 1973, **24**(3): 680)

Resolution 765602 adopted 23 September 1976 prohibiting smoking in the clinics and hospital of the Faculty of Medicine by physicians, students, and technical and administrative personnel; requiring inclusion of smoking histories in patient charts; establishing smoking cessation programmes in the hospital; intensifying education against tobacco in the maternal and child clinics; and increasing information on smoking and its risks at all levels of instruction — professional, middle-level, and primary education

Decree No. 407/981 of 17 December 1980 prohibiting the smoking of tobacco products in any form in buses used for interdepartmental transport of passengers

Law No. 15361 of 24 December 1982 adopting provisions on the advertising and marketing of cigarettes, cigars, and tobacco products (IDHL, 1983, **34**(3): 539)

Decree No. 263983 of 22 July 1983 regulating the marketing and advertising of tobacco products

Law No. 15656 of 10 October 1984 extending the interval for publishing the maximum contents of nicotine and tar by cigarette manufacturers and importers (IDHL, 1988, **39**(2): 396)

Resolution of the Chamber of Deputies dated 9 May 1989 prohibiting smoking in the plenary sessions and working committee meetings of the Chamber of Deputies

Ministry of Public Health, Special Order No. 3904 (undated) prohibiting smoking in the hospitals of the Ministry of Public Health by patients and their visitors, and by physicians, students, and technical and administrative personnel while on duty and in contact with patients, and calling for intensified education on tobacco especially in the maternal and child health clinics, and requiring inclusion of information on smoking in clinical histories in the hospital

URUGUAY (MONTEVIDEO)

Decree No. 16.750 of 21 March 1975 prohibiting smoking by bus drivers for school children

Decree No. 19.067 of March 1979 concerning requirements for theatrical performances, including authorization for the sale of non-alcoholic drinks, cigarettes, and other items in theatres

Decree 407/981 of 12 August 1981 concerning smoking on interdepartmental passenger transportation

VENEZUELA

Law of 13 September 1978 prescribing the tax on cigarettes and tobacco products (IDHL, 1979, **30**(4): 925)

Decree No. 3007 of 2 January 1979 prescribing regulations for the implementation of the law prescribing the tax on cigarettes and tobacco products (IDHL, 1979, **30**(4): 925)

Decree No. 849 of 21 November 1980 prohibiting the transmission by television stations of any commercial advertising which directly or indirectly encourages the consumption of cigarettes and other products derived from tobacco manufacture (IDHL, 1982, **33**(3): 499)

Decree No. 996 of 19 March 1981 prohibiting the transmission by radio stations of any commercial advertising which directly or indirectly encourages the consumption of cigarettes and other products derived from tobacco (IDHL, 1982, **33**(3): 499)

Resolution of 23 October 1984 establishing a Standing Honorary National Council attached to the Division of Chronic Disease of the Ministry of Health and Social Welfare for studying health problems associated with smoking and with a view to formulating policies for the prevention of smoking and the organic diseases resulting therefrom (IDHL, 1986, **37**(2): 276–277)

Resolution of 1985 of the Venezuelan Institute of Social Security prohibiting smoking in administrative and medical care facilities.

VIET NAM

Law of 30 June 1989 on the protection of public health (IDHL, 1990, **41**(1): 15–27)

YUGOSLAVIA

Decree of 29 November 1972 to promulgate the Law on the wholesomeness of foodstuffs and consumer goods (IDHL, 1974, **25**(1): 249)

Annex 4

Effect of legislation on tobacco consumption

Table A4.1 Annual average rates of change in the percentage of adults smoking according to tobacco advertising restrictions in force, 1970–86

Country and year of ban	Age group studied	Years of study	% who smoke		Annual percentage change over study period	
			beginning	end	per country	per group
Enforced tobacco advertising ban						
Iceland, 1972	18–69	1985–86	40.0	36.2	− 9.5	average
Finland, 1978	15–64	1978–86	25.8	25.5	− 0.1	− 3.6
Norway, 1975	16–74	1973–86	41.5	34.5	− 1.1	
Portugal, 1983	na	1983–84	na	23.5	na	
Tobacco promotion in few media						
Belgium	15 +	1980–87	41.5	32.0	− 3.3	
France	15 +	1976–83	44	39	− 1.6	
Italy (enforced ban)	14 +	1980–83	34.9	31.1	− 3.6	average
New Zealand	15 +	1976–86	35	30	− 1.4	− 2.5
Singapore	15 +	1977–84	23	19	− 2.5	
Sweden	16 +	1976–85	38.5	29.6	− 2.6	
Tobacco promotion in most media						
Australia	16 +	1972–83	38.0	33.5	− 1.1	
Austria	15 +	1972–81	28	27	− 1.4	
Belgium	15 +	1970–79	20.2	21.3	+ 0.6	
Canada	15 +	1970–86	45	32	− 1.8	
Denmark	15 +	1970–79	57.9	48.9	− 1.7	
France	15 +	1970–76	53.1	46.7	− 2.0	average
Federal Republic of Germany	15 +	1970–84	41.7	36	− 1.0	− 1.2
Ireland	15 +	1973–82	43	35	− 2.1	
Netherlands	15 +	1970–86	58.5	38.0	− 2.2	
Switzerland	15 +	1972–81	34.6	37.5·	+ 0.9	
United Kingdom	16 +	1972–86	46	33	− 2.0	
United States	17 +	1970–86	36.6	26.5	− 1.7	
Tobacco promotion in all media						
Greece	15 +	1985	na	21.5	na	
Japan	20 +	1970–86	46.6	37.6	− 1.2	− 1.2
Spain	15 +	1970–87	na	40.5	na	

Source: *Health or tobacco. An end to tobacco advertising and promotion.* Wellington, Toxic Substances Board, 1989.
na = data not available.

Fig. A4.1 Norway: per capita consumption of cigarettes and smoking tobacco by people aged 15 years and over

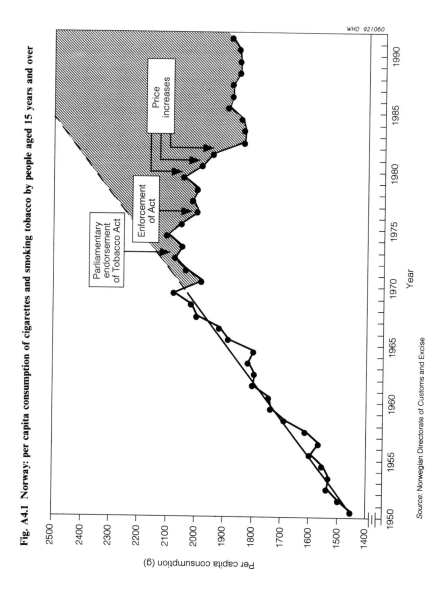

Source: Norwegian Directorate of Customs and Excise

Fig. A4.2. Finland: per capita consumption of tobacco products by adults (moving three-year averages)

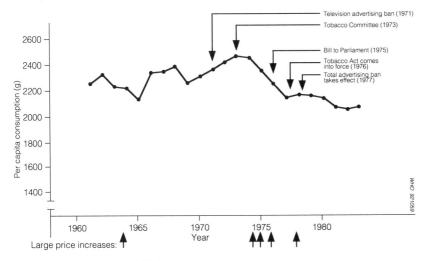

Source: National Board of Health, Finland.

293

Annex 5

Health warnings on tobacco products

Fig. A5.1 Health warnings on tobacco products in Iceland

1. Smoking during pregnancy endangers the health of mother and child.

DIRECTOR GENERAL OF PUBLIC HEALTH.

2. Smoking may damage your arteries and cause heart attack.

DIRECTOR GENERAL OF PUBLIC HEALTH.

3. Protect children from tobacco smoke.

DIRECTOR GENERAL OF PUBLIC HEALTH.

4. If you stop smoking you improve your health and increase your life expectancy.

DIRECTOR GENERAL OF PUBLIC HEALTH.

5. Smoking is a health problem you can help to solve.

DIRECTOR GENERAL OF PUBLIC HEALTH.

6. Hundreds of Icelanders die each year due to smoking.

DIRECTOR GENERAL OF PUBLIC HEALTH.

7. Tobacco smoke pollutes the air and is a health hazard.

DIRECTOR GENERAL OF PUBLIC HEALTH.

8. Snuff and chewing-tobacco may damage the mucous membranes.

DIRECTOR GENERAL OF PUBLIC HEALTH.

295

Fig. A5.2 Health warnings on tobacco packages in Norway

Each brand has to carry these warnings equally distributed on the packets placed on the market. All the warnings are signed by the Directorate of Health, and have a common introduction: "Daily cigarette smoking is dangerous to health".

SMOKING AND CANCER
Smokers run greater risk of cancer, e.g., of lungs, throat and bladder.

SMOKING AND INFANTS
Infants who are exposed to tobacco smoke get pneumonia and bronchitis more often.

SMOKERS CONTRACT PEPTIC ULCER MORE OFTEN THAN NON-SMOKERS
The ulcer heals more quickly if they stop smoking.

CARDIOVASCULAR DISEASES
Smokers run greater risk of myocardial infarction and other cardiovascular diseases

THE MORE YOU SMOKE, THE GREATER THE DANGER TO HEALTH

TO YOU, WHO ARE YOUNG
The earlier you start to smoke, the greater the risk of getting ill.

SMOKING AND EMPHYSEMA
Smoking is an important cause of pulmonary emphysema, a disease which ruptures alveoli and reduces breathing capacity.

SMOKER'S COUGH IN THE MORNING
is often a sign of health damage. If you quit smoking, the cough may disappear.

SMOKING DAMAGES THE LUNGS
It starts with smoker's cough and may end up with lung cancer or another serious disease.

SMOKING DURING PREGNANCY MAY DAMAGE THE CHILD

YOU, WHO HAVE SMOKED FOR A LONG TIME
If you quit smoking, you reduce the risk of serious disease.

PEOPLE WHO QUIT SMOKING, RAPIDLY IMPROVE IN FITNESS

Fig. A5.3 Health warnings on tobacco products in Sweden

- Do not expose your colleagues to tobacco smoke. It is harmful and irritating. *National Board of Health and Welfare.*

- Tobacco smoke contains many carcinogens. The smoke in passive smoking, which affects those in the vicinity of the smoker, contains the highest level of carcinogens. *National Board of Health and Welfare.*

- Tobacco smoking lowers resistance to infections, including those of the respiratory tract. *National Board of Health and Welfare.*

- Do not smoke when children are present. Smoke irritates their respiratory tract. *National Board of Health and Welfare.*

- If you are pregnant or breast-feeding, do not smoke; both you and your child may be harmed. *National Board of Health and Welfare.*

- In 1983, 779 persons died in traffic accidents and at least 8000 from tobacco smoking. *National Board of Health and Welfare.*

- Lung cancer among women will soon be commoner than breast cancer. Smoking is the cause. *National Board of Health and Welfare.*

- Almost all persons who suffer from arteriosclerosis affecting the blood vessels of the legs and have difficulty in walking are smokers. *National Board of Health and Welfare.*

- It is practically only smokers who have a heart attack before they are 50. *National Board of Health and Welfare.*

- Smoking heightens the risk of inflammation of the gums. This can lead to loss of teeth. *National Board of Health and Welfare.*

- If one person smokes, everyone smokes. Most tobacco smoke enters the air breathed by everyone. Your smoking may harm others. *National Board of Health and Welfare.*

- The combination of smoking and contraceptive pills heightens the risk of a heart attack for women over 30. *National Board of Health and Welfare.*